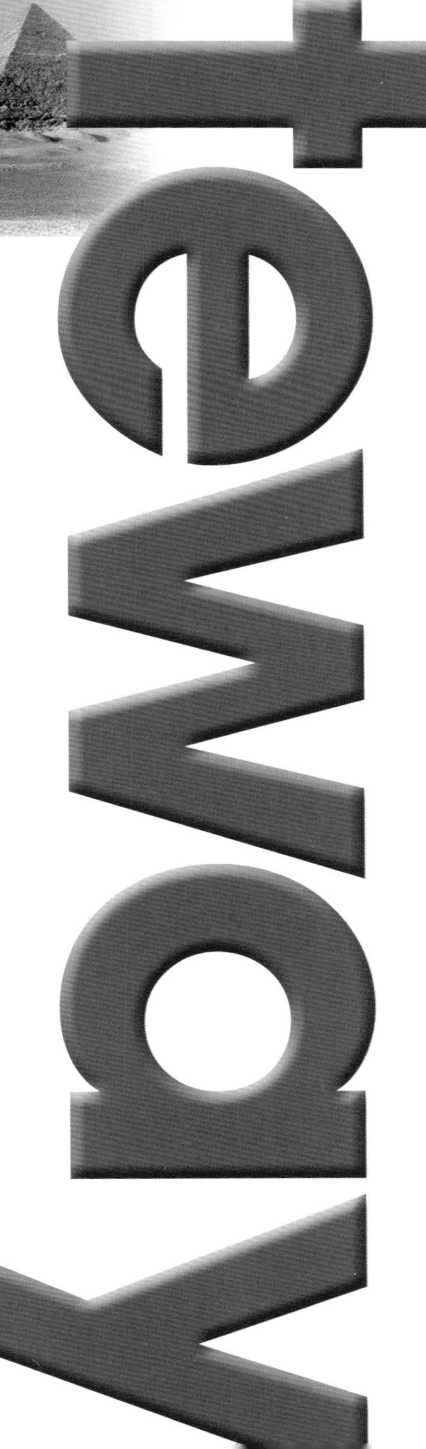

A2

Student's Book

David Spencer

ontents

A2

Grammar ▸ To be ▸ Subject pronouns ▸ Possessive adjectives ▸ *Have got* ▸ Demonstrative pronouns ▸ Possessive *'s*
Listening ▸ The alphabet and spelling ▸ Introductions – questions and answers ▸ Describing people

Listening	Writing	Speaking	Exam success/Study skills
School lessons Everyday activities Eton College Education and lifestyle	School timetables Everyday routines Making notes An informal email	Giving opinions Describing a school timetable Describing routines Talking about yourself	Grammar: Using the grammar reference Listening: Understanding basic information Reading: True/false/not mentioned Speaking: Giving personal information
Free-time activities Describing places in a town New Zealand: radio programme Saturday routines Phoning a cinema	Questions: Present simple Project: group presentation Announcement for a club	Comparing free-time activities Collecting Pair interviews: weekend routines Talking about frequency Asking for information on the phone	Reading: Prediction activities Speaking: Confidence in English Listening: Matching activities Writing: Answering the question
Furniture and rooms Types of homes Present actions Expressions on the phone Telephone numbers	Describing and asking about a room Jobs around the house Describing what people are doing Article describing a place	Describing accommodation Pair interviews: your living room Find the differences Types ofa homes Describing pictures Role-play: On the phone Your ideal bedroom	Use of English: Multiple-choice cloze Writing: Checking your work Vocabulary: Keeping a record Listening: Before you listen
Physical activities Ability Completing notes: Kin-ball Understanding directions	Rules for sports and games Questions with adverbs of manner Writing a questionnaire	Pair interviews: Ability Discussing sport, music and fitness School obligations Role-play: Asking for and giving directions	Speaking: Evaluating your performance Reading: Understanding gist; Multiple-choice Speaking: Negotiating
Ordering food and drink *The Orange* by Wendy Cope The problem of chewing gum: radio programme Menus and prices	Food and drink habits Making notes Formal and informal invitations	Food and drink preferences Roleplay: In a café	Reading: Using a dictionary; missing sentences Listening: First and second listenings Writing: Formal and informal style

Starter unit

Grammar ▸ *To be* ▸ Subject pronouns and Possessive adjectives ▸ *Have got* ▸ Possessive 's ▸ Demonstrative pronouns
Vocabulary ▸ Classroom objects ▸ Colours ▸ Some English-speaking countries and nationalities ▸ Days, months and ordinal numbers ▸ The family ▸ Basic descriptions
Speaking ▸ The alphabet and spelling ▸ Classroom expressions ▸ Saying hello ▸ Telling the time

▸ Vocabulary

Classroom objects

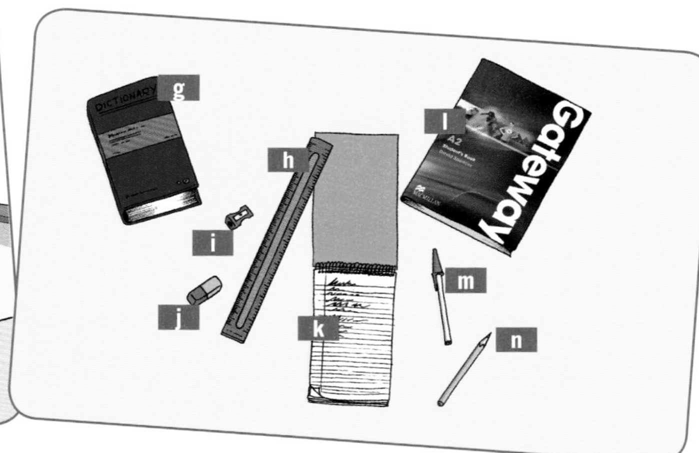

1a Work with a partner. Match the objects in the pictures with these words.

board board rubber CD player chair
computer desk dictionary notebook pen
pencil pencil sharpener rubber ruler
textbook

1b 1.01 Listen and repeat.

2a SPEAKING Work with a partner. Student A: Draw an object from the classroom. Student B: Say the name of the object.

2b Change roles and repeat.

Colours

3 SPEAKING Work with a partner. Look at the pictures and say the name of the classroom object that is:

1 black 2 white 3 red
4 blue 5 brown
6 green 7 yellow 8 grey
9 pink 10 purple 11 orange

▸ Speaking

The alphabet and spelling

1a PRONUNCIATION 1.02 Listen. Why are the letters in different lists?

Grey: A H J K
Green: B C D E G P T V
Red: F L M N S X Z
White: I Y
Yellow: O
Blue: Q U W
Dark blue: R

1b Listen again and practise saying the lists.

2 LISTENING 1.03 Listen and write the letters. What are the five words?

3 Write each word from 2 in numerals.
FOUR = 4

Classroom expressions

4 Look at these classroom expressions. Translate them into your language.

1 How do you spell that?
2 Can you repeat that, please?
3 What does *pencil case* mean?
4 I'm sorry, I don't understand.
5 How do you say that in English?

5 SPEAKING Ask your partner to spell other numbers. Use classroom expressions from 4 if necessary.

How do you spell 7?

S-E-V-E-N. How do you spell 15?

Can you repeat that, please?

Vocabulary

Some English-speaking countries and nationalities

1a Complete the table with these words.

American Australian England Canadian Ireland

Capital city	Country	Nationality
London	1	British or English
Dublin	2	Irish
Washington DC	United States of America	3
Ottawa	Canada	4
Canberra	Australia	5

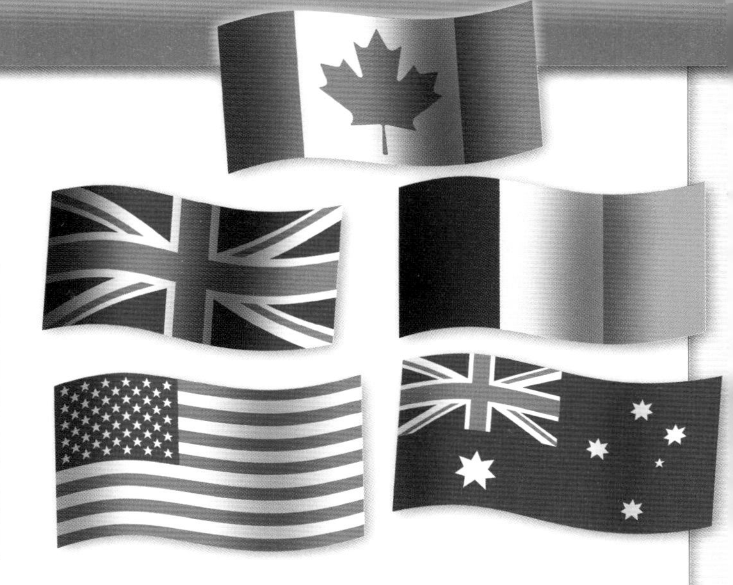

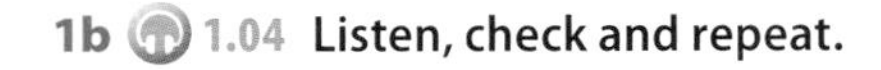

1b 1.04 Listen, check and repeat.

2 Work with a partner. Write a list of other English-speaking countries. How many can you think of?

Speaking *Saying hello*

1 LISTENING **1.05 Listen and complete the dialogue.**

BOY: Hi, I'm Thomas. What's your name?
GIRL: I'm (a) .... Nice to meet you.
BOY: Nice to meet you too. How do you spell your name?
GIRL: (b) ....
BOY: Are you English?
GIRL: No, I'm not. I'm American.
BOY: How old are you?
GIRL: I'm 16. And you?
BOY: I'm 16 too. This is my friend. His name's Luke. He's (c) ....

2 SPEAKING **Work with a partner. Practise the dialogue in 1.**

3a Match the questions (1–4) with the answers (a–d).

1 What's your name? a No, I'm Australian.
2 How do you spell your name? b I'm 17.
3 Are you English? c E-M-I-L-Y.
4 How old are you? d I'm Emily.

3b 1.06 Listen, check and repeat.

4 LISTENING **1.07 Listen to the dialogues and choose the correct alternative.**

1 Name: *Amy/Amie*
Nationality: *English/American/Australian*
Age: *16/17*

2 Name: *Keiron/Kieran*
Age: *15/16*
Nationality: *English/American/Australian*

5a SPEAKING **Work with a partner. Change the names, ages and nationalities in the dialogue in 1. Make them true for you and your partner. Practise the dialogue.**

5b SPEAKING **Act out the dialogue for the class.**

Hi, I'm Adam. What's your name?

I'm Bianka. Nice to meet you.

GRAMMAR GUIDE

To be

1a Look at the sentences and complete the verb table below.

1 I**'m** Thomas.
2 **Are** you English?
3 Yes, I **am**.
4 No, I**'m not**.
5 She **is** my friend.
6 His name **is** Luke.

Affirmative
I (**a**) .... English.
You/We/They **are** English.
He/She/It (**b**) .... English.
Negative
I (**c**) .... Australian.
You/We/They **aren't** Australian.
He/She/It **isn't** Australian.
Question
Am I Canadian?
(**d**) .... you/we/they Canadian?
Is he/she/it Canadian?
Short answers
Yes, I (**e**) ....
No, I (**f**) ....
Yes, you/we/they **are**.
No, you/we/they **aren't**.
Yes, he/she/it **is**.
No, he/she/it **isn't**.

1b Match the long forms with their contractions.

Long forms: 1 are 2 are not 3 is 4 am 5 am not 6 is not

Contractions: a 'm b 're c 's d 'm not e aren't f isn't

GRAMMAR REFERENCE ▸ page 12

2 Complete the sentences with the correct form of the verb *to be*. Make true sentences in the affirmative or negative.

1 Wayne Rooney .... from England.
2 I .... a student.
3 We .... 15.
4 Will Smith and Johnny Depp .... American.
5 My name .... Peter.

3 LISTENING 1.08 **Look at the table. Then listen and read the dialogue. Who is the person?**

Country	BRITAIN								USA							
City	LONDON				BRISTOL				NEW YORK				BOSTON			
Age	15		16		14		17		13		18		15		17	
Name	Smith	Jones	Willis	Kent	Ali	Finn	Ross	Dale	Marks	West	Dent	Cross	North	Mills	Storm	Last

A: Are you from Britain?
B: No, I'm not.
A: Are you from the USA?
B: Yes, I am.
A: Are you from Boston?
B: Yes, I am.
A: Are you 17?
B: Yes, I am.
A: Is your surname Last?
B: No, it isn't.
A: Is it ....?
B: Yes, it is!

4 SPEAKING **Work with a partner. Choose a person from the table in 3. Can your partner discover who you are?**

Are you from Britain?

Yes, I am.

GRAMMAR GUIDE

Subject pronouns and possessive adjectives

5 Look at the sentences. Match the subject pronouns (1–7) with the possesive adjectives (a–g).

1 **I**'m British.
2 **You**'re American.
3 **He**'s Australian.
4 **She**'s German.
5 **It**'s my cat.
6 **We**'re students.
7 **They**'re 16.

a **Her** name is Eva.
b **Your** name is Zak.
c **Their** names are Scott and Lily.
d **My** name is Jack.
e **His** name is Taylor.
f **Our** names are Holly and Emma.
g **Its** name is Tiger.

GRAMMAR REFERENCE ▸ page 12

6 Choose the correct alternative.

Hi! (**a**) I/My name is Katie and this is my classroom. Is (**b**) you/your classroom similar? In the photo you can see three other students. (**c**) His/Their names are Ruby, Danny and Andrew. (**d**) They/Their are 15. (**e**) Our/Your teacher is Miss Smith. (**f**) His/Her first name is Helen. (**g**) He/She is from a big city. (**h**) His/Its name is Birmingham and (**i**) it/its is in the middle of England.

▶ Speaking *Telling the time*

1 Use the clock on the right to help you complete the times.

1  It's seven ....

2  It's .... past eight.

3 

It's .... to ten.

4  It's twenty .... six.

5 

It's .... nine.

6  It's ....

2 SPEAKING Write five times and ask your partner the time.

7.20 / 9.30 / 2.15 / 12.50 / 11.05

What time is it?

It's twenty past seven.

3 SPEAKING Work with a partner. Ask and answer the questions.

1 What time is it now?
2 What time does this class start?
3 What time does this class end?

▶ Vocabulary

Days, months and ordinal numbers

1a Complete the table with these words.

eleventh February fifth July June March May
ninth November October second September seventh
sixth Sunday tenth third Thursday Tuesday Wednesday

Days	Months	Ordinal numbers
1 Monday	1 January	1st first
2	2	2nd ....
3	3	3rd ....
4	4 April	4th fourth
5 Friday	5	5th ....
6 Saturday	6	6th ....
7	7	7th ....
	8 August	8th eighth
	9	9th ....
	10	10th ....
	11	11th ....
	12 December	12th twelfth
		13th thirteenth

1b 1.09 Listen, check and repeat.

2 SPEAKING Work with a partner. Say these ordinal numbers.

1 16th
2 19th
3 21st
4 22nd
5 23rd
6 25th
7 30th
8 31st

3 SPEAKING Work with a partner. Ask and answer the questions.

1 What date is New Year's Day?
2 What day is your favourite day of the week?
3 What is your favourite month?
4 What date is it today?
5 What date is your birthday?
6 What date is it tomorrow?

What date is New Year's Day?

It's the first of January.

What day is your favourite day of the week?

The family

1 Look at the Jones family tree and read the sentences. Check that you understand the words in red.

Mandy has got one **brother** but she hasn't got a **sister**. Mandy's **father** is Carl and her **mother** is Denise. Jake is Mandy's **uncle**. Jake's **wife** is Jenny. She is Mandy's **aunt**. Joe's **grandparents** are Frank and Martha. Frank is Joe's **grandfather** and Martha is his **grandmother**. Joe and Kate are Mandy's **cousins**. Mandy is Jake's **niece** and Kevin is Jake's **nephew**. Carl is Denise's **husband**. Frank has got four **grandchildren** – two **granddaughters** and two **grandsons**. Joe is Jake's **son** and Kate is Jake's **daughter**.

2 Look at the family tree and complete the sentences.

1 Kate is Joe's ....
2 Joe is Carl's ....
3 Denise and Carl are Joe's .... and ....
4 Frank is Kate's ....
5 Kate is Martha's ....

3 SPEAKING Work with a partner. Draw your family tree and describe it to your partner.

I've got two brothers. Their names are Aidan and Ben.

Basic descriptions

4 Who do the words describe, Jake or Carl?

blue eyes – Jake

Jake

beard
blue eyes
brown eyes
dark hair
fair hair
glasses
long hair
moustache
short
short hair
tall
thin

Carl

5 LISTENING 1.10 Look again at the Jones family tree and listen to this description. Is it Mandy, Kevin, Joe or Kate Jones?

6 Write a description of one of the other Jones cousins. Read it to your partner. Do they know who it is?

GRAMMAR GUIDE

Have got

1 Look at the sentences and complete the verb table below.

1 Mandy **has got** one brother.
2 She **hasn't got** a sister.
3 **Has** Mandy **got** cousins?
4 Yes, she **has**.

Affirmative
I/You/We/They **have got** three cousins.
He/She/It (**a**) .... three cousins.
Negative
I/You/We/They (**b**) .... three cousins.
He/She/It **hasn't got** three cousins.
Question
Have I/you/we/they **got** three cousins?
(**c**) .... he/she/it .... three cousins?
Short answers
Yes, I/you/we/they **have**. No, I/you/we/they **haven't**.
Yes, he/she/it (**d**) .... No, he/she/it **hasn't**.

GRAMMAR REFERENCE ▸ page 12

2 Complete the sentences with the correct form of *have got*. Write true sentences in the affirmative or negative.

1 I .... a sister.
2 We .... a cat.
3 My mother .... blue eyes.
4 I .... short hair.
5 My friend .... red hair.

3 Complete the questions with the correct form of *have got*.

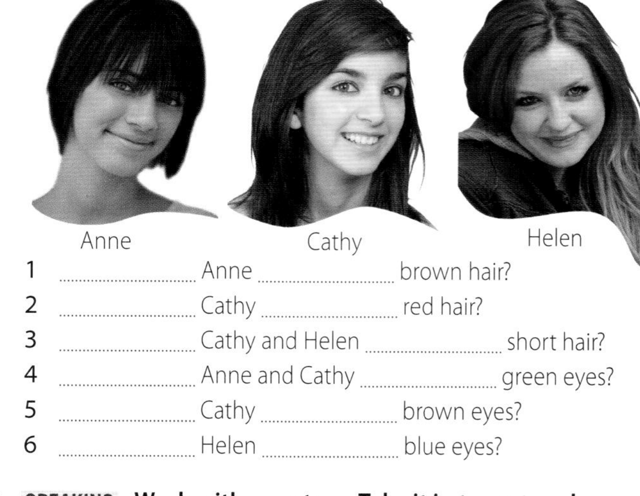
Anne Cathy Helen

1 .... Anne .... brown hair?
2 .... Cathy .... red hair?
3 .... Cathy and Helen .... short hair?
4 .... Anne and Cathy .... green eyes?
5 .... Cathy .... brown eyes?
6 .... Helen .... blue eyes?

4 SPEAKING Work with a partner. Take it in turns to ask and answer the questions in 3.

Has Anne got brown hair?

Yes, she has.

GRAMMAR GUIDE

Possessive 's

5 Look at the sentences and decide if statements 1 and 2 are true (T) or false (F).

a Mandy**'s** grandparents are Frank and Martha.
b Her grandparents**'** names are Frank and Martha.
c Her brother**'s** eyes are brown.
d Her parents**'** names are Denise and Carl.
e Jake is Jenny**'s** husband.

1 After singular names or nouns, we add apostrophe (*'s*) to show possession or a family relationship. T/F
2 After plural nouns ending in *-s*, we just add an apostrophe (*'*) to show possession. T/F

GRAMMAR REFERENCE ▸ page 12

6 Put the apostrophe in the correct place in the sentences about the Jonas Brothers.

1 The brothers names are Joe, Nick and Kevin.
2 Nicks hair is usually long.
3 Their parents names are Denise and Kevin.
4 Their uncles name is Josh.
5 Joshs wife is called Angela.
6 Their grandfathers name is Albert.
7 Nick and the other boys aunt is a singer.

GRAMMAR GUIDE

Demonstrative pronouns

7a Look at the pictures and sentences.

1 **This** is my sister.

2 **That**'s my cousin.

3 **These** are my parents.

4 **Those** are my grandparents.

GRAMMAR REFERENCE ▸ page 12

7b Look at the pictures and complete the phrases with *this, that, these* or *those*.

1 .... boy

2 .... boys

3 .... boys

4 .... boy

Language reference and revision

Grammar reference

To be

Form

Affirmative	I'**m (am)** American. You/We/They'**re (are)** American. He/She/It'**s (is)** American.
Negative	I'**m not (am not)** American. You/We/They **aren't (are not)** American. He/She/It **isn't (is not)** American.
Question	**Am** I American? **Are** you/we/they American? **Is** he/she/it American?
Short answers	Yes, I **am**. No, I'**m not**. Yes, you/we/they **are**. No, you/we/they **aren't**. Yes, he/she/it **is**. No, he/she/it **isn't**.

Use

- We use the verb **to be** to describe a person's nationality, age, appearance, etc.
- We do not use contractions (*'m, 're, 's*, etc.) in short answers.

Subject pronouns

Form

Singular	Plural
I	we
you	you
he/she/it	they

Use

I'm 15.
She's a student.
We are Swiss.

Possessive adjectives

Form

Singular	Plural
my	our
your	your
his/her/its	their

Use

My name is Robert.
Where is your school?
Their mother is Spanish.

Have got

Form

Affirmative	I/You/We/They'**ve got (have got)** brown eyes. He/She/ It'**s got (has got)** brown eyes.
Negative	I/You/We/They **haven't got (have not got)** brown eyes. He/She/ It **hasn't got (has not got)** brown eyes.
Question	**Have** I/you/we/they **got** brown eyes? **Has** he/she/it **got** brown eyes?
Short answers	Yes, I/you/we/they **have**. No, I/you/we/they **haven't**. Yes, he/she/it **has**. No, he/she/it **hasn't**.

Use

- We use **have got** to talk about the things we possess.

Possessive 's

Form

Jack'**s** sister My brother'**s** hair My parents**'** names
My brothers**'** names

Use

- We use **'s** to indicate possession or a family relationship.
- When a noun is plural and ends with an **-s**, we just add an apostrophe (') to the end of the word.

Demonstrative pronouns

Form

Singular	Plural
This is my father.	**These** are my parents.
That is my brother.	**Those** are my cousins.

Use

- We use **this** and **these** for people and objects which are close to the speaker.
- We use **that** and **those** for people and objects that are distant from the speaker.

Vocabulary

1 Classroom objects

board board rubber CD player chair computer desk dictionary notebook pen pencil pencil sharpener rubber ruler textbook

2 Colours

black blue brown dark blue green grey orange pink purple red white yellow

3 Days

Monday Tuesday Wednesday Thursday Friday Saturday Sunday

4 Months

January February March April May June July August September October November December

5 Ordinal numbers

first second third fourth fifth sixth seventh eighth ninth tenth eleventh twelfth thirteenth fourteenth fifteenth sixteenth seventeenth eighteenth nineteenth twentieth twenty-first thirty-first

6 The family

aunt brother cousin daughter father grandchildren granddaughter grandfather grandmother grandparents grandson husband mother nephew niece parent sister son uncle wife

7 Basic descriptions

blue/brown/green eyes short/long/dark/fair/ black/red hair tall short thin beard glasses moustache

Grammar revision

To be

1 Complete the dialogue with the correct form of *to be*.

HARRY: (a) .... you American?
MEGAN: No, I (b) .... I (c) .... British.
HARRY: (d) .... Alex English?
MEGAN: No, he (e) .... He (f) .... from Australia.

WORKBOOK ▶ page 4

/ 6 points

Have got

2 Complete the dialogue with the correct form of *have got*.

JOE: (a) .... you .... a sister?
SAM: Yes, I (b) .... I (c) .... one sister.
JOE: (d) .... she .... dark hair?
SAM: No, she (e) .... Her hair is fair. And she (f) .... brown eyes. Her eyes are blue.

WORKBOOK ▶ page 7

/ 6 points

Subject pronouns, possessive adjectives, possessive 's, demonstrative pronouns

3 Choose the correct alternative.

1 I'm a student. My/Our name is Felipe.
2 She's my sister. His/Her name is Olivia.
3 I've got three books. It/They are on the table.
4 This/These are my parents.
5 The boy's/boys' name is Max.
6 Jamie is Becky's/Beckys' brother.

WORKBOOK ▶ page 4, 7

/ 6 points

Vocabulary revision

Classroom objects

1 Name the classroom objects.

1 .... 2 .... 3 .... 4 .... 5 .... 6 ....

WORKBOOK ▶ page 2

/ 6 points

Days, months, ordinal numbers

2 Complete the lists.

1 first, second, ..., fourth
2 Monday, ..., Wednesday
3 April, May, ..., July
4 sixth, seventh, ..., ninth
5 Friday, ..., Sunday

WORKBOOK ▶ page 5

/ 5 points

The family

3 Write the correct words.

1 Your father's brother is your ....
2 Your father's mother is your ....
3 Your aunt's son is your ....
4 Your father's wife is your ....
5 You are your grandfather's ....
6 You are your aunt's ....

WORKBOOK ▶ page 6

/ 6 points

Basic descriptions

4 Complete the description with some of these words.

beard dark fair glasses long moustache short tall

This man is (a) ....
He's got (b) .... hair.
His hair is (c) ....
He's got a (d) ....
and he's got (e) ....

WORKBOOK ▶ page 6

/ 5 points

Total / 40 points

1 Back to school

Grammar ‣ Present simple affirmative ‣ Prepositions of time ‣ Present simple negative ‣ Object pronouns
Vocabulary ‣ School subjects ‣ School activities ‣ Everyday activities
Speaking ‣ Talking about yourself
Writing ‣ An informal email

‣ Vocabulary

School subjects

1a Work with a partner. Match the pictures with some of these words. Check that you understand the other words. Use your dictionary if necessary.

art biology chemistry English French
geography German history
information and communication technology (ICT)
maths music physical education (PE)
physics Spanish

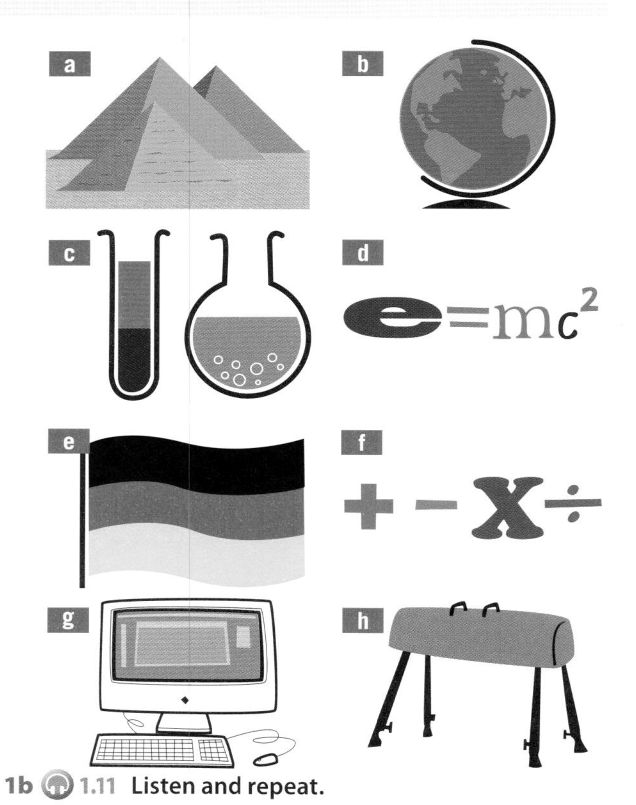

1b 🎧 1.11 **Listen and repeat.**

2 LISTENING 🎧 1.12 **Listen to five school lessons. What is the school subject of each lesson?**

1 ....
2 ....
3 ....
4 ....
5 ....

3 SPEAKING **Work with a partner. Give your opinion of different school subjects. Use these expressions.**

I love it./It's great. 🙂🙂
I like it./It's good. 🙂
It's OK./It's not bad. 😐
I don't like it. 🙁
I hate it./I can't stand it. 🙁🙁

I love PE.

I think it's OK. I don't like history.

I hate it!

School activities

4 Match the pictures with some of these words.

ask/answer a question do homework finish (school/classes)
have a break have lunch sit stand
start (school/classes)

5 Complete the sentences with information about you.

1 I start school at ....
2 I have a break at ....
3 I have lunch at ....
4 I finish school at ....
5 I do homework .... days a week.

6a SPEAKING **Look at this school timetable. Work in five groups. Write *your* school timetable. Each group writes a different day. Write the names of the lessons.**

	Lesson 1	MORNING BREAK	Lesson 2	Lesson 3	LUNCH	Lesson 4	ERNOON BREAK	Lesson
Mon	History		Science	Science		Maths		RE
Tues	Geography		PE	PE		Graphics		Math
Wed	Art		English	English		Music		H
Thur	Science		Geography	[illegible]				
Fri								

6b SPEAKING **Present your timetable to the class.**

On Monday our first lesson is at five to nine. It's PE.

1 Work with a partner. Look at the photo and answer the questions.

1 Who is in the photo?
2 Is the school similar to your school?

2 Read the text. What's your opinion of school life in Japan?

a I think it's great.
b I think it's good.
c It's OK.
d I don't like it.

Typical school life in Japan

Japanese secondary students study typical subjects – maths, English, history, biology, chemistry, PE. A student normally studies ten to fourteen subjects. Students start their first class at half past eight. There are about 30 students in each class.

The students are in the same classroom all day. The teacher goes from one classroom to another at the start and end of the class, not the students.

At the start and end of the class, the students stand for the teacher. When the teacher goes, the students talk with their friends for ten minutes and take their books out of their desks for the next class.

The students have lunch in their classroom. They have a cold lunch, made at home by their parents, or they have a hot lunch made at school. Lunch is 45 minutes and there is no other break, except the ten minutes at the end of the class.

Japanese students finish classes at quarter to four. But when they finish, they clean the desks, the windows and, the board. After they finish class, the students go to after-school clubs.

3 Read the text again. Are these sentences true (T) or false (F) or is the information not mentioned (NM) in the text?

1 Japanese students have very unusual school subjects. T/F/NM
2 In PE classes, they have 45 students with one teacher. T/F/NM
3 The students stand for the teacher at the start of the lesson. T/F/NM
4 The students answer ten questions in a class. T/F/NM
5 The students have lunch in the school cafeteria. T/F/NM
6 The students have a break in the afternoon. T/F/NM
7 Japanese students clean their classroom. T/F/NM
8 Japanese students do homework at six o'clock. T/F/NM

EXAM SUCCESS

In exercise 3, is it more important to give your opinion or to understand the information in the text?

EXAM SUCCESS ▸ page 158

4 Match the underlined words in the text with these pictures and definitions.

1 equal to something
2 not hot
3

4 normal, usual
5

5 SPEAKING What about *you*?

1 What things in Japanese schools are similar to your school?
2 What things are different?

We start at half past eight, like in Japan.

We aren't in the same classroom all day.

GRAMMAR GUIDE

Present simple affirmative

1a Look at the sentences. When do verbs in the present simple finish in *-s*?

1 They **study** typical subjects.
2 We **clean** the classroom.
3 Teachers **teach** and students **learn**.
4 You **go** from one classroom to another.
5 I **finish** classes at quarter to four.
6 It **starts** at half past eight.
7 He **studies** history.
8 School **finishes** at quarter to four.
9 She **does** her homework.

1b Are these sentences true (T) or false (F)?

1 We use the present simple to talk about regular or routine actions. T/F
2 We use the present simple to talk about things that are always or usually true. T/F

GRAMMAR REFERENCE ▶ page 24

2a PRONUNCIATION 1.13 **Look at the verbs and listen. Can you hear the difference in their endings?**

1 /s/ starts likes asks
2 /z/ cleans goes does
3 /ɪz/ finishes watches relaxes

2b Listen again and practise saying the words.

3 Complete the sentences with the present simple form of these verbs.

answer ask do finish go
hate love start write

1 Our school .... at nine o'clock in the morning.
2 My friend .... emails every day.
3 She .... her homework at the weekend.
4 I .... English. It's my favourite subject.
5 My sister .... French. She can't understand a word!
6 When school .... at four o'clock, we .... home.
7 Usually the teacher .... questions and the students .... them.

4 Complete the text with the present simple form of the verbs given.

I (**a**) .... (love) my school. My first class (**b**) .... (start) at 7 o'clock in the morning and it's nuclear physics. My friends and I (**c**) .... (ask) the teacher really difficult questions. After two hours, the teacher (**d**) .... (leave) and our next class is all about the history of the universe. One of my friends, Oscar, (**e**) .... (know) lots about this subject because his mother (**f**) .... (write) encyclopaedias. Oscar (**g**) .... (read) 100 pages a day. It's terrible when school (**h**) .... (finish) but in the evening we (**i**) .... (do) homework for two or three hours. Yes, we all think that our School for Geniuses is great!

GRAMMAR GUIDE

Prepositions of time

5 Look at the sentences and complete the rules with *on*, *at* or *in*.

a Students start their first class **at** half past eight.
b They go to school **on** Saturday.
c They go **in** the morning.
d We start school **in** September.
e School starts **on** 7th September.
f We do homework **at** night.
g They have classes **at** the weekend.
h The next Olympic Games is **in** 2012.

1 We use .... with days.
2 We use .... with times.
3 We use .... with months.
4 We use .... with dates.
5 We use .... with parts of the day (*morning, afternoon, evening*).
6 We use .... with *night* and *the weekend*.
7 We use .... with years.

GRAMMAR REFERENCE ▸ page 24

6a Use the table to write true sentences. Remember to put the verb in the correct form.

Subject	Verb	Object	Preposition of time	
I	go	(to) school		
My mum	study	(to) work		*(time)*
My friends	clean	English	on	*(day)*
My family and I	learn	the house	in	*(month)*
My teacher	watch	homework	at	*(date)*
My good friend	start	French		*(part of the day, or night)*
	speak	the TV		
	finish	DVDs		
	do	to school		

6b SPEAKING Compare sentences with other students. Which sentences are similar?

I go to school at quarter to nine.

So does my friend!

My mum watches DVDs in the evening.

▸ STUDY SKILLS

What can you do to practise new grammar that you learn? **STUDY SKILLS ▸ page 156**

Everyday activities

1a Work with a partner. Match the pictures with some of these phrases. Check that you understand the other phrases.

get (un)dressed   get up   go to bed
go to school by bike/bus/car/train   have a shower
have breakfast/lunch/dinner
make breakfast/lunch/dinner
play football/tennis/computer games   walk to school

1b 1.14 Listen and repeat.

2 SPEAKING Work in small groups. Take it in turns to talk about a typical day.

I get up at half past seven.

I have a shower first. Then I have breakfast.

I walk to school at eight o'clock.

3 LISTENING 1.15 Listen and match the speakers (1–5) with the activities (a–e).

1 Speaker 1   a play tennis
2 Speaker 2   b have lunch at home
3 Speaker 3   c make dinner
4 Speaker 4   d do homework in the evening
5 Speaker 5   e go to bed at 11 pm

School life in the UK

International cultural knowledge
Secondary schools in England

1 **Look at this table of the English education system. What things are similar or different in your country?**

2 **Read the text. Are secondary schools in your country similar to English schools?**

Age on 1st Sept	School
3	Nursery school (not compulsory)
4	Primary school (Infants)
5	Primary school (Infants)
6	Primary school (Infants)
7	Primary school (Juniors)
8	Primary school (Juniors)
9	Primary school (Juniors)
10	Primary school (Juniors)
11	Secondary school
12	Secondary school
13	Secondary school
14	Secondary school
15	Secondary school
16	Secondary school (Sixth Form)/ Sixth Form College (not compulsory)
17	Secondary school (Sixth Form)/ Sixth Form College (not compulsory)

FACT FILE:
Secondary schools in England

- Everybody studies English, maths and science up to the age of 16. These subjects are compulsory. In the first years of secondary school, students have 12 different subjects.
- 90% of students go to *comprehensive schools*. Comprehensive schools are state schools which are open to all students.
- In England, private schools are called *public schools*, or *independent schools*. Independent schools are very expensive. Only 7% of students go to these schools.
- There is one subject in English schools that isn't very usual in other countries. It's called Design and Technology (D & T). When you study this subject, you study different things like food, textiles and materials and electronic products.
- In England, parents can teach their children at home. This is called *home schooling*. About 50,000 children study at home and not at school.
- At 16, English students take national exams called GCSEs. GCSE means General Certificate of Secondary Education.
- After GCSEs, it is possible to finish your studies. Students who stay at school study in the *sixth form*. You study the subjects you like and no subjects are compulsory. Students do just three or four subjects. They take national exams in these subjects. The exams are called *A levels* (Advanced levels).
- English secondary school students normally call their teachers *Sir* (for men) or *Miss* (for women).

3 **Match the words with the correct information.**

Word	Information
a D & T	1 The last part of secondary school, for students from 16 to 18.
b A level	2 You pay to go to this type of school. .
c GCSE	3 You do these national exams when you finish Sixth Form.
d public school	4 This subject looks at things like clothes and food.
e comprehensive school	5 You do these national exams when you are 16.
f home schooling	6 These are state schools. They are for all students.
g Sixth form	7 This is when students have lessons at home, not at school.

4 SPEAKING **What about *you*?**

1 What is your opinion of secondary schools in England?

2 Choose three things that are interesting about secondary schools in England. Make notes about your ideas. Then talk to your partner.

You only do three or four subjects when you're 16 or 17. I think that's good.

I think D & T is an unusual subject.

Cross-curricular – History
A famous English secondary school

5 **Look at the photos of an English secondary school called Eton College. Is Eton similar to your school? Why/Why not?**

6a **Read the quiz about Eton and guess the answers.**

1 Eton College is approximately ...
- a 370 years old.
- b 450 years old.
- c 570 years old.

2 The age of students is between ...
- a 13 and 18.
- b 11 and 18.
- c 3 and 18.

3 The school is for ...
- a boys only.
- b boys, but girls study there when they are 16.
- c boys *and* girls.

4 Old Eton students include ...
- a eight prime ministers from African and Asian countries.
- b British prime ministers.
- c famous secret agents.

5 These people have special clothes to wear at Eton:
- a young students.
- b all students.
- c students and teachers.

6 All Eton students study ...
- a Latin for one year or more.
- b at Oxford or Cambridge.
- c in small classrooms.

7 Eton is important in the history of ...
- a rugby.
- b football.
- c the Olympic Games.

6b LISTENING 1.16 **Listen to some information about Eton. Check your answers to the quiz.**

7 **Listen again. Are the statements true (T) or false (F)?**

1 Students go home every day when school finishes. T/F
2 It costs approximately £30,000 a year to study at Eton. T/F
3 The students have a special name for teachers. T/F
4 The Eton Wall Game is similar to football. T/F
5 There is an old school in England called Rugby School. T/F

8 SPEAKING **What about you?**

1 What schools are famous in your town or country?
2 In your opinion, is an all-boys school or an all-girls school a good thing? Why/Why not?

1 **Work with a partner. Look at the pictures and talk about them. Where are the people?**

5

2 LISTENING 1.17 **Listen to four people talking about education. Match the people (A–D) and the pictures in 1. There are five pictures but only four speakers.**

A ....

B ....

C ....

D ....

▶ STUDY SKILLS

Is it necessary to understand everything the first time that you listen to a text? STUDY SKILLS ▶ page 156

3 **Listen again. Answer the questions with A, B, C or D.**

Who…

1 is part of a big class? A/B/C/D
2 has a parent for their teacher? A/B/C/D
3 doesn't go to school every day because they work too? A/B/C/D
4 lives a long way from their teacher? A/B/C/D
5 doesn't have time to go to school? A/B/C/D
6 says they aren't happy with their classes? A/B/C/D

▶ Grammar in context

GRAMMAR GUIDE

Present simple negative

1 **Look at the sentences and complete the rules with *don't* or *doesn't*.**

a I **don't** have time to go to school.
b You **don't** talk to other students.
c He **doesn't** go every day.
d We **don't** walk to school.
e They **don't** live in a city.

1 After *he/she/it* we use ....
2 After *I/you/we/they* we use ....

After *don't* or *doesn't* we use the verb without *-s*.

GRAMMAR REFERENCE ▶ page 24

2 **Complete the sentences with *don't* or *doesn't*.**

1 I .... get up at six am.
2 Megan and Lucy .... watch football on TV.
3 Andy .... play football.
4 His father .... go to work by car.
5 You .... walk to school.
6 Ryan and I .... do our homework on Sunday.
7 That student .... listen to the teacher.
8 I .... clean my bedroom.

3 **Make the sentences negative.**

1 I go to school in a Ferrari.
I don't go to school in a Ferrari.
2 My cousin reads ten books a day.
3 My grandmother plays computer games.
4 Her parents watch TV at 7 am.
5 You speak French.
6 Sam and Leo go to bed at ten o'clock.
7 His brother makes the dinner.
8 She watches TV in the afternoon.

4 **Look at the pictures. Write sentences with the affirmative or negative form of the present simple.**

1

Lucas .... a big breakfast. (have)

2

My dad .... work at 3 o'clock. (start)

3

I .... at five o'clock. (get up)

4

At school we .... computer games. (play)

5

He .... to school by car. (go)

5a **Write true sentences about you and your routines. Use the words in the table to help you. Make the sentences affirmative or negative.**

I don't have a shower at night.
I have a shower in the morning.

Verb	Noun
play	TV
have	computer games
	school
get up	bed
watch	football
go to	shower
	lunch
do	homework

5b SPEAKING **Work with a partner. Read your sentences to your partner. Then tell the class about your partner.**

Anne doesn't have a shower at night.
She has a shower in the morning.

GRAMMAR GUIDE

Object pronouns

6a **Look at the sentences. Are the words in green and red subject or object pronouns?**

a She talks to **me**. I listen to **her**.
b They like **us**. We like **them**.
c He hates **you**. You don't like **him**.

6b **Match the subject and object pronouns in the table.**

Subject pronoun	Object pronoun
1 I	a you
2 you	b her
3 he	c it
4 she	d me
5 it	e them
6 we	f him
7 they	g us

GRAMMAR REFERENCE ▸ page 24

7 **Write the sentences again using an object pronoun.**

1 I like *Mary*. I like ....
2 She loves *football*. She loves ....
3 We listen to *our teachers*. We listen to ....
4 The teachers speak to *me and the other students*.
The teachers speak to ....
5 They hate *Mr Smith*. They hate ....

1 LISTENING 1.18 **Listen to a new student introducing himself to the class. Complete the notes with these words.**

art computer games fifteen PE school science tennis twenty university

Name: Adam Miller
From: Ontario, Canada
Parents' names: Jack and Alice Ontario, Canada
Brothers and sisters: Katie – (**a**) .... years old – studies at (**b**) ....
Olivia – (**c**) .... years old – studies at this (**d**) ....
Favourite subjects: (**e**) ...., (**f**) .... and music
Doesn't really like: (**g**) ....
After school: plays (**h**) ...., doesn't play (**i**) ....

2a What does Adam say to the teacher? Complete the dialogue with the sentences (1–6) below. One answer does not appear in the dialogue.

TEACHER: You're new in the class this year. Tell us something about yourself. What's your name and where are you from?
ADAM: (**a**) ....
TEACHER: Tell us about your family.
ADAM: (**b**) ....
TEACHER: What about school? What are your favourite subjects?
ADAM: (**c**) ....
TEACHER: What about physics and chemistry?
ADAM: (**d**) ....
TEACHER: And after school?
ADAM: (**e**) ....

1 I play tennis. I don't play computer games because I don't like them much.
2 I get up at quarter to eight. I have a shower and get dressed. I have breakfast and then I go to school by car with my dad.
3 My parents' names are Jack and Alice. I've got two sisters. Their names are Katie and Olivia. Katie is 20 years old. She studies at university. Olivia is 15. She comes to this school.
4 They're OK, but they aren't my favourite subjects. I don't really like science.
5 I love sport so I really like PE. And I like art and music. I'm good at art. I like drawing and painting.
6 My name's Adam, Adam Miller. I'm from Ontario, in Canada.

2b SPEAKING **Work with a partner. One of you is the teacher and the other is the student. Practise the completed dialogue.**

3 Look at the dialogue again and find an example sentence for each word in the Speaking Bank.

▸ Speaking Bank

Useful words for linking ideas

- Addition: *and* *I have a shower and get dressed.*
- Contrast: *but* ....
- Reason: *because* ....
- Consequence: *so* ....

4 Complete the sentences with *and, but, because* or *so*.

1 I love history .... I hate geography.
2 I don't like PE .... I'm very bad at sport.
3 I get up, I have a shower .... I get dressed.
4 My maths teacher is very good .... I understand everything.
5 I walk to school .... my house is just five minutes away.
6 I speak French .... I don't speak Spanish.
7 My friend is American .... she speaks English.

5a SPEAKING **Work in pairs. Student A: You are the teacher. Ask the questions in 2. Student B: You are the student. Use the information on page 167.**

5b When you finish, change roles. Student A: Use the information on page 167.

Practice makes perfect

6a SPEAKING **Make notes about your family, the school subjects you like/don't like and what you do after school.**

6b Work with a partner. One of you is the teacher and asks questions. The other person talks about themselves.

▸ EXAM SUCCESS

What topics connected with personal information are typical in a speaking exam? For example, your name, your age …

EXAM SUCCESS ▸ page 158

Developing writing *An informal email*

1 Read the email from Mark. Find Mark in the photo.

Message

From: Mark <Mark@mailnet.com>
To: info@mailpals.com
Subject: About me

Hi!

a My name's Mark Johnson. I'm from England. I've got two brothers. We live in Birmingham.

b Here's a photo of me with my family. I've got blue eyes and fair hair. My hair is short. I'm thin but I'm not very tall.

c I go to a big comprehensive school called Newfield. My favourite subjects are ICT and Spanish. I don't like maths or physics! I have Spanish on Mondays and Wednesdays. And I have physics on Tuesdays and Fridays.

d I get up at half past seven on school days. I walk to school because it's only ten minutes away. After school I play football. I have dinner with my parents at about half past six.

Write back soon. Tell me about yourself.

Best wishes,

Mark

2 Look at the email. Which paragraph (a–d) …

1 gives basic information about Mark and his family? ....
2 talks about Mark and school? ....
3 gives a physical description of Mark? ....
4 gives information about Mark's daily routine? ....

3a Look at the email again. When do we use capital letters in English? Choose the correct answers.

1 with names and surnames
2 with cities
3 with countries
4 with nationalities and languages
5 for members of the family
6 with days and months
7 with the first person singular pronoun
8 at the start of a sentence

3b Which rules for capital letters are different in your language?

4 Write the sentences again using capital letters where necessary.

1 the capital of scotland is edinburgh.
2 my name is susan johnson and i'm from australia.
3 his brother studies english in manchester.
4 is robert british or american?
5 on tuesday, i study french.

5 Look at Mark's email again and complete the information in the Writing Bank.

Writing Bank

Useful words and expressions in informal emails

- Begin with ....
- Use contractions, ..., not *I have got*.
- To finish, write *Write back* .... and *Best* ....

Practice makes perfect

6 Look at the task and write the email. Include all the information. Use Mark's email as a model and use capital letters and words and expressions from the Writing Bank.

You receive an email from a boy in England. Reply to the email. Include information about:

- your family
- your hair, eyes, etc.
- your likes and dislikes at school
- your routine

Language reference and revision

Grammar reference

Present simple affirmative

Form

Affirmative	I/You/We/They **start** at 9 o'clock. He/She/It **starts** at 9 o'clock.

Spelling

- We usually add **s** to the verb.
  like – likes walk – walks
- We add **es** to verbs that end in **-s, -sh, -ch, -x**
  watch – watches wash – washes
  kiss – kisses
- We add **es** to the verbs **go** and **do**.
  go – goes do – does
- With verbs that end in **consonant** + **y**, we omit the **y** and add **ies**.
  study – studies cry – cries
- With verbs that end in vowel + **y**, we add **s**.
  play – plays say – says

Use

We use the present simple to talk about:

1 regular habits and routines.
We study maths on Mondays.
He watches DVDs every weekend

2 permanent situations.
Teachers teach and students learn.
Babies cry if they are hungry.
I go to bed when I am ill.

Prepositions of time

We use:

in with parts of the day
in the morning, in the afternoon, in the evening
with months
in September, in December
with years
in 1999, in 2011

on with days
on Monday, on Sunday
with dates
on 20th January, 6th November

at with times
at 6 o'clock, at ten to eleven
with **night** and **the weekend**
at night, at the weekend

Present simple negative

Form

Negative	I/You/We/They **don't (do not) start** at 9 o'clock. He/She/It **doesn't (does not) start** at 9 o'clock.

- We use ***doesn't*** with the third person singular (***he/she/it***).
- After ***don't*** or ***doesn't*** we use the base form of the verb (without **-s**), e.g. ***go, clean, start***.

Object pronouns

Singular	Plural
me	us
you	you
him/her/it	them

Use

He watches it on TV.
He listens to me.
She talks to them.

Vocabulary

1 School subjects

art biology chemistry English
French geography German history
information and communication technology (ICT)
maths music physical education (PE)
physics Spanish

2 School activities

ask/answer a question
do homework
finish (school/classes)
have a break
have lunch
sit stand
start (school/classes)

3 Everyday activities

get (un)dressed get up go to bed
go to school by bike/bus/car/train
have a shower
have breakfast/lunch/dinner
make breakfast/lunch/dinner
play football/tennis/computer games
walk to school

4 Other words and phrases ▶ page 146

▶ Grammar revision

Present simple affirmative

1 Look at the pictures and write about what Ethan does on Sunday. Use the correct form of these verb phrases.

do homework get up go to bed
have a shower play football watch TV

1 Ethan and his friends

....
on Sunday morning.

2 Ethan

....
at half past ten on Sunday.

3 Ethan and his brother

....
at half past nine on Sunday.

4 Ethan

....
after football.

5 Ethan

....
on Sunday afternoon.

6 Ethan and his brother

....
at 7 pm on Sunday evening.

WORKBOOK ▶ page 12 / 6 points

Prepositions of time

2 Complete the sentences with *in*, *on* or *at*.

1 I get up .... ten o'clock.
2 .... Saturday I go to bed late.
3 I read .... night.
4 It's my birthday .... 7th February.
5 I have English lessons .... the evening.

WORKBOOK ▶ page 12 / 5 points

Present simple negative

3 Write sentences using the negative form of the present simple.

1 Usain Bolt/play tennis. ....
2 I/get up in the afternoon. ....
3 My parents/do homework. ....
4 We/go to school on Sunday. ....
5 You/finish school at 10 pm. ....
6 My grandfather/watch TV all day. ....

WORKBOOK ▶ page 15 / 6 points

Object pronouns

4 Look at the subject pronouns and write the correct object pronouns.

1 I .... 3 we .... 5 she ....
2 he .... 4 you .... 6 they ....

WORKBOOK ▶ page 15 / 6 points

▶ Vocabulary revision

School subjects

1 Write the school subjects that match the pictures.

1 
....

2 
....

3 
....

4 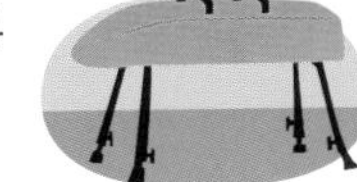
....

5 
....

6 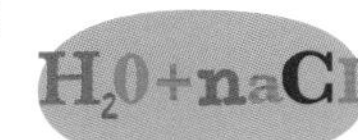
....

WORKBOOK ▶ page 10 / 6 points

School activities

2 Write verbs in the correct form to complete the activities.

1 Many people s.............. school at 9 o'clock in the morning.
2 When school f.............., the students go home.
3 A lot of students h.............. lunch at school.
4 I d.............. my homework in the evening.
5 After three classes, we h.............. a break.

WORKBOOK ▶ page 10 / 5 points

Everyday activities

3 Complete the everyday activities with vowels.

1 h...v... a sh...w...r
2 g... t... b...d
3 h...v... br...kf...st
4 m...k... d...nn...r
5 g...t ...ndr...ss...d
6 g... t... sch......l by b...s

WORKBOOK ▶ page 13 / 6 points

Total / 40 points

2 Time out

Grammar ▸ Present simple – questions and short answers ▸ Question words ▸ Adverbs of frequency ▸ Articles
Vocabulary ▸ Free-time activities ▸ Places to go in a town
Speaking ▸ Asking for information on the phone
Writing ▸ An announcement

▸ Vocabulary

Free-time activities

1a Work with a partner. Match the photos with some of these words. Check that you understand the other words.

chat online collect things dance do sport
draw go out with friends listen to music
play a musical instrument read surf the Internet
take photos watch films

1b 1.19 Listen and repeat.

2 What free-time activity or activities are associated with these words?

1. camera
2. pencil
3. CD
4. DVD
5. books, comics and magazines
6. guitar, piano
7. ball
8. computer

3 SPEAKING Tell your partner when you do the free-time activities in 1.

I surf the Internet at the weekend.

I read at night.

I don't collect things.

I listen to music when I do my homework.

4 LISTENING 1.20 Listen to four dialogues. Match the dialogues with the free-time activities (a–g).

1. Dialogue 1 ....
2. Dialogue 2 ....
3. Dialogue 3 ....
4. Dialogue 4 ....

a watching films
b listening to music
c surfing the Internet
d taking photos
e drawing
f chatting online
g dancing

5 Complete the sentences with true information about you and your free-time activities.

1. I love ....*doing sport*.... .
2. I like ....
3. I think .... is OK.
4. I don't like ....
5. I hate ....

6 SPEAKING Work with a partner. Compare your answers from 5. How similar are you?

I love surfing the Internet.

I like surfing the Internet but I love watching films.

1 Work with a partner. Look at the photo and the title of the text. What can you see? What do you think this person's hobby is?

STUDY SKILLS

How do photos, pictures and titles help you before you read a text? STUDY SKILLS ▸ page 156

2 Read this interview with the teenager in the photo. What is her hobby? Why is the book *Twilight* special for her?

Your hobbies

Emma, what's your special hobby?

I collect books.

Why do you collect books? Do you like reading?

Yes, I do. I love reading. But I don't read the books in my collection.

Why not?

I have two copies of my favourite books – one to collect and one to read.

Have you got a favourite book in your collection?

Yes, I've got a copy of *Twilight* by Stephenie Meyer. People pay $4,000 for this book now.

Why do people pay so much?

Because the book is very popular, especially because of the film. And this copy is very difficult to find. It's a first edition. It's got the author's signature and the date of the book's publication. Now there are millions of copies of *Twilight* in the world. But I think only seventy thousand copies exist of the first edition. The good thing is that these books aren't expensive if you buy them when they first appear.

How do you know if a book is a first edition?

On one of the first pages, the books usually have a list of numbers. For example, 2 4 6 8 10 9 7 5 3 1. If the list contains the number 1, it's a first edition.

Does your copy of *Twilight* have your name in it?

No, it doesn't. If a book has a name in it, other collectors don't want to buy it. But that isn't very important to me. This book is special for me because I love the story. I only collect books that I love reading.

3 Read the text again and choose the correct alternative.

1. Emma *likes/doesn't like* reading.
2. Emma's copy of *Twilight* *is/is not* valuable because it's one of the first copies.
3. New first editions *are/are not* normally very expensive.
4. A book with the numbers 4 6 8 10 9 7 5 3 *is/is not* a first edition.
5. Collectors *like/don't like* buying a book with another person's name in it.
6. Emma only *collects/doesn't collect* copies of her favourite books.

4 Match the underlined words in the text with the definitions.

1. how a person signs their name *signature*
2. when a book first appears
3. one of the first printed copies of a book
4. not easy or not simple
5. a group of things you collect
6. people who collect things

5 SPEAKING What about *you*?

Do you collect anything? What?

I collect comics.

I don't like collecting.

GRAMMAR GUIDE

Present simple – yes/no questions and short answers

1a Look at the questions and short answers. Match questions 1 and 2 with the answers (a and b).

1 **Do** you **like** reading?
2 **Does** the book **have** your name in it?

a Yes, it **does**./No, it **doesn't**.
b Yes, I **do**./No, I **don't**.

1b Are these sentences true (T) or false (F)?

1 We use **does** with *he/she/it* and **do** with the other subject pronouns. T/F
2 In questions, **do** or **does** comes before the subject. T/F
3 In short answers, we repeat the main verb. T/F

GRAMMAR REFERENCE ▸ page 36

2 Complete the questions with *Do* or *Does*.

1 .... you like reading?
2 .... your mum read magazines?
3 .... your friends read comics?
4 .... this book have your name in it?
5 .... people read a lot in your country?
6 .... you read when you have a break at school?
7 .... your teacher give you books to read for homework?

3 SPEAKING Work with a partner. Ask and answer the questions in 2. Use short answers to reply.

4a SPEAKING Look at these activities. Prepare questions to ask people in your class.

Do you get up at six o'clock?

4b Ask different people in the class the questions. Find a different person in the class for each activity. Write their name in the square.

GRAMMAR GUIDE

Present simple – wh- questions and question words

5a Look at the questions. Notice where question words like *Why*, *What* and *How* go in a question.

a **Why do** you **collect** books?
b **How do** you **know** if it's a first edition?

5b Look at the question words (1–7). Check that you understand their meaning.

1 Why?
2 How?
3 What?
4 Which?
5 Who?
6 When?
7 Where?

GRAMMAR REFERENCE ▸ page 36

6a Complete the questions with the correct word in 5b.

1 .... do you do at the weekend?
I go out with my friends.
2 .... do you go?
I go to the cinema.
3 .... do you go there?
Because I love watching films.
4 .... do you go there?
I go by bus.
5 .... do you go there?
Usually on Saturday evening, at about 6 o'clock.
6 .... do you go with?
I go with my friends, Steve and Maddy.
7 .... films do you watch, adventure or comedy?
We watch adventure films.

6b 1.21 Listen, check and repeat the questions.

7a SPEAKING Use some of the questions from 6 to interview your partner about what they do at the weekend. Prepare five more questions to ask your partner about what they do in their free time.

7b Ask your partner the questions.

7c Now tell the class about your partner.

Anne plays netball at the weekend. She plays at school. She also goes to …

Places to go in a town

1a **Work with a partner. Match the photos with some of these words. Check that you understand the other words. Use your dictionary if necessary.**

cinema fast-food restaurant library museum
park shopping centre sports centre
stadium swimming pool theatre

1b 🎧 1.22 **Listen and repeat.**

2a **Read the descriptions. Which places are described?**

1. You can buy things there. *shopping centre*
2. You can read books and take books out there.
3. You can watch films there.
4. You can eat burgers or pizzas there.
5. You can swim there.
6. You can play basketball or football there.
7. You can see a play or listen to concerts there.
8. You can watch football matches, sports events or concerts there.
9. You can see paintings and old objects and learn about history there.
10. You can walk, play sport, meet friends and see trees and flowers there.

2b 🎧 1.23 **Listen and check.**

3a PRONUNCIATION 🎧 **Listen to the words again and put them in the correct column.**

●	● • •	• ● •	● • • •	● ● • •
	cinema			fast-food restaurant

3b SPEAKING **Practise saying the words with the correct stress.**

4 SPEAKING **Tell your partner three places from 1 that you like and three places from 1 you don't like.**

I like the cinema but I don't like the theatre.

I like sport so I love going to the park.

Time out in New Zealand

Cross-curricular – Geography
New Zealand facts

1 **Work with a partner. Read this information about New Zealand. Can you find any information which is NOT correct? If you don't know, guess.**

2 LISTENING 1.24 **Listen to a radio programme about New Zealand. Find and change all the incorrect information in 1.**

3 **Now write correct information about New Zealand for these topics.**

1 Geographic location
2 Size
3 Capital city/other important cities
4 Geography of the country
5 Language(s)
6 National symbol(s)

4 **Work in groups. Each group should choose a different country.**

1 In your group, make notes on the topics in 3 for your country.
2 Each member of the group chooses one of the topics. Find out more information about the topic and look for pictures.
3 In your group, decide how to present your information to the rest of the class. Prepare it and present it.

New Zealand FACT FILE

- New Zealand is in the Atlantic Ocean.
- It is 2,000 kilometres from Australia.
- New Zealand has three big islands. Everyone calls the islands North Island, East Island and South Island. But officially, they do not have names.
- The capital city of New Zealand is Auckland.
- New Zealand is the same size as Italy or the United Kingdom.
- New Zealand has three mountains which are 3,000 metres high, or more. It also has a volcano.
- Abel Tasman, from the Netherlands, is an important person in the history of New Zealand. He is the first European to see New Zealand, in 1742. The name New Zealand comes from Zeeland, a province of the Netherlands.
- In 1769, the British explorer Captain Cook arrives in New Zealand. In 1840, New Zealand becomes a British colony. Today it is independent.
- The original people of New Zealand are called Maoris.
- The macaca bird is a symbol of New Zealand. People use this name for a fruit too, but this fruit is originally from China.
- 98% of people in New Zealand speak English. The second official language is Maori.

INSIDE INFORMATION

- New Zealand is one of only three countries in the world that has TWO national anthems. One is *God save the Queen*. The other is *God defend New Zealand*.
- A Maori native name for New Zealand is Aotearoa. It means Land of the Long White Cloud.

Culture
Free time in New Zealand

5 **Look at the people in the photos. Do you know any of them?**

6 **Look at the table. Read the text below and match the person with *what they do, what they are famous for* and *their photo*.**

Who?	What?	Famous for?	Photo?
1 Peter Jackson	the New Zealand rugby team	first person to get to the top of Mount Everest	a
2 Kiri Te Kanawa	a film director	the *Lord of the Rings* films	b
3 All Blacks	an actor	a special Maori dance called the Haka	c
4 Russell Crowe	an opera singer	the film *Gladiator*	d
5 The Flight of the Conchords	a music group	make funny songs	e
6 Sir Edmund Hilary	a climber	singing for 600 million people	f

Cinema in New Zealand

The film director Peter Jackson is from New Zealand. He is the director of the *Lord of the Rings* films.

The actor Russell Crowe was born in New Zealand. He has an Oscar for the film *Gladiator*. He now lives in Australia.

Sport in New Zealand

New Zealanders love sport. Rugby is the unofficial national sport. The New Zealand rugby players are called the All Blacks because they wear black shirts. Before they play, they do a Maori dance called the Haka.

Cricket and swimming are popular, and extreme sports are popular too. New Zealand is the home of bungee jumping!

Climbing mountains is another popular hobby. Sir Edmund Hillary, the first man to climb Everest, was born in New Zealand.

Music in New Zealand

Kiri Te Kanawa is a very famous opera singer from New Zealand. She comes from a Maori family. She is famous for singing at the wedding of Prince Charles and Princess Diana in front of 600 million people!

The Flight of the Conchords is a comedy music group from New Zealand. They are very popular in Britain and the USA.

WORD BOOSTER

Match the words and pictures.

1 rugby 2 bungee jumping 3 climb 4 funny

a 
b 
c 
d 

7 SPEAKING **What about *you*?**
Look at the question. Make notes about your answers. Then talk to your partner.

Think about people from your country who are famous for cinema, sport and music. Who are your favourites and why?

I like Roger Federer because he's a very good tennis player.

Listening

1 SPEAKING Work with a partner. Think of a typical Saturday morning. What do you do? Where do you go?

I play football on Saturday morning.

EXAM SUCCESS

In this listening exercise, you match people with the correct information. Why is it important to read the names and information BEFORE you listen?

EXAM SUCCESS ▸ page 158

2 LISTENING 1.25 Listen to two people talking about where their friends go on Saturday morning. Match the people (1–5) with the places (a–e).

1 Sam	a shopping centre
2 Matthew	b park
3 Ben	c museum
4 Isabel	d sports centre
5 Sophia	e library

3 Look at the information. Which person in 2 does each sentence describe? Listen again if necessary.

1 This person always plays basketball on Saturday morning. ....
2 This person never swims on Saturday morning. ....
3 This person often does his homework in a library. ....
4 This person hardly ever goes to the sports centre. ....
5 This person sometimes goes to the park. ....

Grammar in context

GRAMMAR GUIDE

Adverbs of frequency

1a Look at the sentences. The words in bold say how often we do something. We call them adverbs of frequency. Put them in order from 0% to 100%.

1 I **always** go to the library.
2 I **never** go to the library.
3 I **often** go to the library.
4 I **usually** go to the library.
5 I **hardly ever** go to the library.
6 I **sometimes** go to the library.

0%
a *never*
b ....
c ....
d ....
e ....
f ....
100%

1b Look at the sentences and choose the correct alternative.

a I'm **always** here.
b They **never** walk to school.
c He's **usually** here.

1 Adverbs of frequency come before/after *to be*.
2 Adverbs of frequency come before/after main verbs (e.g. *go, swim, play*).

GRAMMAR REFERENCE ▸ page 36

2 SPEAKING Work with a partner. Ask and answer the questions. Answer with *Yes* or *No* and an adverb of frequency.

1 Do you go to the theatre? *Yes, sometimes.*
2 Do you walk to school?
3 Do you go to bed at 11 pm?
4 Do you make your breakfast?
5 Do you do your homework on Sunday?

3 Write the sentences again with an adverb of frequency in the correct place. Make the sentences true for you.

1 I dance. *I hardly ever dance.*
2 I go to the theatre.
3 I am late for class.
4 I do my homework.
5 I go out with my friends on Friday.

4a SPEAKING Work with a partner. Guess your partner's answers in 3. Write them down.

I think Maria often dances.

4b See if you are correct.

I think you often dance.

No, I never dance!

4c Tell the class about you and your partner.

Maria never dances but I often dance.

GRAMMAR GUIDE

Articles

5a Look at the sentences and complete the rules with *a/an* or *the*.

a I go to **a** sports centre.
b **The** sports centre is in Cannon Street.

1 We use .... the first time we talk about something.
2 We use .... when we mention something again, for the second or third time.

5b Put these expressions in the correct columns below.

play basketball/tennis/football
play the guitar/piano/violin
watch TV
see a film
at night
in the morning/afternoon/evening
have breakfast/lunch/dinner
go to school/work/church
at the weekend

Article (*a/an, the*)	*No article*
play the guitar/piano/violin	play basketball/tennis/ football

GRAMMAR REFERENCE ▸ page 36

6 Complete the sentences with *the, a, an* or no article (0).

1 I have .... favourite restaurant. .... restaurant is in King Street.
2 Why don't we watch .... TV tonight?
3 My brother plays .... violin.
4 I don't go to .... school on Saturday.
5 I play in .... basketball team. The name of .... team is the Giants.
6 They play .... football on Friday.
7 Where do you go at .... weekend?
8 I don't want to read. I want to watch .... exciting film.

7 Look at the pictures. What do the people usually do on Saturdays? Write sentences. Do you need *a/an, the* or no article (0)?

1 go/work

2 play/piano

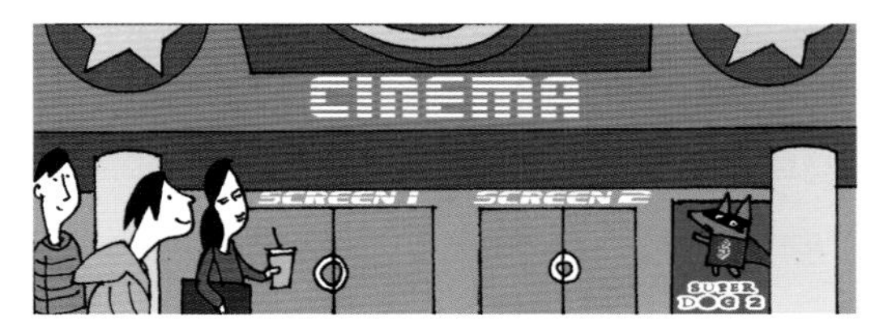

3 see/film

4 eat/lunch/in/Italian restaurant

5 play/basketball

6 watch/TV

8 Read the sentences and correct the mistakes with articles.

1 He goes to school at weekend.
2 I've got a computer. But a computer is quite old.
3 My sister plays the guitar on the Saturday.
4 She plays the tennis at a big sports centre.
5 We usually watch TV in evening.
6 I read a book before I go to sleep at the night.
7 Ann: Have you got the brother?
Ben: Yes, I've got one brother and one sister.

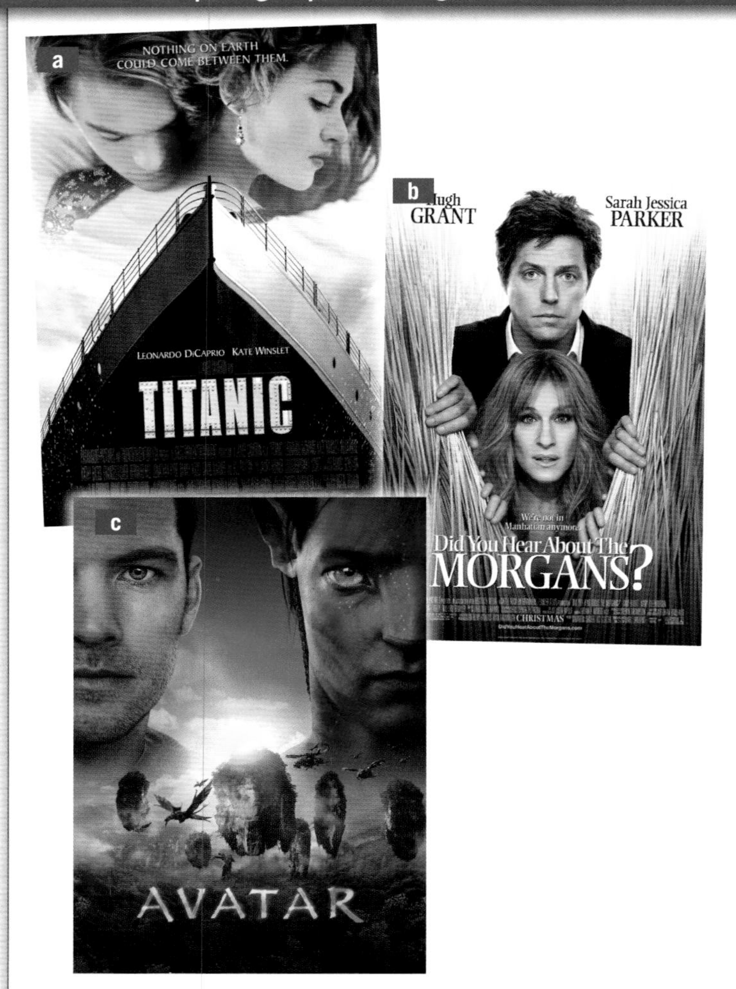

1 SPEAKING **Work with a partner. Look at the film posters. Do you know the films? Which film do you prefer?**

2a LISTENING 1.26 **Listen to a girl making a telephone call to a cinema. Complete the dialogue.**

INFORMATION DESK: Good afternoon. This is Neon Cinema.
KATE: Good afternoon. I'd like some information, please.
INFORMATION DESK: Certainly. How can I help you?
KATE: Can you tell me what time the new (**a**) .... film is on?
INFORMATION DESK: Yes, let's see. It's on at 4.20, (**b**) .... and (**c**) ....
KATE: Sorry, can you repeat that?
INFORMATION DESK: Yes, of course. 4.20, (**d**) .... and (**e**) ....
KATE: How long is the film?
INFORMATION DESK: One hour and (**f**) .... minutes.
KATE: Uh-huh. How much are the tickets?
INFORMATION DESK: Adults are (**g**) £...................., and children under 15 are (**h**) £.....................
KATE: OK. Thanks for your help.
INFORMATION DESK: You're welcome. Thank you for calling.

2b SPEAKING **Work with a partner. Student A is Kate and Student B is the information desk. Practise reading the dialogue out loud.**

3 **Complete the expressions in the Speaking Bank. Who says them – the person asking for information (A) or the person giving information (G)?**

Speaking Bank

Useful expressions to ask for and give information on the phone

- I'd .... some information, please.
- How can I .... you?
- Can you .... me what time the film starts?
- How .... is the film?
- How .... are the tickets?
- Thanks for .... help.
- .... welcome.
- .... you for calling.

Practice makes perfect

4a SPEAKING **Work with a partner. Look at the task and use the diagram below to prepare the dialogue.**

You are in the UK. You want to see a film. Ring the cinema for information about the film. Tell them the title and find out:

- times
- the length of the film
- the price of the tickets for adults and for children

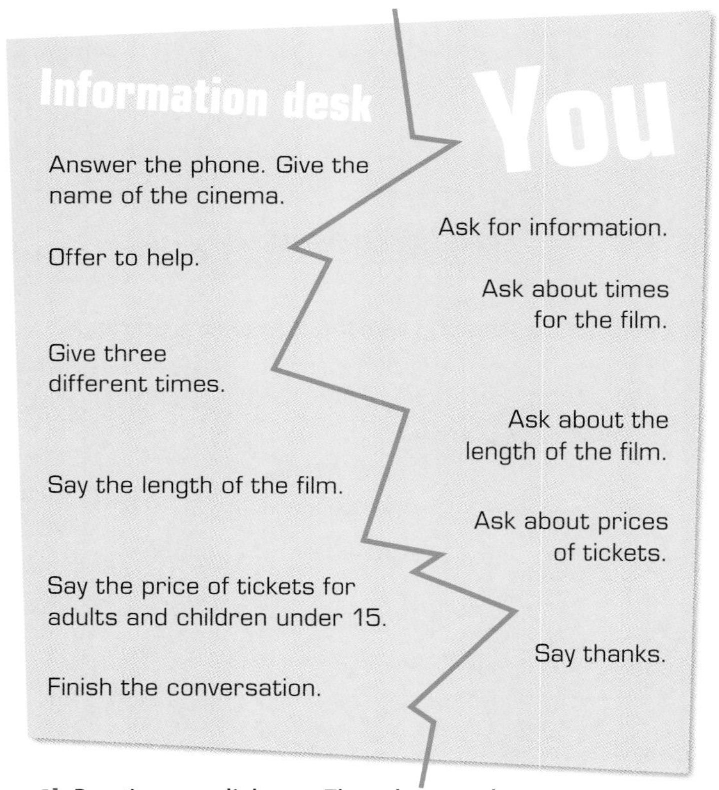

4b **Practise your dialogue. Then change roles.**

STUDY SKILLS

What can you do to practise speaking English as much as possible?
STUDY SKILLS ▸ page 156

1 Read the two announcements. Which club do you prefer? Why?

The School Book Club

Do you like reading? If you do, come and join the School Book Club now!

We meet once a week to talk about new books. Bring a book and tell us about it!

The School Book Club meets in the school library on Wednesday at 5 pm.

For more information, call Charlotte on 0761 327 4997 or visit our new website.

Mark's Music Club

Are you mad about music? If the answer is yes, Mark's Music Club is the place for you!

We usually meet on Friday at 6 pm, at Mark's house. Bring your favourite CDs and introduce us to your favourite groups or singers. The idea is to start our own radio station. So why not be a DJ for the day?!

Call Mark on 0234 765 9753

Don't sit there! Call him NOW!

2 Read the announcements again and answer these questions.

	The School Book Club	Mark's Music Club
1 Where does the club meet?	*The school library*	
2 When does the club meet?		
3 What do they do in the club?		
4 How do you get more information about the club?		

3 Put these sentences from the announcements in the correct place in the Writing Bank.

1 We usually meet on Friday at 6 pm, at Mark's house.
2 Don't sit there!
3 Bring a book.
4 Are you mad about music?
5 Call him now!

Writing Bank

Useful language in announcements

- Use short questions to make people interested.
  (a) ....
- Give the essential information in clear sentences.
  (b) ....
- Use imperatives. They tell people what to do.
  (c) .... and (d) .... Or they tell people what not to do. (e) ....

4 Look again at the announcements in 1. Underline all the imperatives that you find.

Practice makes perfect

5a Work with a partner and choose a club. Look at the task. Decide what information to include.

> Write an announcement for a club. The club can be for any free-time activity, for example sport, computers, photography, art, films, dance, collecting ...
> Include information about:
> - where you meet
> - when you meet
> - what you do
> - how you can get more information
>
> Write 50–70 words.

5b Individually, write your announcement. Use the announcements in 1 and the Writing Bank to help you.

5c Display your announcements in the classroom. Which clubs are popular?

EXAM SUCCESS

Does your announcement contain all the necessary information and the correct number of words?

EXAM SUCCESS ▸ page 158

Language reference and revision

Grammar reference

Present simple – yes/no questions and short answers

Form

Yes/no questions	**Do** I/you/we/they **work**? **Does** he/she/it **work**?
Short answers	Yes, I/you/we/they **do**. No, I/you/we/they **don't**. Yes, he/she/it **does**. No, he/she/it **doesn't.**

Use

- We only use **does** with *he/she/it*.
- **Do** and **Does** come before the subject.
  Does the book... ? Do I... ?
- In short answers we do not repeat the main verb.
  Do you work? Yes, I do.

Present simple – wh- questions and question words

Form

Wh- questions	**Where** do I/you/we/they work? **Why** does he/she/it work?

- *Wh-* questions contain question words like **who**, **what**, **which**, **where**, **when**, **why**, **how**.
- The question word comes at the start of the question.

Adverbs of frequency

Use

- We use adverbs of frequency to say if something happens often or not.
- The usual position for adverbs of frequency is before the main verb.
  I usually walk to school.
- Adverbs of frequency go after the verb *to be*.
  I'm always happy.
  He's often at home.

100%
always
usually
often
sometimes
hardly ever
never
0%

Articles

A/An

- We use **a/an** when we mention something for the first time, or to say that the person or thing is one of a number of things or people.
  I go to a sports centre. I often watch a film on Saturday.

No article

- We do not use an article when we are talking about people or things in general.
  I like music. Films are good.
- We do not use an article in these cases.
  play basketball/football/tennis
  have breakfast/lunch/dinner
  go to school/work/church
  watch TV
  at night

The

- We use **the** to talk about something or somebody mentioned before.
  I go to a sports centre. The sports centre is really big.
- We also use **the** to talk about a specific thing.
  The film on TV tonight is great.
- We also use **the** in these cases.
  play the guitar/piano/violin
  in the morning/afternoon/evening
  at the weekend

Vocabulary

1 Free-time activities

chat online collect things dance do sport draw go out with friends listen to music play a musical instrument read surf the Internet take photos watch films

2 Places to go in a town

cinema fast-food restaurant library museum park shopping centre sports centre stadium swimming pool theatre

3 Other words and phrases ▶ page 147

Grammar revision

Present simple – questions, question words and short answers

1 Complete the sentences.

BETH: (**a**) .... you go to school on Saturday morning?
JAKE: No, I (**b**) ....
BETH: (**c**) .... do you do?
JAKE: I watch TV or I read.
BETH: (**d**) .... do you watch TV?
JAKE: Because I love watching films.
BETH: (**e**) .... your brother like watching films?
JAKE: Yes, he (**f**) ....
BETH: Does he (**g**) .... football?
JAKE: No, he (**h**) .... He hates it.

WORKBOOK ▶ page 20

/ 8 points

Adverbs of frequency

2 Put the words in order to make sentences. Then put the sentences in order of frequency. 1 = 100%, 6 = 0%.

a watch TV I never ☐
b magazines She usually reads ☐
c bus by go sometimes They ☐
d We ever hardly school to walk ☐
e is happy Joe always ☐
f my are friends My house often at ☐

WORKBOOK ▶ page 23

/ 6 points

Articles

3 Choose the correct alternative.

1 I usually play *the/0* football.
2 My sister plays *the/a* guitar.
3 I go to *0/the* school at quarter to nine.
4 Excuse me. Have you got *a/the* pencil?
5 *A/The* pencil on the table is Mike's.
6 We have *0/the* breakfast at eight o'clock.

WORKBOOK ▶ page 23

/ 6 points

Vocabulary revision

Free-time activities

1 Complete the sentences with these words.

collect comics draw instrument
online sport surfs takes
to watches with

1 He .... photos with a digital camera.
2 I want to play a musical .... one day.
3 She likes listening .... music.
4 I like using the computer and chatting ....
5 At the weekend I go out .... my friends.
6 He always .... the Internet on Saturday.
7 They .... football shirts from around the world. They've got fifty!
8 She likes doing .... – basketball, tennis, table tennis …
9 My sister .... two or three films at the weekend – on TV and at the cinema.
10 I .... pictures in my free time. I use special pencils.
11 He doesn't read books but he likes ....

WORKBOOK ▶ page 18

/ 11 points

Places to go in a town

2 Write the names of the places.

1
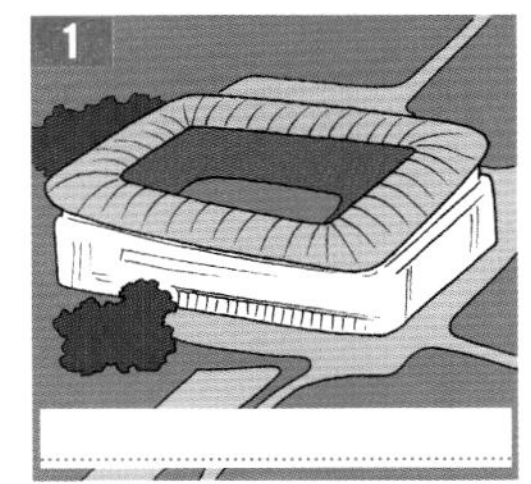
....

2

....

3

....

4

....

5

....

6

....

7

....

8

....

9

....

WORKBOOK ▶ page 21

/ 9 points

Total ***/ 40 points***

Gateway to exams *Units 1–2*

Reading

Tip For Reading Exams

In *True/False/Not mentioned* activities, remember …

To answer the questions, look for the information in the text. Do not answer with your opinion.

EXAM SUCCESS ▶ page 158

1 Read about this school.

1 Why is the school special?
2 Do you like the school? Why/Why not?

Every summer, 15-year-old Luke Jones goes to school. But he doesn't study maths, English or history at this school. The school is a special football academy and Luke studies how to play football. Football is Luke's favourite free-time activity. One day, he wants to be a professional football player.

Luke's parents take him to the academy. It's inside a special sports centre. But his mum and dad don't stay because the teachers don't want parents to watch the lessons.

Luke's first lesson begins at 9 o'clock. It's a training session. Luke does exercises with the ball. At 11 o'clock, the students stop and have water, fruit and an energy bar. From 11.45 to 12.45, they play football again. At 12.45, Luke and his friends have lunch.

After lunch, from 1.45 to 2.30, they don't play football. They play other sports. But from 2.30 to 3.30, they have a football match. Then it's time to have a shower and go home. Luke usually goes home by bus. In the evening Luke watches football on TV or he sometimes plays one of his computer games. It's always a computer game about football, of course!

2 Read the text again. Are these sentences true (T) or false (F) or is the information not mentioned (NM) in the text?

1 Luke doesn't like maths, English or history. T/F/NM
2 Luke goes to the academy by bus. T/F/NM
3 Luke has his football lessons in a sports centre. T/F/NM
4 Luke's mum and dad watch him in the training sessions. T/F/NM
5 Luke and the other students have a break in the morning. T/F/NM
6 They don't play football in the afternoon. T/F/NM
7 Luke has his shower at home. T/F/NM
8 Luke has three football computer games. T/F/NM

3 **What about *you*?**

The football academy is Luke's idea of a perfect school. What is a perfect school for *you*?

▶ Listening

▶ Tip For Listening Exams

In matching activities, remember …

Read the names and information BEFORE you listen. They can give you an idea of what will appear in the conversation.

EXAM SUCCESS ▶ page 158

4 1.27 Listen to Mel and her dad talking about presents that she has got for her friends. Match the presents A–H with the friends 1–5.

PRESENTS	FRIENDS	
A book	Mark	1
B digital camera		
C CD	Simon	2
D pencils		
E DVD	Pat	3
F comics		
G computer game	Jenny	4
H ball	Barbara	5

5 **What about *you*?**

Look again at the presents. Which one is your favourite? Why?

▶ Speaking

▶ Tip For Speaking Exams

In activities where you give personal information, remember …

Be prepared to say and spell your name and to talk about your age, where you are from, where you live, school, your typical routine, your likes and dislikes …

EXAM SUCCESS ▶ page 158

6 Match the beginnings of the questions (1–8) with the ends (a–h).

1 How do you spell your	**a** to school?
2 Are you	**b** your free time?
3 What time do you	**c** British?
4 How do you go	**d** subjects?
5 What subjects do	**e** at the weekend?
6 What are your favourite	**f** you study?
7 What do you do in	**g** start school?
8 Where do you go	**h** surname?

7 Work with a partner. Take it in turns to ask and answer the questions in 6.

▶ Writing

▶ Tip For Writing Exams

In writing exams, remember …

Put all the necessary information in your text and write the correct number of words.

EXAM SUCCESS ▶ page 158

8 Write an informal email to a friend. Describe somebody in your family. Include this information:

- name and description (age, hair, eyes …)
- free-time activities – likes
- free-time activities – dislikes

Write 50–70 words.

▶ 'Can Do' Progress Check

CEF

1 **How well can you do these things in English now? Give yourself a mark from 1 to 4.**

1 = I can do it very well.
2 = I can do it quite well.
3 = I have some problems.
4 = I can't do it.

a I can talk about routine actions using the present simple. ☐
b I can ask for and give basic personal information. ☐
c I can talk about school and everyday activities. ☐
d I can understand simple texts about life at school. ☐
e I can write a short informal email. ☐
f I can say how often I do things using adverbs of frequency. ☐
g I can talk about what I do and where I go in my free time. ☐
h I can understand short texts about free-time activities. ☐
i I can ask for basic information on the phone. ☐
j I can write short announcements. ☐

2 **Now decide what you need to do to improve.**

1 Look again at my book/notes.
2 Do more practice exercises. ⇨ WORKBOOK page 26–27
3 Ask for help.
4 Other: ____________

3 Coming home

Grammar ▸ *There is/There are* ▸ Prepositions of place ▸ Present continuous
Vocabulary ▸ Rooms ▸ Household objects and furniture ▸ Jobs around the house
Speaking ▸ Expressions on the phone
Writing ▸ Describing a place

▸ Vocabulary

Rooms

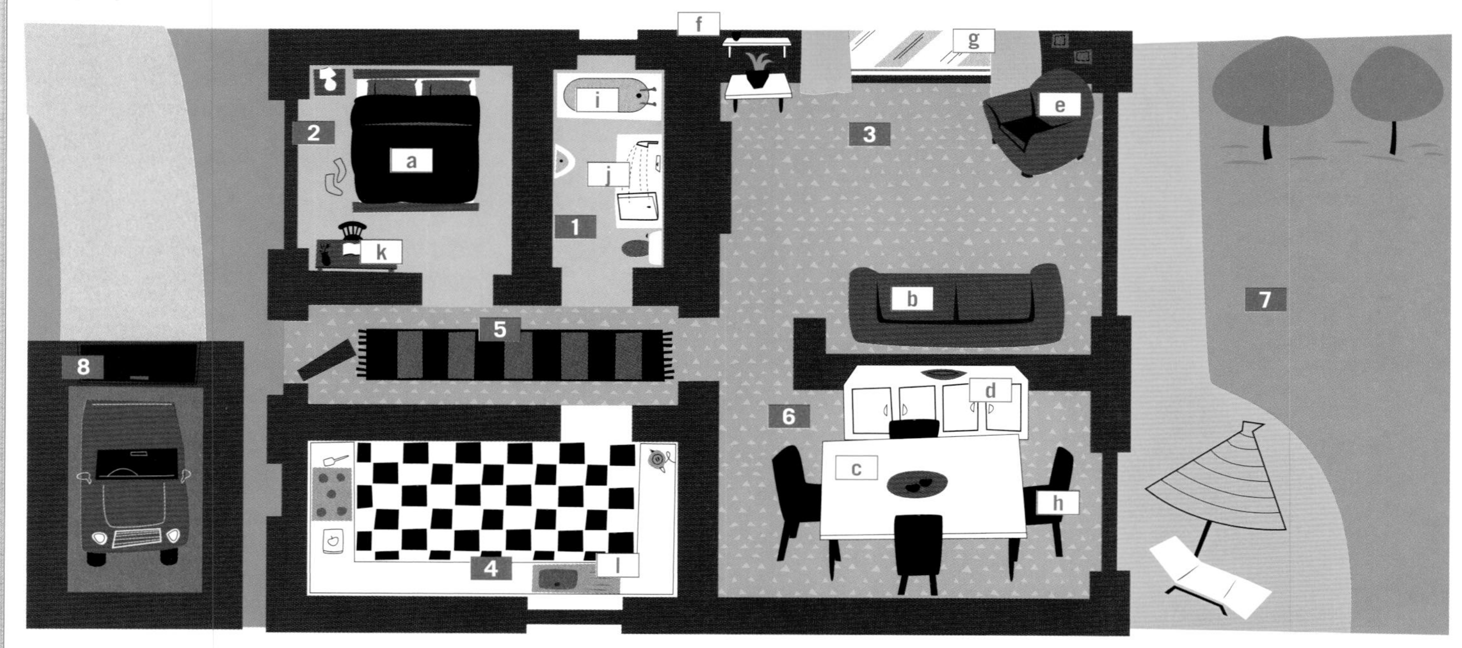

1a Work with a partner. Match the rooms (1–8) with these words.

bathroom bedroom
dining room garage garden
hall kitchen living room

1b 1.28 Listen and repeat.

2 Name the rooms.

1 You cook there.
2 You have a shower there.
3 It's outside. Children play there. It usually has flowers.
4 When you go into a house, you are there.
5 You put the car there.
6 You watch TV there.
7 You sleep there.
8 You eat there.

3 SPEAKING Work with a partner. Tell your partner what rooms your house or flat has or hasn't got.

My flat has got six rooms. It's got two bedrooms. It hasn't got a garden …

Household objects and furniture

4a SPEAKING Work with a partner. Match the objects (a–l) in the picture with some of these words. Use your dictionary if necessary.

armchair bath bed CD player chair clock computer cooker
cupboard desk DVD player fridge games console lamp/light
microwave phone poster radiator shelf shower sink sofa
table toilet TV washing machine window

4b 1.29 Listen and repeat.

4c Where do you find these objects in your house?

I've got a CD player in my bedroom, and a clock. I think we've got clocks in all the rooms.

We haven't. We've got a clock in the living room and the kitchen. And the CD player is in the living room.

5 LISTENING 1.30 Listen to someone describing their flat. Complete this diagram with the furniture and objects that they have.

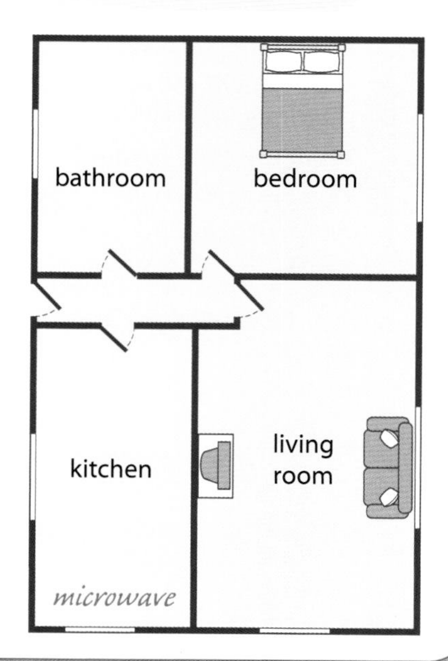

6 SPEAKING Work in small groups. Talk about what you've got in your bedroom.

I've got a desk and two chairs …

▸ STUDY SKILLS

Do you write down new vocabulary? Where do you write it? How do you organise the vocabulary? STUDY SKILLS ▸ page 156

Reading

1 Work with a partner. Look at the photos and answer the questions.

1 Which part of the world do you think this woman lives in?
2 What type of house do you think she's got?

2 Read the text and check your answers in 1.

AT HOME WITH ELLEN LONG

Ellen Long is a famous American actress and model. Her husband, Ricardo Medál, is a top football player. They have a spectacular new home in Dallas. (5)

Ellen knows what she likes in a house. She loves coffee cups on the table, shoes next to the bed. She doesn't like people who say: 'Oh, look at this beautiful sofa – but don't sit down, (10) don't sit down!' When she sees a space where there aren't pictures or lamps, she always puts something there. Ellen also loves colour. She likes rooms to have purple or yellow walls. (15)

There are six bedrooms and seven bathrooms in her house. Here Ellen answers questions about the house.

EXCLUSIVE INTERVIEW!

Do you collect anything?
(20) Yes. I've got three or four hundred shoes!

What is there to read in your living room?
A Spanish magazine called (25) 'Football Today'. Ricardo is Spanish.

What is there in your garage?
My car, of course! I've got a lovely little sports car.

(30) **Is there a cinema in your house?**
Yes, there is. And in the cinema, there's a big statue of an alien. It's from a film and Ricardo loves it.

3 Read the text again. Does Ellen (not Ricardo) like these things or not? Put the line where you find the answer.

1 shoes
2 football magazines
3 statues of aliens
4 colourful walls
5 spaces in the house where there are no pictures or lamps
6 objects on tables, not inside cupboards or wardrobes

4 Look at the underlined words in the text. What do you think they mean? Check in your dictionary.

5 SPEAKING What about *you*?

What do you think of Ellen's house and her ideas about houses?

I'm similar to Ellen. I like comfortable houses.

And I like big houses!

GRAMMAR GUIDE

There is/There are

1 Look at the sentences and complete the table.

1 **There's** a big statue of an alien.
2 **There are** five bedrooms in her house.
3 No, **there aren't**.
4 **There aren't** pictures or lamps.
5 **Is there** a cinema in your new house?
6 Yes, **there is**.

	Singular	Plural
Affirmative	(a)	(b) ....
Negative	**There isn't** a swimming pool.	(c) ....
Question	(d)	**Are there** five bedrooms?
Short answer	(e) ..../ No, **there isn't**.	Yes, **there are**./ (f) ....

GRAMMAR REFERENCE ▶ page 50

2 Complete the sentences about the room that you are in now. Use *is, are, isn't* or *aren't*.

1 There .... a blackboard.
2 There .... fifty chairs.
3 There .... an armchair.
4 There .... three computers.
5 There .... a clock on the wall.
6 There .... a sink.
7 There .... more than fifteen desks.

3a SPEAKING Prepare questions to ask your partner about their living room.

Is there a computer in your living room?
Are there pictures in your living room?
How many pictures are there?

3b Use the questions to interview your partner. Then tell the class about your partner's living room.

GRAMMAR GUIDE

Prepositions of place

4 Match the sentences (a–h) with the pictures (1–8).

There's a cat ...

a **on** the table.
b **under** the table.
c **near** the table.
d **behind** the table.
e **in front of** the table.
f **next to** the table.
g **in** the sink.
h **above** the table.

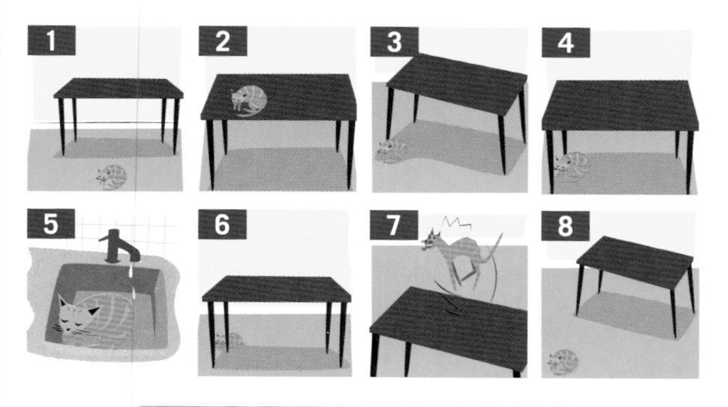

GRAMMAR REFERENCE ▶ page 50

5 Read about Tony Hawk's house. Choose the best word (A, B or C) for each gap.

Tony Hawk is the king of skateboarding. So it's no surprise that there (**1**) .... a big skate park next (**2**) .... his house. He likes basketball too. There (**3**) .... two basketball courts. And he has an outdoor swimming pool. Tony likes relaxing (**4**) .... the water. There's (**5**) .... really big living room in the house, with three different games consoles, all connected to an enormous plasma TV. Tony spends a lot of time (**6**) .... the TV because he loves playing new computer games. He always has lots of skateboard games (**7**) .... the table – they're his favourite!

	A	B	C
1	A is	B are	C isn't
2	A of	B to	C in
3	A aren't	B isn't	C are
4	A on	B in	C to
5	A a	B 0	C the
6	A under	B on	C in front of
7	A on	B in	C under

EXAM SUCCESS

In this type of exercise, there is a text with spaces. You fill the spaces in the text with one of three words. Is it a good idea to stop and think about the spaces the first time you read? Why/Why not?

EXAM SUCCESS ▶ page 158

6 Look at picture A and complete the sentences with the correct prepositions.

1 The cat is .... the chair.
2 The cupboard is .... the fridge.
3 The table is .... the fridge.
4 There are two books .... the table.
5 The microwave is .... the cupboard.
6 The mouse is .... the cupboard.

7 SPEAKING Work with a partner. Look at pictures A and B. What differences can you find?

In picture B, there isn't a cat under the chair. But there is a dog under the table.

Jobs around the house

1a Work with a partner. Match the pictures with some of these phrases. Check that you understand the other phrases.

cook   do the ironing   do the shopping
do the washing   lay the table   make the bed
take the rubbish out   tidy up   wash the dishes

1b 1.31 Listen and repeat.

2 Write six sentences saying how often you do these jobs around the house. Make two of your sentences *false*.

I always take the rubbish out.
I usually make my bed.

3 SPEAKING Work in small groups. Say your sentences. Can the other students guess which two sentences are false?

I always take the rubbish out.

I think it's false. I think you hardly ever take the rubbish out.

You're right!

INSIDE INFORMATION

- There are three basic styles of house in Great Britain: detached (when a house is independent from other houses), semi-detached (when two houses are together), and terraced (when the houses are all in a line).
- Another typical type of house is a bungalow. This is a one-storey house where all the rooms are on the same level.
- People also live in flats. These are a set of rooms on one floor of a big building. We call this building a block of flats.

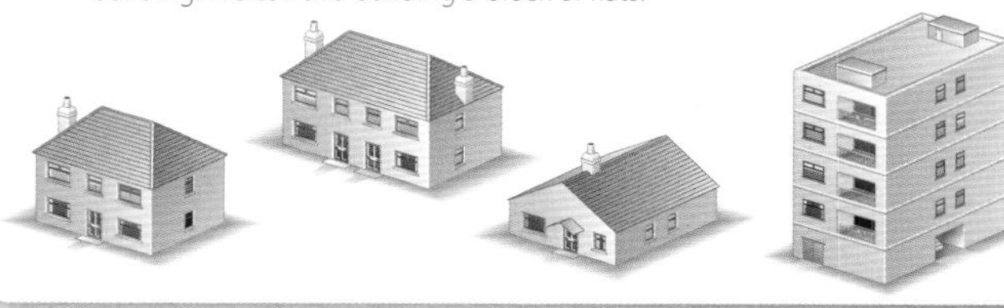

International cultural knowledge
An Englishman's home

1 **Look at the photos of different British homes. Work with a partner. Say which you like and dislike.**

2 LISTENING 1.32 **Listen to people talking about where they live. Put the photos in 1 in the order that you hear about them.**

1 .... 2 .... 3 .... 4 ....

▸ WORD BOOSTER

Match the words with the photos in 1.

1 hall of residence ....
2 cottage ....
3 semi-detached house ....
4 houseboat ....

3 **Listen again. Which person (Speaker 1–4) ...**

1 says there are 15,000 people in a similar situation to them? ....
2 has only got one room? ....
3 lives in a very small village? ....
4 uses a kitchen with other people? ....
5 has lots of friends where they live? ....
6 has got three bedrooms and two gardens? ....
7 lives in a place with 120 people? ....

4 SPEAKING **What about *you*?**

1 Which types of house are similar or different to houses in your country?
2 Which type of house is similar to yours?

We've got semi-detached houses and blocks of flats.

We haven't got houseboats.

Cross-curricular – Science
Eco-homes

5 Work with a partner. Look at the pictures and find these things. Use your dictionary if necessary

glass	grass	plants	pollution	nature	the Sun
ventilation	water tank				

6 Read this text. Match each paragraph (1–4) with a picture (a–d).

1 Earth is our home. But it has problems with pollution. That's why the British government wants the houses of the future to be eco-homes that help nature.

2 Eco-homes often have plants or grass on them so that they are part of nature. The plants and grass are also good because they make the house warm in the winter and cool in the summer. Some new eco-homes have plants on them that produce food!

3 Houses need energy to make radiators, cookers and other household objects work. Eco-homes usually have lots of glass and windows. The sun passes through the windows, makes things inside the house warm and gives the house energy. In the summer, eco-homes aren't hot because they use natural ventilation. Air comes through the big, open windows and makes the house cool.

4 Grey water is important in eco-homes. There is usually a big tank in the house or in the garden. The tank holds the grey water, which is old water from the shower, sink or washing machine. Eco-homes use this water again, for example in the toilet, or for the garden.

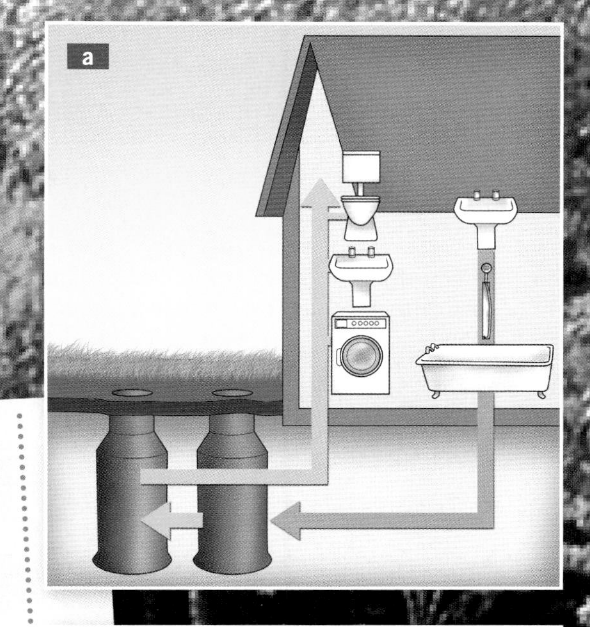
a

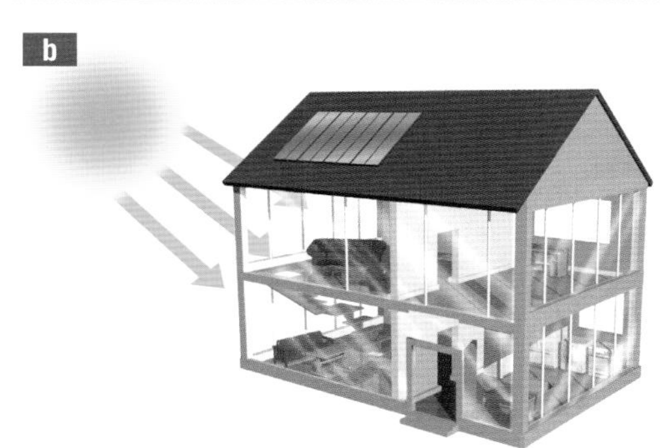
b

c

d

▸ WORD BOOSTER

Match the words and descriptions.

1	warm	a	40ºC
2	winter	b	20ºC
3	cool	c	10ºC
4	summer	d	period of the year when it is hot
5	energy	e	period of the year when it is cold
6	hot	f	electricity or other type of power

7 Read the text again and answer the questions.

1 Why are eco-homes good?
2 Why is it good to have plants and grass on a house?
3 Why do eco-homes have a lot of glass and windows?
4 What is grey water?
5 Why is grey water useful?

8 What about *you*?

1 Do you think eco-homes are a good idea? Why/Why not?
2 Do you know any eco-homes?

I think that eco-homes are a good idea but they're very unusual!

1 **Work with a partner. Describe the pictures. What can you see?**

STUDY SKILLS

How can looking at the pictures help you when you listen to a text? STUDY SKILLS ▸ page 156

2a LISTENING 1.33 **Listen to four dialogues and tick (✓) the correct picture. There is one question for each dialogue.**

1 What is Sarah doing at the moment?

2 What are Danny and Mike doing?

3 What is Matt doing?

4 What is Olivia doing on the computer?

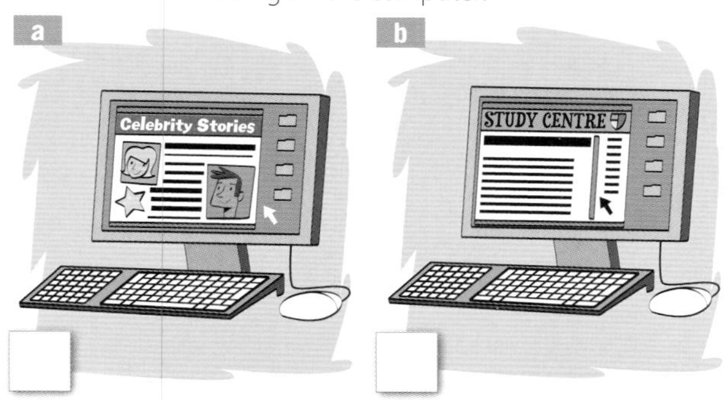

2b **Listen again and check your answers.**

GRAMMAR GUIDE

Present continuous

1 Look at the sentences and choose the correct alternative.

a I**'m** cook**ing** pasta with tomatoes.
b You**'re** read**ing** about your favourite actor.
c We **aren't** play**ing** computer games.
d **Are** you us**ing** the computer?
e Yes, I **am**./No, I**'m not**.

1 We make the present continuous with the verb be/have and the *-ing* form of the main verb.
2 We use the present continuous to talk about routines/things that are happening now.

GRAMMAR REFERENCE ▸ page 50

2a Look at the spelling rules for the *-ing* form of the verb.

Most verbs: add *-ing*	Verbs ending in consonant + *e*: take away *e* and add *-ing*	Some verbs ending in one vowel + one consonant: double the consonant and add *-ing*
play – playing	*write – writing*	*run – running*
cook – cooking	*make – making*	*swim – swimming*

2b Now write the *-ing* form of these verbs in the correct place in the table.

chat dance do eat have put sit
study take tidy wash

3a PRONUNCIATION 1.34 **Listen to the pronunciation of the *-ing* form of the words in the table. Do we say PLAYing or playING?**

3b **Listen again and repeat the words with the correct stress.**

4 Look at the picture and write about what the people are doing. Use these verbs in the present continuous.

cook do the ironing draw eat play tennis
read a magazine take the rubbish out
wash the dishes

1 Dexter ....
2 Hannah ....
3 Lucas and Isaac ....
4 Jason ....
5 Josh ....
6 Megan and Katie ....
7 Billy ....
8 Emma and Poppy ....

5 Put the words in order to make questions.

1 doing are Emma What and Poppy?
2 drawing Billy is What?
3 Lucas Isaac basketball Are playing and?
4 Hannah Is the rubbish out taking?
5 is Jason doing What?
6 eating Emma What is?
7 Who doing is the ironing?
8 Dexter is What doing?

6 SPEAKING Work in small groups. One person asks the questions in 5. The others answer but *do not look* at the picture.

What are Emma and Poppy doing?

I think they're eating.

No, I think they're cooking.

1 LISTENING 1.35 **Listen to three phone conversations. In which conversation is it possible for Jessica to speak to Tom? What problems does she have in the other two conversations?**

2 **Listen again and complete the conversations with the sentences below.**

CONVERSATION 1

MR. HARRIS:	(a) ....
JESSICA:	Hello. Is that Mr. Harris?
MR. HARRIS:	(b) ....
JESSICA:	Hello. This is Jessica, Tom's friend. (c) ....
MR. HARRIS:	No, he isn't. He's having his piano lesson at the moment.
JESSICA:	(d) ....
MR. HARRIS:	Yes, of course.
JESSICA:	Can you tell him to call me?
MR. HARRIS:	OK.
JESSICA:	Thanks.

1 Is Tom there? 2 Can I leave him a message?
3 Yes, speaking. 4 Hello, 453 720.

CONVERSATION 2

LEO:	Hello?
JESSICA:	Hello. (a) ....
LEO:	No, it's Leo.
JESSICA:	Oh, hi, Leo. It's Jessica. (b) ....
LEO:	Yes, he is. (c) .... I'll get him.
JESSICA:	Thanks.

1 Is Tom there?
2 Hang on a minute.
3 Is that Tom?

CONVERSATION 3

MAN:	Hello. 453 736.
JESSICA:	Tom? Is that you? (a) ....
MAN:	Sorry. (b) ....
JESSICA:	Tom, Tom Harris.
MAN:	Sorry. (c) ....

1 Who are you calling?
2 You've got the wrong number.
3 This is Jessica.

3a 1.36 **Look at these telephone numbers. Listen to how we say them.**

1 0161 482 6530 =
oh one six one, four eight two, six five three oh
2 0253 669 5558 =
oh two five three, double six nine, double five five eight

3b **Listen again and repeat the numbers.**

4 SPEAKING **Work with a partner. Take it in turns to say these telephone numbers.**

1 0649 445 6777
2 9866 328 8822
3 9219 0042 6519
4 7511 1165 0862

5a SPEAKING **Write down three phone numbers.**

5b **Say your numbers to your partner. Can they write them down correctly?**

6 **Look at the expressions in the Speaking Bank. Who says them – the person making the call (C) or the person who is answering the phone (A)?**

Speaking Bank

Useful expressions on the phone

- Hello, 677 432856. ....
- Hello, is that Ann? ....
- Yes, speaking./No, it's Isabel. ....
- Is Katy there? ....
- Sorry, you've got the wrong number. ....
- Hang on a minute. I'll get him/her. ....
- Can I leave a message? ....
- Do you want to leave a message? ....

Practice makes perfect

7a SPEAKING **Work with a partner. Do this role-play using the phone expressions from the Speaking Bank.**

Student A: You are Monica's sister/brother. Look at page 167.
Student B: You are Monica's friend. Look at page 160.

7b **Now change roles and do the role-play again.**

1 Imagine your ideal bedroom. Would you like to have these objects in your room? Give a mark from 0 to 5 for each object (0 = I don't want it, 5 = I really want it).

1 posters	☐	5 a DVD player	☐
2 a computer	☐	6 a games console	☐
3 a TV	☐	7 a microwave	☐
4 a CD player	☐	8 a fridge	☐

2 SPEAKING Work with a partner. Compare your answers. Are there other things you would like in an ideal bedroom?

3 Four British teenagers describe their ideal bedrooms. Read the descriptions. Who wants the bedroom in the photo?

4 SPEAKING Work with a partner. Tell them which bedroom you like. Tell them which bedroom you don't like. Explain your decisions.

I like Charlie's bedroom because I like playing computer games.

I love the cinema bedroom! I like watching films and eating popcorn.

5 Look at the Writing Bank. Complete the list of adjectives that appear in the descriptions. Check that you understand them. Use your dictionary if necessary.

Writing Bank

Using adjectives

- Adjectives help us to write interesting descriptions. Here are some useful adjectives to describe a place:
  ideal, enormous, spectacular, big,
  ……………………………………
- Adjectives usually come:
  before the noun they describe:
  It's a spectacular swimming pool.
  after the verb *to be*:
  The swimming pool is spectacular.

Practice makes perfect

6a Look at the task.

> An English magazine wants teenagers to describe their ideal bedrooms. Write an article about your ideal bedroom. Include information about the furniture and other objects.

6b Write your article. Remember to use adjectives to describe the room and the furniture.

EXAM SUCCESS

When you finish writing a text in an English exam, what things do you need to check before you give it to the teacher?

EXAM SUCCESS ▸ page 158

We wanted to know what the ideal teenager bedroom was like so we spoke to four teenagers about their dream room. We wanted to know about size, objects, furniture… everything! Well, we got four very different answers…

Emma
My ideal bedroom has got enormous windows and a spectacular view of a big swimming pool. When I wake up, the first thing I do is swim in the pool.

Jasmine
My ideal bedroom has got bright pink walls and an armchair. I sit in the armchair in the morning, open my notebook and write stories. I listen to beautiful music on my CD player and when I open the window I always hear birds singing.

Charlie
On the walls of my ideal bedroom I've got posters of my favourite football players and on my desk there's a huge computer with Internet access. Next to the desk there are two sofas for my friends when they come and visit me. There's a TV and a games console. When my friends are here, we play.

Edward
My ideal bedroom is a cinema. I've got a really comfortable bed. On the wall there's an enormous TV connected to a DVD player. Next to my bed there's a fridge with cold drinks. There's also a microwave to make popcorn!

Language reference and revision

Grammar reference

There is/There are

Form

	singular	plural
Affirmative	**There's** a bedroom.	**There are** two bedrooms.
Negative	**There isn't** a kitchen.	**There aren't** two kitchens.
Question	**Is there** a bedroom?	**Are there** two bedrooms?
Short answers	Yes, **there is**./No, **there isn't**.	Yes, **there are**./No, **there aren't**.

Prepositions of place

on

under

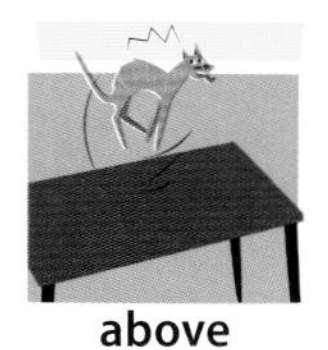

above

near

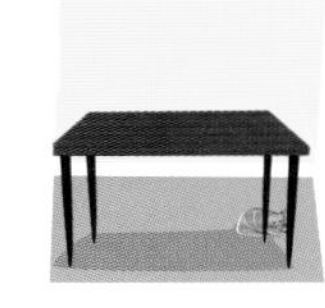

behind

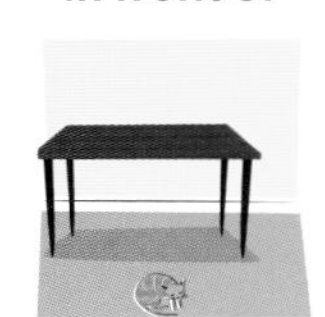

in front of

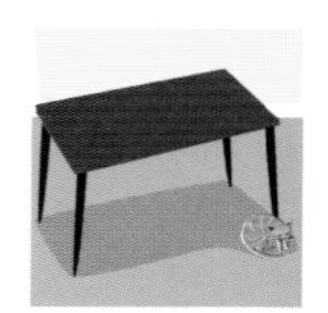

next to

in

Present continuous

Form

Affirmative	subject + **am/are/is** + verb+**-*ing*** *We're tidying up.*
Negative	subject + **am not/aren't/isn't** + verb+**-*ing*** *She isn't cooking.*
Question form	**Am/Are/Is** + subject + verb+**-ing**? *Are they making the bed?*
Short answers	Yes, subject + **am/are/is**. No, subject + **am not/aren't/isn't**. *Yes, I am.* *No, they aren't.*

Spelling

See page 161 for rules about spelling the **-*ing*** form.

Use

- We use the present continuous to talk about actions that are happening now.
  She can't answer the phone. She's doing her homework.

Vocabulary

1 Rooms

bathroom
bedroom
dining room
garage   garden
hall   kitchen
living room

2 Household objects and Furniture

armchair   bath   bed   CD player   chair   clock
computer   cooker   cupboard   desk   DVD player
fridge   games console   lamp/light   microwave
phone   poster   radiator   shelf   shower   sink
sofa   table   toilet   TV   washing machine
window

3 Jobs around the house

cook   do the ironing
do the shopping   do the washing
lay the table   make the bed
take the rubbish out   tidy up
wash the dishes

4 Other words and phrases ▶ page 148

Grammar revision

There is/There are

1 Look at the picture and complete the sentences with *There is, There are, There isn't* or *There aren't*.

1 .... a poster of a rock group.
2 .... three mobile phones.
3 .... a CD player.
4 .... two dogs.
5 .... two tables.
6 .... a lamp.
7 .... an armchair.

WORKBOOK ▶ page 30   **/7 points**

Prepositions of place

2 Look at the picture in 1. Are the sentences *true* (T) or *false* (F)? Change the prepositions in the false sentences.

1 The mobile phones are on the table. T/F
2 The games console is on the table. T/F
3 The dogs are in the sofa. T/F
4 The lamp is behind the sofa. T/F
5 The sofa is under the poster. T/F
6 The armchair is behind the sofa. T/F

WORKBOOK ▶ page 30   **/6 points**

Present continuous

3 Complete the sentences with the present continuous form of the verbs given.

1 A: Where's Joe?
B: He .... (have) a shower.
2 Kate isn't here at the moment. She .... (take) the rubbish out.
3 Ethan and I .... (not watch) the TV. We .... (read) a magazine.
4 .... you .... (surf) the Net?
5 A: .... your mum .... (cook) the dinner?
B: Yes, she ....

WORKBOOK ▶ page 33   **/7 points**

Vocabulary revision

Rooms

1 Which room do you usually use for these activities?

1 making the breakfast: ....
2 eating with family and friends: ....
3 having a shower: ....
4 entering the house: ....
5 watching TV: ....
6 parking the car: ....

WORKBOOK ▶ page 28   **/6 points**

Jobs around the house

2 Complete the jobs around the house with these words.

do do lay make take tidy wash

1 .... the rubbish out
2 .... the shopping
3 .... up
4 .... the table
5 .... the bed
6 .... the dishes
7 .... the washing

WORKBOOK ▶ page 31   **/7 points**

Furniture and household objects

3 Write the names of the objects.

1 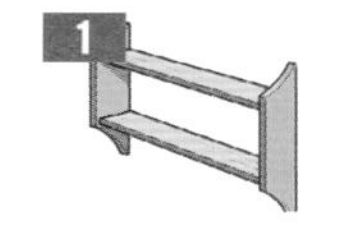 ....
2 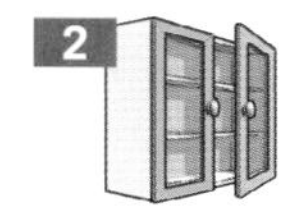 ....
3  ....
4 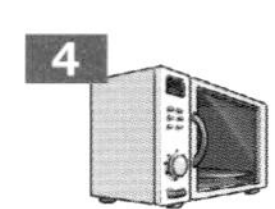 ....
5  ....
6 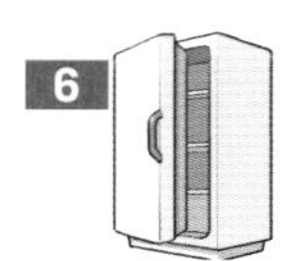 ....
7  ....

WORKBOOK ▶ page 28   **/7 points**

Total   **/40 points**

4 Body building

Grammar ▸ *Can/Can't* ▸ Adverbs of manner ▸ *Have to/Don't have to/Must/Mustn't*
Vocabulary ▸ Parts of the body ▸ Basic physical activities ▸ Sports
Speaking ▸ Giving directions
Writing ▸ A questionnaire

▸ Vocabulary

Parts of the body

1a Work with a partner. Match the parts of the body with these words.

arm back chest ear eye face finger
foot hand head leg mouth neck nose
shoulder stomach toe tooth

1b 1.37 Listen and repeat.

2 Complete the sentences with parts of the body.

1 On the end of your leg is your ....
2 On the end of your foot you have five ....
3 Adults usually have 32 ....
4 You use your .... to listen.
5 You use your .... to read.
6 On the end of your arm is your ....
7 Your hand has five ....
8 When you eat, the food goes to your ....

Basic physical activities

3 Work with a partner. Match the pictures with some of these words. Check that you understand the other words. Use your dictionary if necessary.

climb dive fall hit jump kick rest
ride (a horse/bike) run skate ski swim

4 LISTENING 1.38 Listen. What activities do you hear?

1 ....
2 ....
3 ....
4 ....
5 ....
6 ....
7 ....

5 Write down one or more physical activities you associate with these words. Use your dictionary if necessary.

1 mountains *climb, ski, fall*
2 triathlons
3 football
4 the winter
5 water
6 martial arts
7 the holidays

6 SPEAKING Work in small groups. Read out the activity or activities for one of the words in 5. Who can guess the word?

run, dive, swim, ride a bike, rest.

Triathlons?

Yes.

Reading

1 Read this text and choose a good title.

1. How avalanches start
2. How to survive an avalanche
3. Accidents in the mountains

....

OK, so you can ski really well and you can climb mountains easily. But, can you survive an avalanche? Avalanches are when snow suddenly falls down a mountain. 150 people die in avalanches each year. People usually start them by accident when they are skiing or climbing in the mountains.

There are things that you can do to survive an avalanche. First, always check the weather carefully before you go to the mountains. Take rescue signals or transmitters. They help people to know where you are. And take decisions about what to do before an avalanche starts. When the avalanche comes, you can't talk about what to do; there's no time.

When the avalanche begins, the first thing to do is to leave all your things as fast as you can. Skis or a big, heavy bag can pull you down under the snow. Next, move your hands, arms and legs and start 'swimming'. You do this to stay above the snow. If possible, jump to one side to escape the avalanche. And when the avalanche comes, close your mouth. Snow can get in quickly and stop you from getting air.

If the snow covers you, make a space in front of your mouth immediately so that you can breathe. If you can, put your arms up above the snow to show people where you are. If you can't, wait calmly and patiently. Don't shout and don't panic. People can't hear you when you're under the snow.

STUDY SKILLS

What is important when you read a text for the first time: to understand everything or to get a general understanding of what the text is about? STUDY SKILLS ▸ page 156

2 Read the text again and choose the best answers.

1. What is an avalanche?
   a. Another name for snow.
   b. A person who can climb mountains easily.
   c. When snow suddenly falls down a mountain.
2. What is the usual cause of avalanches?
   a. Snow and wind.
   b. People doing sport and other activities.
   c. People who fall down the mountain.
3. Why is it important to take decisions before the avalanche starts?
   a. Because the weather often changes.
   b. Because you need to decide to bring your skiis.
   c. Because when the avalanche begins it's difficult to speak.
4. When the avalanche arrives, it's a good idea to …
   a. jump up and down.
   b. take off your equipment.
   c. call to members of your group.
5. When you are under the snow, the important thing is to …
   a. have air.
   b. make people hear you.
   c. keep moving.

EXAM SUCCESS

Look at your answers in 2. Have you got an answer for each question? EXAM SUCCESS ▸ page 158

3 Work with a partner. Why does the text talk about …

1. skiing? *Some people start avalanches when they are skiing.*
2. carrying big bags?
3. swimming?
4. jumping?
5. waiting?

4 Match the underlined words in the text with the definitions.

1. say something so a lot of people can hear you
2. weighing a lot
3. in a relaxed, slow way
4. to happen without being planned
5. things that send or communicate messages
6. go away from a bad or difficult situation

5 SPEAKING What about *you*?

Do you like snow and the mountains? Why/Why not?

I like snow and the mountains because I like skiing.

I don't like skiing but I like snow in winter.

GRAMMAR GUIDE

Can/Can't

1 Look at the sentences and decide if the statements below are *true* (T) or *false* (F).

a You **can** ski really well.
b People **can't** hear you when you're under the snow.
c **Can** she climb mountains?
d Yes, she **can**./No, she **can't**.

1 The forms of **can/can't** do not change with different subject pronouns *I, you, he, she, we, they.* T/F
2 We use **do/does** to make questions with *can.* T/F
3 We use **can/can't** to talk about ability and possibility. T/F

GRAMMAR REFERENCE ▸ page 62

2a PRONUNCIATION 1.39 **Listen to these sentences. Which sound is long, *can* or *can't*?**

1 I **can** speak Spanish.
2 I **can't** speak Spanish.

2b 1.40 **Listen to the sentences. Put a tick (✓) if the people can do the activity. Put a cross (✗) if they can't.**

1 .... 2 .... 3 .... 4 .... 5 ....

2c 1.41 **Listen and repeat the sentences.**

1 I can read.
2 I can't get up at six.
3 We can't understand.
4 John can do his homework.
5 We can speak English.

3 Complete the sentences with *can* or *can't* and these verbs.

chat cook hit play play ride swim

1 My sister .... I never eat the things she makes.
2 My friend .... the guitar but he isn't in a group.
3 I .... tennis. I don't have a racket and I don't know the rules.
4 Jamie and Becky .... under the water. They go 15 metres without air!
5 You .... the ball with your hand in football.
6 Liam is only four but he .... a bike. He's good at it.
7 We .... online at home because we haven't got a computer.

4a SPEAKING **What *can* or *can't* you do? Write the activities in the correct column. Use these words.**

climb cook draw play ride a bike/horse
sing skate ski speak German swim

	I CAN	I CAN'T
MY PARTNER CAN		
MY PARTNER CAN'T		

4b Work with a partner. Ask your partner questions to find out what they *can* or *can't* do. Write the activities in the correct squares.

Can you cook?

Yes, I can./ No, I can't.

GRAMMAR GUIDE

Adverbs of manner

5 Look at the sentences and answer the questions.

a You can ski really **well**.
b You can climb mountains **easily**.
c Check the weather **carefully**.
d Leave your things **fast**.
e Snow can get in **quickly**.
f Wait **calmly** and **patiently**.

1 Do adverbs of manner describe *how* we do something or *how often* we do something?
....
2 Do adverbs of manner go with the verb *to be* or with other verbs?
....
3 What are the two last letters in regular adverbs?
....
4 Are these adverbs regular or irregular?
well fast hard late early
....

GRAMMAR REFERENCE ▸ page 62

6 Complete the sentences with adverbs from the adjectives given.

1. He does exams very .... (fast). He finishes in ten minutes and the other students finish in one hour.
2. He does exams really .... (bad). He only gets one out of ten!
3. Our train leaves at half past eight. Let's wait .... (patient) in this room.
4. He rides his bike .... (slow) and .... (careful) because he doesn't want to have an accident.
5. It's important to dance really .... (good) if you want to work as a dancer.
6. She works very .... (hard) – from 9 to 5, six days a week.

7a SPEAKING Write six questions using adverbs of manner. You can use these adverbs or ones of your choice.

badly calmly carefully fast hard patiently
quickly slowly well

Can you sing well?
Do you usually wait patiently?
Do you ride your bike carefully?

7b Interview another student with your questions.

Can you sing well?

Yes, I can.

Do you usually wait patiently?

No, I don't.

Sports

1 Work with a partner. Match the photos with some of these words. Check that you know the other sports. Use your dictionary if necessary.

baseball basketball cycling fishing
football golf gymnastics ice skating
judo netball rugby sailing
table tennis tennis volleyball

a

b

c

d

e

2 Which sports in 1 do we usually play

1. with a ball?
2. with a racket?
3. with a bat?

3 SPEAKING Work with a partner. Ask and answer the questions.

1. What is your favourite sport?
2. Which sport(s) can you play well?
3. Which sport(s) do you like watching?
4. Which sport(s) do you hate?
5. Who is your favourite sports star or team? Which sport do they do?

Fitness and exercise

Cross-curricular – Physical Education (PE)

Basic concepts

1 Look at the picture. What are the children doing? Do you have a similar class?

2 Work with a partner. Look at these concepts. They are all very important in PE. Do you know what the concepts are? Guess.

1 Aerobic exercise
2 Anaerobic exercise
3 Cool down
4 Heart rate
5 Warm up

3 Read definitions of the concepts in 2 from a PE textbook. Match the concepts 1–5 with the definitions A–E on the right. Use a dictionary if necessary.

4 Read the definitions again. Are these statements *true* (T) or *false* (F)?

1 It is important to stretch before *and* after you do sport. T/F
2 Jogging for 30 minutes is an anaerobic exercise. T/F
3 If you cycle for 20 minutes at medium speed, your body has enough oxygen. T/F
4 Your resting heart rate is similar to your minimum heart rate. T/F
5 Running fast is a good way to warm up. T/F

▸ WORD BOOSTER

Match the words and definitions.

1	heart	a	your heart makes sounds and movements
2	breathing	b	the organ in your chest that pumps blood
3	stretching	c	slowly, little by little
4	period	d	how fast something is
5	beats	e	the process of taking air in and then letting it out
6	speed	f	making parts of your body as long as possible
7	gradually	g	an amount of time

5 SPEAKING What about *you*?

1 Do you think you are fit at the moment? Why/Why not?
2 Do you always warm up and cool down when you do physical exercise?

I don't think I'm very fit.

Why not?

Because I hardly ever do exercise. I'm tired after five minutes!

A We do this after physical exercise. The idea is to slow down our heart and our breathing. It also helps stop problems after exercise. A good way to do this is by running very slowly and gently. Then do gentle stretching.

B This means exercise with oxygen. The body has enough oxygen to do this type of activity for a long period. The exercise is gentle. An example of this type of exercise is swimming slowly for 30 minutes.

C This means exercise without oxygen. The body has not got enough oxygen to do this type of activity for a long period. An example of this type of exercise is running 100 metres as fast as possible.

D This is the number of times your heart beats in a minute. Your resting heart rate is your minimum heart rate when you are relaxed and doing nothing. Your maximum heart rate is the top speed of your heart when you are doing exercise.

E We do this before physical exercise. The idea is to make your muscles warm, to gradually make your heart go fast, and to make your muscles and joints flexible. Stretching and slow, gentle running can help.

i INSIDE INFORMATION

- PE classes in the UK are usually a mixture of practice and theory.
- Common sports in UK secondary schools are swimming, cricket, gymnastics, netball and athletics.
- Secondary students have 90 minutes of PE a week. Some students join after school sports clubs and play football, rugby and hockey.

Popular culture

We got the beat by The Go-Go's

6 Read this short text about music and exercise and answer the questions.

1 How does music help us to do intense physical activity?
2 When is fast music good?
3 Why is slow music good?
4 How can music help us to reduce the oxygen we breathe?
5 How can music motivate us?

Music helps with physical exercise in different ways.

It helps you to think positively. Very hard and intense exercise feels easy with music!

Fast music helps to give you energy before doing sport. Slow music can calm you and help you to concentrate.

You can match the tempo of the music to the tempo of the physical exercise. This controls your movement and can help you to reduce the oxygen you need.

Music can motivate you. The words of some songs are very positive. Sometimes, songs help you to remember moments in films that make you feel good.

▸ WORD BOOSTER

fall in line *get in a line, one person after another*
hang out *go out with friends*
hang around *wait*
quarter after twelve *(American) quarter past twelve*
go-go music/pony/watusi *types of music or dance*
trance *a state caused by hypnosis*
chance *opportunity, possibility*

7 Read the words to the song. Do you think the music will be fast or slow? Read the word booster to check the vocabulary.

See the people walking down the street
Fall in line just watching all their feet
They don't know where they wanna go
But they're walking in time

They got the beat
They got the beat
Yeah
They got the beat

See the kids just getting out of school
They can't wait to hang out and be cool
Hang around 'til quarter after twelve
That's when they fall in line

Kids got the beat
They got the beat
They got the beat
Yeah
Kids got the beat

Go-go music really makes us dance
Do the pony, puts us in a trance
Do the watusi, just give us a chance
That's when we fall in line

We got the beat
We got the beat
We got the beat
Yeah
We got the beat

Everybody get on your feet
We know you can dance to the beat
Jumping, get up
Round and round and round

INSIDE INFORMATION

- This song is from 1981 and is by a group called The Go-Go's.
- The Go-Go's were the first all-woman band to write their songs, play their instruments and have a number one record.
- The song has 150 beats per minute. Experts say this is great for running and fast exercise.

8 1.42 Listen to the song. Do you think this is a good song for physical exercise? Why/Why not?

9 What about *you*?

1 Do you like this song? Why/Why not?
2 Do you listen to music when you do sport or exercise? Why/Why not?

I like the song. It's quite fast.

Yes, and the words are positive.

Listening

1 **Work with a partner. Look at the photo of a Kin-ball game and talk about what you can see. How do you think you play Kin-ball? Guess.**

2 **Read the notes about Kin-ball. What type of information do you think is missing?**

The ball has a diameter of (a) ....

It (b) .... heavy. The colour of the ball is usually (c) ....

There are (d) .... teams in a Kin-ball match. Players have to wear black, (e) .... or (f) ....

When you defend, you must keep the ball in the (g) .... It mustn't hit the (h) ....

A complete Kin-ball match is (i) .... minutes long.

3a LISTENING 1.43 **Listen to two people talking about Kin-ball and complete the notes.**

3b **Listen again and check your answers.**

4 SPEAKING **What about *you*?**

Would you like to play Kin-ball? Why/Why not?

I'd like to play. It looks really fun!

Grammar in context

GRAMMAR GUIDE

Have to, don't have to, must, mustn't

1 **Look at the sentences and complete the statements with *have to, don't have to, must* or *mustn't*.**

a You **have to** play with a really special ball.

b You **don't have to** buy anything to play, just the ball.

c The person who hits the ball first **must** shout *omnikin*.

d The ball **mustn't** hit the floor.

1 We use .... and .... for things that are necessary or obligatory.

2 We use .... for things that are not necessary (but we can do them if we want).

3 We use .... for things that we can't do because we don't have permission.

GRAMMAR REFERENCE ▸ page 62

2 **Complete the sentences with *have to, has to, don't have to* or *doesn't have to*.**

1 You .... be good at football to become a professional.

2 A football player .... be especially tall.

3 Professional football players .... know all the rules of the game.

4 You .... be a boy to play football.

5 Professional footballers .... play football 365 days a year.

6 A professional football player .... run a lot.

7 Professionals .... have short hair.

3 Look at the statements about volleyball and choose the correct alternative.

1 You must/mustn't kick the ball.
2 You must/mustn't hit other players.
3 You must/mustn't respect other players.
4 You must/mustn't follow the rules of the game at all times.
5 The ball must/mustn't go over the net.
6 Players must/mustn't run and hold the ball in their hands.

4 Read the sentences. Write N if the sentence describes a necessary action, NN if it describes an action that is not necessary, or CD if it describes an action that we can't do.

1 You don't have to run fast. *NN*
2 Football players often have to travel.
3 You mustn't play ball sports here.
4 You must do all the exercises.
5 You mustn't kick the other players.
6 Each team has to have eleven players.
7 You don't have to wear a red shirt.

5a SPEAKING Work with a partner. Look at the photos. What rules do you know for these sports? Write sentences with *have to, don't have to, must, mustn't, can* and these words.

ball bat foot hand head hit kick
minutes racket run team touch wear

5b SPEAKING Tell the class your sentences about one of the sports. Can they guess the sport?

6 Look at the sentences and choose the correct alternative. If you think two alternatives are correct, mark both of them.

1 Usually we has to/have to/don't have to go to school on Monday.
2 You must/mustn't/don't have to smoke at school.
3 You must/mustn't/have to study hard to be a doctor.
4 At our school we doesn't have to/don't have to/mustn't wear a uniform.
5 You has to/have to/must speak English in English lessons if you want to speak well.
6 You mustn't/must/don't have to break school furniture.
7 Usually a student hasn't to/doesn't have to/don't have to use a computer to do exams.
8 Students must/don't have to/mustn't hit each other.

7a SPEAKING Work with a partner. Prepare true sentences to talk about things that are necessary, not necessary or not permitted at your school. Use the correct forms of *have to* and *must*. Think about clothes, furniture, sports, excursions, eating and drinking ...

You mustn't arrive late. You have to wear a uniform.

7b Compare your ideas with other students. Do you have the same sentences?

1 SPEAKING **Work with a partner. Match the pictures with these phrases.**

Go past (the cinema). Go straight on. It's between X and Y. It's on the corner (of X and Y). It's on your left. It's on your right. It's opposite (the cinema). Turn left. Turn right. Walk along (X).

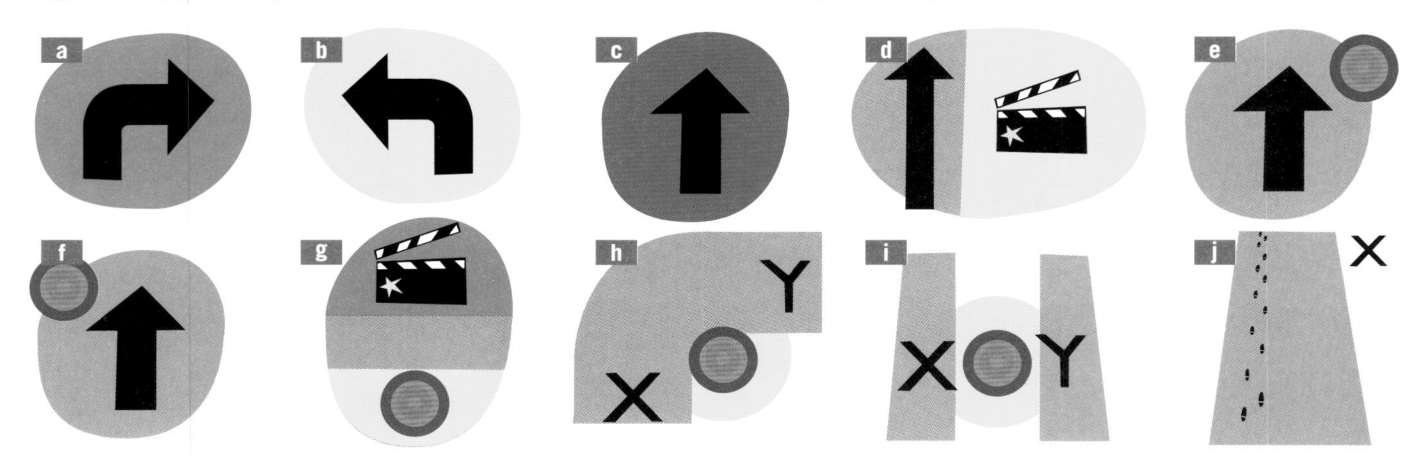

2 LISTENING 1.44 **Look at the map and listen. James is inside the bus station. Where does he want to go?**

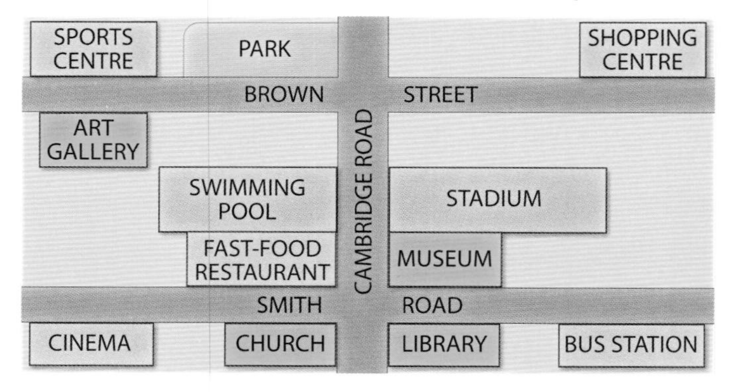

3a Work with a partner and complete the dialogue.

JAMES: Excuse me. Can you tell me how to get to the (**a**) ……………, please?

WOMAN: When you go out of the bus station, turn (**b**) ……………. Walk along Smith Road and then turn (**c**) …………… at Cambridge Road. Go (**d**) ……………. Walk (**e**) …………… the museum and the stadium. Then turn (**f**) …………… at Brown Street. Go past the (**g**) …………… and the (**h**) …………… is on your right, opposite the (**i**) …………….

JAMES: Thanks!

3b Listen again and check your answers.

4a SPEAKING **Use the map in 2. Prepare directions from the bus station to a different place in the town.**

4b Work with a partner. Give your directions, but don't say the name of the place. Can your partner say which place it is?

When you go out of the bus station, turn left. Go straight on. Walk past Cambridge Road and the church. It's on your left.

It's the cinema.

5 Look at the useful expressions in the Speaking Bank. Read the dialogue in 3 and tick the expressions which appear in it.

▸ Speaking Bank

Useful expressions to ask for and give directions

Asking
- Can you tell me how to get to …, please?
- Excuse me, do you know where … is?
- Is there a … near here?

Giving
- Turn right/left.
- Walk along …
- Go straight on.
- Go past …
- It's on the right/left.
- It's on the corner (of … and …).
- It's between … and …
- It's opposite …

Practice makes perfect

6a SPEAKING **Look at the task.**

You are in a town in England. Somebody asks you for directions. Give the directions as clearly as possible. Check that your partner understands.

6b Work with a partner. Do this role-play using expressions from the Speaking Bank to help you. Take it in turns to do the task.

Student A: You are at the bus station and want directions. Look at page 167.

Student B: You are also at the bus station and want directions. Look at page 160.

▸ EXAM SUCCESS

In this type of activity, can you say what you like or do you have to give specific information?

EXAM SUCCESS ▸ page 158

▸ STUDY SKILLS

How do you know if you and your partner are doing a speaking activity well?

STUDY SKILLS ▸ page 156

1 **Match the questions (1–8) with the answers (a–h).**

QUESTIONNAIRE

....

1 How often do you come to this swimming pool?
2 When do you usually come to the pool?
3 How well can you swim?
4 Why do you come to the pool?
5 Is the pool near your house?
6 How do you come here?
7 Do you come to the pool alone or with a friend or member of the family?
8 What is your general opinion of the pool?

a Not very well. I'm a beginner.
b Yes, it's only ten minutes from here.
c I usually come alone, but sometimes my sister comes with me.
d Because I want to learn to swim really well.
e Once or twice a week.
f I walk.
g I think it's great. My instructor is really nice and the pool is clean. Sometimes the water's cold!
h In the afternoon or evening.

2 **Work with a partner. Choose a good title for the questionnaire.**

1 Is our pool cool?
2 Are you a good swimmer?
3 The pool or the gym – which do you prefer?
4 Do you use our pool?

3 **Look at the advice in the Writing Bank. Read this questionnaire written by a student. Does the student follow the advice?**

GYM – YES OR NO?

1 What time you come to the gym?
2 You come with your sister?
3 Who is your favourite sports star?
4 Do you can do gymnastics well?
5 Your house is near to the gym?
6 What does you think of the gym?

Writing Bank

Useful advice for writing questionnaires

- Give your questionnaire an interesting title.
- Make all your questions relevant to the questionnaire.
- If possible, put the questions in order. We usually start with general questions and then we ask specific things. The last question can ask for a general conclusion.
- Be very careful with grammatical mistakes in questions. Do you have the correct word order? Is the auxiliary verb *do* necessary?

4 **Work with a partner and do the tasks.**

1 Correct the mistakes in the questions in 3.
2 Take out any questions that are not relevant.
3 Add one or two relevant questions.

Practice makes perfect

5a **Write a questionnaire to find out what the people in your class think about sport and PE at school. What do they like doing? What don't they like? Use the information in the Writing Bank to help you.**

5b **Give students your questionnaire.**

5c **Report back to the class. Tell them some interesting answers to the questions in your questionnaire.**

Language reference and revision

Grammar reference

Can/Can't

Form

Affirmative	I/You/He/She/We/They **can** swim.
Negative	I/You/He/She/We/They **can't (cannot*)** skate.
Question	**Can** I/you/he/she/we/they ski?
Short answers	Yes, I/you/he/she/we/they **can**. No, I/you/he/she/we/they **can't**.

* We write *cannot* as one word, not two.

Use

- We use **can** to talk about ability.
  She can speak English.
- We also use **can** to talk about possibility.
  I can go out this evening because I don't have homework.

Adverbs of manner

Form

Regular adverbs

- We add **-ly** to the adjective:
  slow – slowly, patient – patiently, careful – carefully
- We sometimes need to change the spelling of the original adjective:
  easy – easily, terrible – terribly

Irregular adverbs

- *good – well, fast – fast, hard – hard, early – early, late – late*

Use

- We use adverbs of manner to describe how we do something. They go with verbs (but not the verb *to be*).
  I walk slowly.

Have to, don't have to

Form

Affirmative	I/You/We/They **have to** wear a uniform at school. He/She **has to** wear a uniform.
Negative	I/You/We/they **don't have to** go to school on Sunday. He/She **doesn't have to** go to school on Sunday.
Question	**Do** I/you/we/they **have to** wear a uniform? **Does** he/she **have to** wear a uniform?
Short answers	Yes, I/you/we/they **do**. No, I/you/we/they **don't**. Yes, he/she **does**. No, he/she **doesn't**.

Use

- We use **have to** to talk about things which are obligatory or necessary.
  You have to speak English in class.
- We use **don't have to** to talk about things which are not obligatory or necessary.
  He doesn't have to speak English.

Must, mustn't

Form

Affirmative	I/You/He/She/We/They **must** come to class on time.
Negative	I/You/He/She/We/They **mustn't** smoke at school.

Use

- We use **must** to talk about things that are necessary or obligatory.
  You must sit down in class.
- We use **mustn't** to talk about things we can't do because we don't have permission.
  You mustn't be late.
- **Must** is not very common in the question form. We usually use **have to**.

Vocabulary

1 Parts of the body

arm back chest ear eye face finger foot hand head leg mouth neck nose shoulder stomach toe tooth

2 Basic physical activities

climb dive fall hit jump kick rest ride (a horse/bike) run skate ski swim

3 Sports

baseball basketball cycling fishing football golf gymnastics ice skating judo netball rugby sailing table tennis tennis volleyball

4 Other words and phrases ▸ page 149

Grammar revision

Can/Can't

1 Write the sentences again with *can* or *can't*. Do not change the meaning.

1 Do you know how to ski?
....?
2 It is impossible for me to come.
....
3 I don't know how to play golf.
....
4 It's possible for her to run marathons.
....
5 They aren't able to swim.
....
6 Is it possible for you to walk?
....?
7 I'm able to ride a bicycle.
....

WORKBOOK ▶ page 38 /7 points

Adverbs of manner

2 Write the adverb for these adjectives.

1 patient ....
2 good ....
3 bad ....
4 fast ....
5 slow ....
6 careful ....
7 hard ....

WORKBOOK ▶ page 38 /7 points

Have to/don't have to/must/mustn't

3 Complete the sentences with *have to, don't have to, must* or *mustn't*. If there are two possibilities, put both.

1 You .... drink and drive a car. It's illegal.
2 You .... have a passport to visit the USA.
3 You .... be born in England to speak English.
4 Smoking is not permitted here. You .... do it.
5 Children under 16 .... go to school.
6 Not all exercises are obligatory. You .... do them all.
7 We .... go by car because there isn't any public transport.

WORKBOOK ▶ page 41 /7 points

Vocabulary revision

Parts of the body

1 Write the names of the parts of the body.

1 .... 2 .... 3 .... 4 .... 5 .... 6 .... 7 ....

WORKBOOK ▶ page 36 /7 points

Basic physical activities

2 Look at the pictures. What physical activities do you usually do with them?

1 .... 2 .... 3 .... 4 .... 5 ....

WORKBOOK ▶ page 36 /5 points

Sports

3 Complete the sports with vowels (*a, e, i, o, u*).

1 j...d...
2 v...ll...yb...ll
3 r...gby
4 gymn...st...cs
5 s...l...ng
6 f...sh...ng
7 b...s...b...ll

WORKBOOK ▶ page 39 /7 points

Total /40 points

Gateway to exams Units 3–4

Reading

Tip For Reading Exams

In multiple-choice activities, remember …

Always answer all the questions. You do not usually lose marks for incorrect answers. EXAM SUCCESS ▸ page 158

1 Work with a partner. What do you know about rugby?

2a You are going to read about a sport called 'underwater rugby'. Work with a partner and write two questions about the sport.

2b Read the text quickly to find the answers.

3 Read the text again. Choose the correct answer (**A**, **B** or **C**) for each question.

Underwater rugby is an unusual sport. People think that it's similar to rugby. It isn't. You play underwater, so you have to be able to swim well.

The game has two halves. Each half is fifteen minutes. In the middle, the game stops and the players have a break for four minutes. There are two teams. One team usually wears white and the other team wears blue or black. Each team has eleven players. But your team can't have eleven players in the water at the same time. Only six people from each team can be in the water. It's very difficult to swim fast under water for a long time. So the other five players are substitutes; they go in and play when the other players get tired.

There are two goals, one at each end of the swimming pool. They are like the baskets in basketball but they are on the bottom of the pool. To score a goal, you must put the ball in the basket. The ball has got salt water inside it. This makes the ball go down in the water, not up. The players mustn't take the ball out of the water. You mustn't attack another player. If you do, you have to be out of the water for two minutes and your team must play with only five people, not six.

1 To play underwater rugby, it's important to be good at
- **A** swimming.
- **B** rugby.
- **C** unusual sports.

2 The players play for
- **A** 15 minutes.
- **B** 30 minutes.
- **C** 34 minutes.

3 You can easily see the different teams because
- **A** one team has men, the other has women.
- **B** they have very different colours.
- **C** one team has to swim fast, but the other doesn't.

4 In a game of underwater rugby, there are usually .... players in the water in total.
- **A** six
- **B** eleven
- **C** twelve

4 **SPEAKING** What about *you*?

Would you like to play underwater rugby? Why/Why not?

Use of English

Tip For Use Of English Exams

In activities where you choose words for gaps, remember …

First, read the complete text. This is to get a general understanding of the text. Don't stop to think about the gaps. EXAM SUCCESS ▸ page 158

5 Read the text about sport. Choose the best word (**A**, **B** or **C**) for each gap.

There **(1)** .... a lot of extreme sports in the world. Extreme sports are usually dangerous. You **(2)** .... have bad accidents when you practise them. You must think **(3)** .... before you decide to do an extreme sport. Some people prefer to just stay at home and watch extreme sports **(4)** .... TV. But you **(5)** .... sit watching TV all day. It's really bad for you too. My parents don't have time for sport during the week and on Saturday they **(6)** .... the shopping and tidy up the house. But on Sunday they get up **(7)** ...., at 7 o'clock, and they go for a run. **(8)** .... the afternoon, they play tennis. Running and tennis aren't extreme sports, but it helps them to stay fit. Me? I do all my exercise in the school gym!

	A	B	C
1	**A** is	**B** isn't	**C** are
2	**A** can	**B** can't	**C** must
3	**A** careful	**B** carefully	**C** good
4	**A** on	**B** in	**C** next to
5	**A** must	**B** mustn't	**C** don't have to
6	**A** do	**B** make	**C** go
7	**A** early	**B** late	**C** lately
8	**A** On	**B** At	**C** In

Speaking

Tip For Speaking Exams

In information role-plays, remember …

You have to communicate specific information. You cannot just say what you like. EXAM SUCCESS ▸ page 158

6 Work with a partner. Look at these expressions for giving directions. For each expression, draw a simple diagram.

1. Turn right.
2. Go straight on.
3. Go past the computer room.
4. It's on the left.
5. It's on the corner.
6. It's between the gym and the canteen.
7. It's opposite the Coach's Room.

7 Work with a partner. Look at the situation below and role-play the dialogue.

1. **Student A:** You are new at this school. Ask for directions to the gym. If you don't understand, ask your partner to repeat.

   Can you tell me how to get to the gym, please?

   Student B: Give directions.
2. Change roles.
   Student B: Ask for directions to the library.
   Student A: Give directions.
3. Now practise asking for directions to other places in the school.

Writing

Tip For Writing Exams

In writing exams, remember …

Read your work carefully when you finish. Check for mistakes with punctuation, capital letters, word order, spelling, tenses and agreement between the subject and verb.

EXAM SUCCESS ▸ page 158

8 What is your favourite room at home? What is there in the room? Why do you like it? Make notes and then tell your partner.

9 An English-speaking friend wants information about your favourite room at home. Write an email. Include a description of the room and say why you like it. Begin:

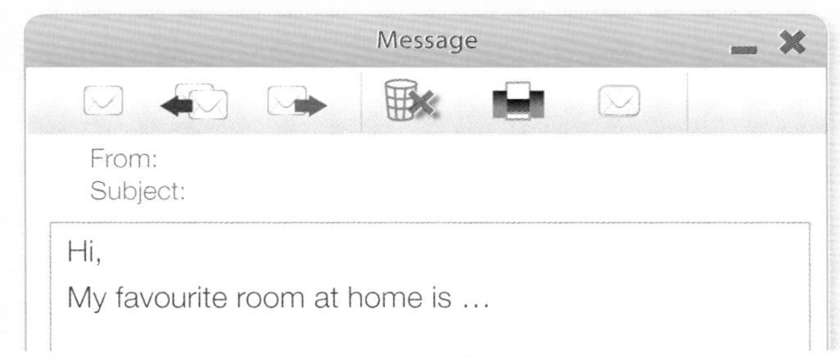

▸ 'Can Do' Progress Check

CEF

1 How well can you do these things in English now? Give yourself a mark from 1 to 4.

1 = I can do it very well.
2 = I can do it quite well.
3 = I have some problems.
4 = I can't do it.

a I can talk about houses and rooms using *There is/There are.* ☐

b I can talk about what's happening now using the present continuous. ☐

c I can understand written and spoken texts about homes. ☐

d I can have a basic conversation on the phone. ☐

e I can write a short description of a room. ☐

f I can talk about abilities and obligations using *can, must, have to,* etc. ☐

g I can name different parts of the body and physical activities. ☐

h I can understand simple written and spoken texts about sports. ☐

i I can ask for and give directions. ☐

j I can write a simple questionnaire. ☐

2 Now decide what you need to do to improve.

1. Look again at my book/notes.
2. Do more practice exercises. ⇨ WORKBOOK page 44–45
3. Ask for help.
4. Other: ....

5 Good food guide

Grammar	▸ Countable and uncountable nouns ▸ *Some, any, a/an* ▸ *A lot of, much, many* ▸ *Should, shouldn't*
Vocabulary	▸ Food ▸ Drink ▸ Containers
Speaking	▸ Ordering food
Writing	▸ An invitation

▸ Vocabulary

Food

1a Work with a partner. Match the photos with some of these words. Check that you understand the other words. Use your dictionary if necessary.

apple banana beans biscuit bread burger butter cake cheese chicken chips egg fish grape ice cream lemon meat melon nuts pizza rice salad salt strawberry sugar tomato

1b 🎧 1.45 Listen and repeat.

2a How often do you eat the food in 1? Put each word into one of these columns.

Often	Not often	Never

2b SPEAKING Work with a partner. Compare your lists. Are they similar?

I often eat bananas, but you never eat them.

No, I hate bananas!

3a PRONUNCIATION Which words in 1 have two syllables? Where is the stress in these words – on the first or second syllable?

Apple

3b 🎧 1.46 Listen, check and repeat.

Drink

4 Match the photos with some of these words.

coffee hot chocolate lemonade milk milkshake mineral water orange juice tea

5 SPEAKING Work with a partner. Find out which drinks your partner likes or doesn't like.

6 LISTENING 🎧 1.47 Listen to four dialogues. Write down the food and drink that the people want.

1 Two .... with ...., ... and ....
2 One .... and one .... coffee.
3 A ...., and a .... with ....
4 One sandwich with .... and one sandwich with ....

7 SPEAKING You and your partner are hungry. Decide which food in 6 you prefer.

I want a pizza!

I'd prefer the burger and chips.

1 Work with a partner. What do you think are the ingredients in:

1 a chicken burger?
2 a strawberry milkshake?

2 Read the text and check your answers in 1.

What's in your food?

It's lunch time. You're hungry. You've got a chicken burger and a strawberry milkshake.

Yum! But have you got any idea what is inside the food you're eating?

Of course, in the chicken burger there's some chicken. There's also some tomato and some cheese, and there's even some healthy salad with it. But there are also some extra ingredients in the chicken. For example, there are at least seven or eight chemical additives. They include salt and sugar, but also preservatives (to stop the food going bad) and antioxidants (to protect the food from oxygen in the air). The people who make burgers can also choose to add chemical flavours. Some chickens also contain hormones. These hormones make the chickens get big quickly. And, don't forget water! Chicken burgers are 45% water. They add extra water to make the chicken look big.

And what's inside that strawberry milkshake? It's got strawberries and milk, right? Wrong! There's some milk and sugar, but there aren't usually any real strawberries in strawberry milkshakes. Strawberries are expensive and they go bad. The solution: scientists create special flavours in laboratories and then they add their secret ingredients – E129, cinnamyl valerate, benzyl isobutyrate …

Mmmm, delicious!

3 Read the text again. Are the sentences true (T) or false (F)?

1 Chicken burgers and milkshakes have got very simple ingredients. T/F
2 There is no chicken in a chicken burger. T/F
3 Antioxidants stop food from going bad. T/F
4 They don't use strawberries in strawberry milkshakes. T/F
5 There is just one problem with real strawberries – they cost a lot of money. T/F
6 The chemicals that scientists create are very important to make a milkshake. T/F

4 Use your dictionary to look up the meaning of the underlined words in the text.

STUDY SKILLS

Look up the word *water* in your dictionary. Is it a noun or a verb or both? Does it have just one meaning or does it have others? When you look up a word in a dictionary, is it a good idea to look only at the first definition? Why/Why not?

STUDY SKILLS ▸ page 156

5 SPEAKING What about *you*?

1 Do you think the food you eat is simple, healthy and natural?
2 Which do you prefer – home-made food, fast food or food from a restaurant?

I eat a lot of fast food. My mum and dad haven't got time to cook.

My mum is usually at home and she cooks really well.

GRAMMAR GUIDE

Countable and uncountable nouns

1a Look at the sentences. In a, the words in bold are countable nouns. In b, the words in bold are uncountable.

a They're eating **burgers** and **chips**.
b They've only got **bread** and **water**.

1b Which list below is of countable nouns? Which list is of uncountable nouns?

1 LIST A: milk, salt, cheese, water
2 LIST B: apple, banana, egg, strawberry

GRAMMAR REFERENCE ▸ page 76

2 Put these food and drink words in the correct column.

~~biscuit~~ bread burger butter cheese
egg meat rice sugar tomato

Countable	Uncountable
biscuit	

GRAMMAR GUIDE

Some, any, a/an

3 Look at the sentences and match the boxes below to make the rules.

a You have **a** chicken burger.
b There aren't **any** strawberries.
c There's **some** cheese.
d Is there **any** milk?
e There are **some** extra ingredients.
f Do you want **an** apple?
g There isn't **any** milk in the fridge.
h She hasn't got **a** banana.

1 We use **a/an** with	a uncountable nouns (*water*) and plural countable nouns (*apples*) in negative sentences and questions.
2 We use **some** with	b singular countable nouns (*apple, banana*) in affirmative and negative sentences and questions.
3 We use **any** with	c uncountable nouns (*water*) and plural countable nouns (*apples*) in affirmative sentences.

GRAMMAR REFERENCE ▸ page 76

4 Look at the picture and complete the sentences with *some, any, a* or *an*.

1 He's got .... tomatoes.
2 He's got .... egg.
3 He hasn't got .... apples.
4 He's got .... bread.
5 He hasn't got .... cheese.
6 He's got .... milk.
7 He hasn't got .... burger.

5 Complete the dialogue with *some, any, a* or *an*.

KATY: Excuse me, have you got (**a**) .... small pizzas with tomatoes?
SHOP ASSISTANT: No, sorry. We haven't got (**b**) .... small pizzas. But, we've got (**c**) .... big pizza with tomatoes.
KATY: Has the pizza got (**d**) .... cheese?
SHOP ASSISTANT: Yes, it has.
KATY: Oh. What about drinks? Have you got (**e**) .... orange juice?
SHOP ASSISTANT: Yes, and we've got (**f**) .... apple juice too.
KATY: OK. I'll take the big pizza and the apple juice please!

6 SPEAKING **Work with a partner. Look at the two fridges. Find differences between them.**

In the first fridge, there's some orange juice.

In the second fridge there isn't any orange juice.

Containers

1a Work with a partner. Match the pictures with the words.

a bottle of water   a can of cola
a carton of orange juice   a cup of coffee
a glass of milk   a packet of biscuits   a slice of pizza

1b 1.48 **Listen and repeat.**

2 Which word(s) in 1 can we usually use with these products?

1 cake .... *a slice of cake*
2 lemonade ....
3 milk ....
4 tea ....
5 rice ....
6 crisps ....
7 apple juice ....

3a Use the words on this page to write seven true sentences about yourself.

I drink five or six glasses of water a day.
I eat three or four slices of pizza a week.

3b SPEAKING **Compare sentences with a partner. Are you similar or different?**

I drink five or six glasses of water a day.

Me too.

I eat three or four slices of pizza a week.

I eat three slices of pizza a day!

Click onto...

Healthy food

Cross-curricular – Science/Biology
Superfoods

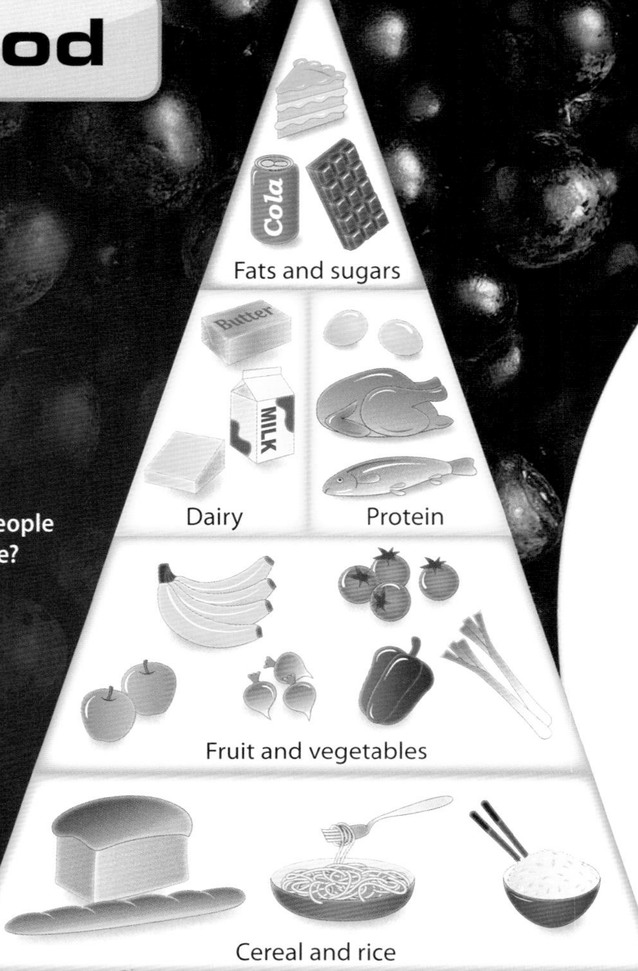

1 Work with a partner. Look at the pyramid.

1 What food can you see?
2 What food can you add to the different sections?
3 Why are the foods divided into the different sections?

2 Blueberries are a fruit originally from North America. Some people call blueberries a *superfood*. What do you think *superfoods* are? Do you think *superfoods* really exist?

3 Read the text. What is the conclusion? Do *superfoods* exist?

4 Read the text again and answer the questions.

1 Do scientists use the name *superfood*? Why/Why not?
2 What type of foods do people usually call *superfoods*?
3 Why are blueberries special?
4 What do antioxidants do?
5 Why do scientists think that just eating *superfoods* doesn't make you healthy?
6 When can supermarkets call foods *superfoods*?
7 Why is the name *superfood* not very useful?

Superfoods – do they exist?

People sometimes talk about *superfoods*. Some types of food are super because they are extremely healthy. But *superfood* is not a scientific name. Some scientists think it's wrong to believe that some foods have special ingredients that can protect us.

Superfoods are usually fruit and vegetables which produce a lot of antioxidants. Colourful fruit like blueberries are a good example. They help to produce antioxidants which help fight heart problems and cancer. Some people now think that if they eat a few blueberries, they are going to be healthy. But scientists say that the important thing is to have a balanced diet, to eat a bit of everything, not just eat one or two superfoods.

Now, shops and food companies have to be careful. The European Union says that they need scientific evidence to call food *superfood*.

But is the name *superfood* useful? A simple carton of milk is super because milk contains calcium and we know that calcium is good for bones. So the real superfoods are milk, apples, oranges, bananas, yoghurt, fish and tea. They are all parts of a good, balanced diet.

▸ WORD BOOSTER

Match the words and definitions.

1 protect
2 contain
3 produce
4 balanced
5 evidence
6 bones

a hard parts of a body that make the skeleton
b something that shows that another thing is true
c to have or to include
d make, create
e all parts are in the correct amounts
f keep in good condition

5 SPEAKING What about *you*?

Do you sometimes eat a particular type of food because you think it's good for you?

I drink orange juice because of the vitamin C.

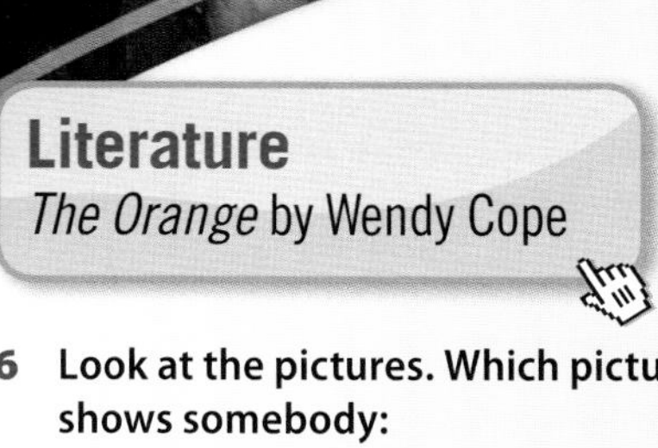

Literature
The Orange by Wendy Cope

6 Look at the pictures. Which picture shows somebody:

1 *peeling* an orange?
2 *sharing* an orange?
3 *enjoying* an orange?

7 You are going to read a poem about the people in the pictures. The poem is in the past. Before you read, match the present and past forms.

Present simple	Past simple
1 is	a bought
2 do	b made
3 make	c peeled
4 get	d shared
5 share	e got
6 have	f was
7 peel	g did
8 buy	h enjoyed
9 enjoy	i had

8a LISTENING 1.49 **Listen to the poem. Is the poem happy or sad?**

8b Work with a partner. Take it in turns to read the poem aloud.

9a SPEAKING **Read what a student says about the poem and answer the questions.**

'This is a beautiful poem. It's very simple but it is very positive. It shows that a small ordinary thing can make us feel good. I think the poet is in love. Everything is different and special, including small, silly things!'

1 Do you agree with the student? Why/Why not?
2 Do *you* like the poem? Why/Why not?

9b Discuss your ideas with other students.

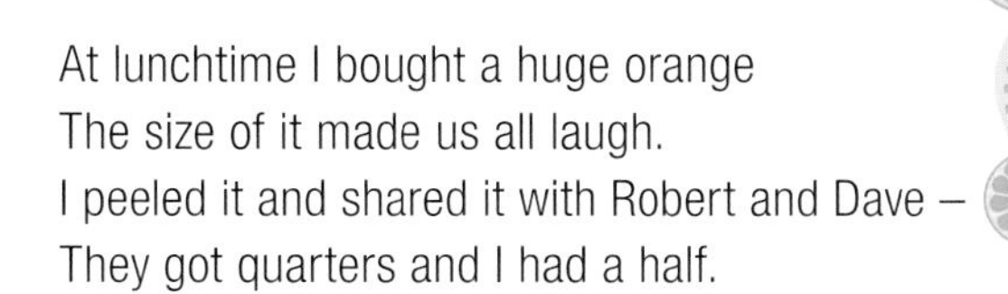

At lunchtime I bought a huge orange
The size of it made us all laugh.
I peeled it and shared it with Robert and Dave –
They got quarters and I had a half.

And that orange it made me so happy,
As ordinary things often do
Just lately. The shopping. A walk in the park
This is peace and contentment. It's new.

The rest of the day was quite easy.
I did all my jobs on my list
And enjoyed them and had some time over.
I love you. I'm glad I exist.

Wendy Cope: "The Orange" from 'Serious Concerns', Faber & Faber, Ltd., 1992

INSIDE INFORMATION

- The poet Wendy Cope was born in 1945 in England.
- She was a student at Oxford University and was a teacher in a primary school.
- Her poems often seem simple and funny but they say serious and important things.
- This poem is from 1992.

WORD BOOSTER

Match the words and definitions.

1 huge	a very big
2 size	b recently
3 lately	c how large or small something is
4 contentment	d happy
5 glad	e a feeling of happiness and satisfaction

10 Work in small groups. Make a list of things that make you happy.

Playing football in the park.
Going to a concert.

1 **Work with a partner. Ask and answer these questions.**

1 Do you like chewing gum?
2 How often do you chew chewing gum?
3 Is chewing gum usually cheap or expensive?
4 Where do people usually put chewing gum when they finish it? Do they always put it in the bin?

2 LISTENING 1.50 **Listen to a radio programme about chewing gum and answer the questions.**

1 What problem with chewing gum do they talk about on the programme?
2 Which speaker doesn't think chewing gum is really a problem – Stephanie, Gary, Thomas or Vanessa?

STUDY SKILLS

The first time you listen to a text, what do you do if there is something you don't understand?

STUDY SKILLS ▸ page 156

3 **Listen again. Match the people (1–4) with their ideas (a–e). One idea is not stated by any of the speakers.**

1 Stephanie
2 Gary
3 Thomas
4 Vanessa

a They should stop selling chewing gum.
b Cans of drink should be expensive too because it costs money to clean them off the street.
c They should use the money from chewing gum to clean the streets.
d People who throw chewing gum on the street should pay fifty pounds.
e The problem isn't the people who eat chewing gum, it's the number of bins.

4 SPEAKING **What about *you*?**

1 Do you think chewing gum is a problem?
2 What do you think is a good solution? One of the ideas in 3, or something different?

I don't think it's a big problem.

I don't agree. There's a lot of chewing gum on the streets.

Grammar in context

GRAMMAR GUIDE

A lot of, much, many

1 **Look at the sentences and decide if the statements below are *true* (T) or *false* (F).**

a How **much** chewing gum is there?
b How **many** teenagers eat chewing gum?
c There is/isn't **a lot of** chewing gum on the streets.
d There are/aren't **a lot of** bins on the street.
e Is there **a lot of** chewing gum on the floor?
f There isn't **much** chewing gum here.
g Not **many** people put their chewing gum in the bin.

1 We use **much** for uncountable nouns and **many** for countable nouns. T/F
2 We usually use **much** and **many** in questions and negative sentences. T/F
3 We use **a lot of** for countable and uncountable nouns. T/F
4 We use **a lot of** in affirmative and negative sentences and in questions. T/F

GRAMMAR REFERENCE ▸ page 76

2 **Complete the sentences with *much, many* or *a lot of*. If you can use two alternatives, write both.**

1 There aren't ………… bottles in the fridge.
2 Are there ………… tomatoes in the fridge?
3 There is ………… water in the bottle.
4 I've got ………… chips on my plate.
5 Have you got ………… juice in your glass?
6 There aren't ………… biscuits.

3a Complete the questions with *How much* or *How many*.

1 .... cola do you drink a week?
2 .... burgers do you eat a month?
3 .... eggs do you eat a week?
4 .... mineral water do you drink?
5 .... apples do you eat a week?
6 .... meat do you eat?
7 .... pizzas do you eat a week?
8 .... juice do you drink a week?
9 .... milk do you drink a day?
10 .... cups of coffee do you drink a day?

3b SPEAKING **Work with a partner. Ask and answer the questions. Choose from these answers:**
A lot
Quite a lot
Not much
Not many
I never eat/drink ....

How much cola do you drink a week?

Quite a lot. Usually six or seven cans. And you?

Not much. I prefer lemonade or juice.

GRAMMAR GUIDE

Should, shouldn't

4 Look at the sentences and choose the corrct alternative.

a You **should** put your chewing gum in the bin.
b You **shouldn't** throw chewing gum on the floor.
c What **should** we do about the problem?

1 We use **should** for something that *is/isn't* a good idea.
2 We use **shouldn't** for something that *is/isn't* a good idea.

GRAMMAR REFERENCE ▶ page 76

5 Complete the sentences with *should* or *shouldn't*.

1 You .... eat fruit and vegetables every day.
2 You .... throw cans and bottles on the floor.
3 People .... eat fast food all the time.
4 We .... be careful about what we eat.
5 Young children .... go to bed very late.

6a SPEAKING **Work with a partner. Make a list of eight things you should or shouldn't do to be healthy.**
You should do exercise three times a week.

6b Tell the class your ideas. Choose the top five ideas.

1 SPEAKING **Work with a partner. Look at the menu and answer the questions.**

1 Would you like to eat at this café? Why/Why not?
2 What do you think *starters, extras, mains* and *desserts* are?

2a LISTENING 1.51 **Listen to how we say the prices for the** ***starters and extras.***

2b Work with a partner and practise saying the prices on the menu.

Three pounds ten or three ten.

3 LISTENING 1.52 **Listen to two people ordering food in the café. You are the waiter. Make a note of their order.**

Table 10: Order.

4a Complete the dialogue with statements 1–8. There are eight statements but only six spaces.

1 Regular or large?
2 Are you ready to order?
3 What do you want?
4 That's £14.40 in total.
5 Would you like a dessert?
6 Here's your change.
7 Can I get you anything to drink?
8 Would you like salad with that?

WAITER: Hello. (**a**) ....
CHLOE: Yes. Could I have a cheeseburger and chips, please?
WAITER: Sure. (**b**) ....
CHLOE: No thanks.
WAITER: And what can I get you?
MATTHEW: What are the chicken fingers?
WAITER: They're small pieces of chicken. You get five.
MATTHEW: I see. I think I'll have the chicken and rice, please.
WAITER: OK, so that's one cheeseburger and chips and one chicken and rice. (**c**) ....
CHLOE: Yes, I'll have a lemonade, please.
MATTHEW: And I'd like a cola.
WAITER: (**d**) ....
MATTHEW: Large please.
WAITER: (**e**) ....
CHLOE: Here you are.
WAITER: Thanks. (**f**) .... I'll bring your food and drinks to your table in a couple of minutes. Enjoy your meal!

4b **Listen again and check your answers.**

The Cheap and Cheerful Café

Menu

Starters and extras
Chicken fingers £3.10
Special salad £2.90
Chips £1.00

Mains
Fish and chips £6.00
Chicken and rice £6.50
Cheese and tomato pizza £5.85
Cheeseburger and chips £5.50

Desserts
Strawberry cheesecake £3.50
Chocolate brownie £3.30
Ice cream (chocolate, strawberry or vanilla) £2.20
Fruit salad £2.90

Drinks
Banana milkshake £1.50
Home-made lemonade £1.10
Cola – regular £1.20
– large £1.30,
Coffee £1.10
Tea £1.10

EXAM SUCCESS

In this type of exercise, should you read the complete dialogue first? Why/Why not?

EXAM SUCCESS ▶ page 159

5 SPEAKING **Work in groups of three. Practise the completed dialogue in 4.**

6 Read the dialogue again and complete the useful expressions in the Speaking Bank.

Speaking Bank

Useful expressions to order food
The waiter

- Can I help you?
- Are you (**a**) .... to order?
- What can I get you?/What would you like?/ Would you like (a salad)?
- Can I (**b**) .... you anything to drink?
- Enjoy your (**c**) ....!
- That's £14.40 in (**d**) ....
- (**e**) .... your change.

The customer

- Could I (**f**) .... a cheeseburger, please?
- I think I (**g**) .... have the chicken and rice.
- I'd (**h**) .... a cola.
- Have you got any lemonade?
- How much is that?/Can we have the bill?

Practice makes perfect

7a SPEAKING **Work in groups of three. Prepare a dialogue where one person is the waiter and the other two people are customers. Use the menu in 1 and the Speaking Bank to help you.**

7b Practise your dialogue. Then act it out for the rest of the class.

1 Look at the photo. Match it with one of the invitations.

a

Hi Sam,

It's my birthday on Saturday and I'm inviting some friends to go out and celebrate. Would you like to come? We're meeting at Fosters, the fast-food restaurant on Green Street, at one o'clock. We're having lunch there and then we're going to the cinema to see a film. Please come!

Let me know if you can make it.

All the best

Max

b

Emma,

We're finally in our new house and we're having a party here to celebrate. It's next Friday. Can you come? You don't have to bring drinks but can you bring some food – pizzas, sandwiches or something? The party's starting at 7 o'clock but you can come when you like.

See you there!

Alice

c

Dear Alfie,

The summer holidays are here! To celebrate, I'm inviting everyone to a picnic in the park on Wednesday afternoon. I've got some food – pizzas, sandwiches, crisps, and things like that. But, please bring your own drinks. Oh, and bring a ball. We can play football. We're starting the picnic at one o'clock. Don't be late!

Hope you can come.

Cheers

Dan

2 Read the invitations and for each invitation answer these questions.

1 Who makes the invitation?
2 Why do they make the invitation?
3 What is the invitation for? A party, a picnic ...?
4 Where should the person go?
5 What day/time should they go?
6 What should they bring?

3 Look at the invitations again and answer the questions.

1 What are typical ways of starting and finishing email messages to friends?
2 Look at this sentence. What tense is it in? In the invitation, is it talking about an action in the present or a future plan/arrangement?

We're meeting at Fosters at one o'clock.

EXAM SUCCESS

When you write to a friend in English, should you use contractions or not? How important is it to write texts in the correct style? EXAM SUCCESS ▸ page 159

4 Look at the invitations again and complete the useful expressions in the Writing Bank.

Writing Bank

Useful expressions in informal invitations

- Would you (a) .... to come?
- Can you come?
- Please come!
- Let me (b) .... if you can/can't (c) .... it.
- (d) .... you can come.
- See you there!
- Please (e) .... (your own drinks).
- Can you (f) .... (some food)?
- It's starting at (one o'clock).
- (g) .... be late!

Practice makes perfect

5a Look at the task.

> You are in Britain. Write an invitation. Invite a friend to a celebration that you are planning. Include all the important information.

5b Make notes about:

- what you want to celebrate: a birthday, moving to a new house, the start of the holidays ...
- what you want to do: go out somewhere, have a party, have a picnic/barbecue ...
- where you should meet
- what day/time you should meet
- what people should bring: food, drink ...

5c Write your invitation.

5d Give your invitation to another student. Can they answer all the questions in 2 for your invitation?

Language reference and revision

Grammar reference

Countable and uncountable nouns

- We can **count** *apples, bananas, eggs, burgers* and *chips* and so there is a singular and plural form. They are **countable** nouns.
- We cannot count some things and so we do not usually use a plural form. For example, *milk, water, bread, salt, cheese*. They are **uncountable** nouns.

Some, any, a/an

Use

- We use **some** with uncountable nouns and with plural countable nouns, in affirmative sentences.
  I've got some apples.
  We've got some water.
- We use **any** with uncountable nouns and with plural countable nouns, in negative sentences and questions.
  I haven't got any milk.
  He hasn't got any apples.
  Have you got any orange juice?
  Are there any bananas?
- We use **a/an** with singular countable nouns in affirmative and negative sentences and in questions. **An** goes before a vowel sound.
  I haven't got a burger.
  He's got an egg.
  Have you got an MP3 player?

A lot of, much, many

Use

- We use **much**, **many** and **a lot (of)** to talk about big quantities.
- We often use **much** in negative sentences and questions, with uncountable nouns.
  I haven't got much lemonade.
  Have you got much water?
- We often use **many** in negative sentences and questions, with plural countable nouns.
  I haven't got many chips.
  Have you got many eggs?
- We use **a lot of** in affirmative and negative sentences and in questions, with countable and uncountable nouns.
  I've got a lot of apples.
  I haven't got a lot of tomatoes.
  Have you got a lot of water?
- We use **of** when **a lot** comes before a noun. But when there is no noun after **a lot** we do not use **of**.
  I've got a lot of bananas.
  Are there any bananas? Yes, there are a lot.

Should, shouldn't

Form

Affirmative	You **should** eat fruit and vegetables.
Negative	You **shouldn't** eat a lot of cakes and chocolate.
Question	**Should** I eat fish?
Short answers	Yes, I **should**./No, I **shouldn't**.

Use

- We use **should** to talk about things that it is a good idea to do.
  You should drink milk because it's good for you.
- We use **shouldn't** to talk about things that it is not a good idea to do.
  You shouldn't eat a lot of sugar because it's bad for your teeth.

Vocabulary

1 Food

apple banana bean biscuit
bread burger butter cake
cheese chicken chips egg
fish grape ice cream lemon
meat melon nuts pizza
rice salad salt strawberry
sugar tomato

2 Drink

coffee hot chocolate lemonade
milk milkshake mineral water
orange juice tea

3 Containers

bottle can carton cup
glass packet slice

4 Other words and phrases ▶ page 151

Grammar revision

Countable and uncountable nouns

1 Write C (Countable) or U (Uncountable) for each word.

1 bread ....
2 salt ....
3 sugar ....
4 biscuit ....
5 rice ....
6 cheese ....
7 burger ....
8 milk ....

WORKBOOK ▶ page 48

/ 4 points

Some, any, a/an

2 Look at the picture. Complete the sentences with the correct form of *There is/are* and *some, any, a* or *an*.

1 There .... bread.
2 There .... bananas.
3 There .... egg.
4 There .... apples.
5 There .... water.
6 There .... milk.

WORKBOOK ▶ page 48

/ 6 points

A lot of, much, many

3 Choose the correct alternative. If both alternatives are correct, mark both.

1 There are *a lot of/much* biscuits in the packet.
2 There isn't *much/many* milk in the fridge.
3 Is there *a lot of/much* water in the bottle?
4 Have you got *many/much* tomatoes?
5 There's *a lot of/many* rice.

WORKBOOK ▶ page 51

/ 5 points

Should, shouldn't

4 Write complete sentences giving good advice. Use *should* or *shouldn't*.

1 You/write carefully in exams. ....
2 Young children/watch very violent films. ....
3 You/wash your hands before you cook. ....
4 People/help their friends. ....
5 You/talk when the teacher is talking. ....
6 Everyone/eat some fruit every day. ....
7 You/drink a lot of cola because it's bad for your teeth.
....

WORKBOOK ▶ page 51

/ 7 points

Vocabulary revision

Food

1 Complete the sentences with these words.

bread burgers chickens chips eggs
ice cream pizzas rice tomatoes

1 People eat a lot of .... in Asia.
2 You make .... with potatoes.
3 Omelettes are made from ....
4 .... are originally from Italy.
5 To make a sandwich you always need ....
6 You get eggs from ....

WORKBOOK ▶ page 46

/ 6 points

Containers

2 Name the objects.

1 a .... of ....
2 a .... of ....
3 a .... of ....
4 a .... of ....
5 a .... of ....
6 a .... of ....

WORKBOOK ▶ page 49

Drink

3 Write the names of the drinks.

1  ....
2  ....
3  ....
4  ....
5  ....
6 ....

WORKBOOK ▶ page 46

/ 6 points

Total */ 40 points*

6 Tourist attractions

Grammar ▸ Past simple of *to be* and *can*
▸ Past simple affirmative – regular and irregular verbs
Vocabulary ▸ Countries and nationalities ▸ Words connected with tourism
▸ Transport
Speaking ▸ Talking about a holiday
Writing ▸ A postcard

▸ Vocabulary

Countries and nationalities

1a Work with a partner. Match the flags with some of these countries. If you don't know, guess.

Argentina Brazil Czech Republic Egypt France Great Britain Ireland Italy
Japan Poland Russia Slovakia South Africa Spain Switzerland the USA Turkey

1b 2.01 **Listen and repeat.**

2a Match the countries in 1 with these nationalities.

Russian Swiss Irish French
Czech British Turkish
South African Argentinian Spanish
American Egyptian Polish
Slovakian Brazilian Japanese
Italian

Argentina – Argentinian

2b 2.02 **Listen, check and repeat.**

3a SPEAKING **Write down the name of one famous person (fictional or non-fictional) for as many of the nationalities as possible.**

Argentinian – Diego Maradona
French – Nicolas Sarkozy ...

3b Work in small groups. Take it in turns to say the names of a famous person. Can the others say the correct nationality?

Roger Federer.

Is he German?

I think he's Swiss.

Yes, that's right.

Words connected with tourism

4 Match the definitions with these words.

guidebook luggage hotel tickets sightseeing passport
package holiday train/boat/plane trip/excursion

1 the bags you take on holiday
2 a book that gives tourist information
3 types of transport for land, water, and air
4 a building where you pay to stay in a room
5 an official document for travelling with your photo and your nationality
6 when you go to a place and then come back
7 travelling around to visit monuments and other interesting sights
8 papers that show you can use a type of transport or enter a place
9 a holiday where everything is included – the transport, hotel, etc.

5 LISTENING 2.03 **Listen. What is the subject of each dialogue? Choose the correct alternative.**

1 passport/guidebook/luggage
2 hotel/package holiday/sightseeing
3 guidebook/trip/tickets

6 SPEAKING **Work with a partner. Ask and answer the questions.**

1 Have you got a passport? Do you like your passport photo?
2 What do you think of package holidays?
3 Which do you prefer, travelling by train, plane or boat? Why?
4 Do you like sightseeing? Why/Why not?
5 How much luggage do you usually take when you go on holiday?
6 Do you usually take a guidebook when you go on holiday? Why/Why not?

Have you got a passport?

Yes, I have.

Do you like your passport photo?

No, I hate it. I'm very young in the photo.

1 Work with a partner. Look at the poster and talk about what you can see.

The first person to have the idea of package holidays was probably Thomas Cook. Cook was born in Great Britain in 1808. His first organised trip was in 1841. He took a group of 500 people 19 kilometres by train. The price of the excursion was one shilling.

This first trip was a success. The next trip was an excursion to Liverpool. This time, the price also included the hotel. People loved the idea. They could travel easily, without worrying about finding a place to stay. Before their trip, they knew exactly how much it was going to cost. Before, travel and tourism were only for the rich. But not now.

1855 was the year of Cook's first foreign excursion. In the 1860s, there were organised trips to Switzerland, Italy, Egypt and the United States. His Swiss trips were especially popular.

Cook's travel agency was a great success. The base for their operations was a shop in London. Customers could also buy guide books and luggage there.

1872 was the first year of Thomas Cook's 'round the world tour'. The route was via the USA, Japan, China and India. The length of the trip was 212 days. The price of a ticket was 200 guineas, which is about £80,000 in today's money! That wasn't cheap!

Nowadays, the Thomas Cook company doesn't belong to Cook's family but it is still in business. The company has over 45 planes, 800 shops, and 19,000 people working for it.

2 Read the text and choose the best title.

1 The life of Thomas Cook
2 The first trip around the world
3 Thomas Cook and the beginning of modern tourism

3 Read the text again and explain the importance of these years.

1 1808: *Thomas Cook was born in 1808.*
2 1841: ....
3 1855: ....
4 1860s: ....
5 1872: ....

4 Answer the questions with information from the text.

1 Why was Thomas Cook an important person in the history of tourism?
2 What was special about Thomas Cook's excursion to Liverpool?
3 Why was Thomas Cook's idea popular?
4 Where was the centre of Thomas Cook's business?
5 What do you know about the Thomas Cook company today?

5 Match the underlined words in the text with these definitions.

1 people who have a lot of money
2 with good results
3 road or path you use to go from one place to another
4 not costing a lot of money
5 going through one place to arrive at another
6 how much something costs
7 a business that helps people to plan holidays
8 today

6 SPEAKING What about *you*?

Which country in the text would you most like to visit? Why?

I'd like to visit Egypt.

Why?

I want to see the pyramids.

GRAMMAR GUIDE

Past simple of to be

1 Look at the sentences and complete the verb table.

1 His first trip **was** in 1841.
2 The ticket **wasn't** cheap.
3 The ticket and food **were** included in the price.
4 Because of Cook, travel and tourism **weren't** only for the rich.
5 **Was** Thomas Cook British? Yes, he **was**.

Affirmative	
I was You were He/She/It (**a**) .... We were You were They (**b**)	in the USA in 2006.
Negative	
I wasn't You weren't He/She/It (**c**) .... We weren't You weren't They (**d**)	in the USA in 2006.
Question	
(**e**) .... I/he/she/it (**f**) .... you/we/they	in the USA in 2006?
Short answers	
Yes, I/he/she/it (**g**) .... No, I/he/she/it (**h**) .... Yes, we/you/they (**i**) .... No, we/you/they (**j**)	

GRAMMAR REFERENCE ▸ page 88

2 Complete the dialogue with *was, wasn't, were* or *weren't*.

Mia: Hi, Ryan. Where (**a**) .... you last week? You (**b**) .... at school. Why not?
Ryan: I (**c**) .... in the USA. My dad (**d**) .... there on business.
Mia: (**e**) .... you in New York?
Ryan: No, we (**f**) .... We (**g**) .... in Washington DC.
Mia: (**h**) .... it warm there?
Ryan: No, it (**i**) .... It (**j**) .... really cold!

3 Look at the list of top 10 tourist attractions. Complete the sentences with the correct past forms of *to be*.

Top 10 tourist attractions

1 Times Square, New York City
2 National Mall and Memorial Parks, Washington DC
3 Disney World, Orlando
4 Trafalgar Square, London
5 Disneyland, California
6 Niagara Falls, Ontario
7 Fisherman's Wharf, San Francisco
8 Tokyo Disneyland, Urayasu
9 Notre Dame de Paris, Paris
10 Disneyland Paris, Paris

2008

1 In 2008, Times Square .... the number one tourist attraction in the world.
2 Six of the top ten tourist attractions .... in North America.
3 The Eiffel Tower .... in the top ten.
4 One attraction in the top ten .... in Great Britain.
5 Trafalgar Square .... number five in the list.
6 The Great Wall of China and the Grand Canyon .... in the top ten.
7 One of the top ten attractions .... in North America or Europe.
8 Two of the top ten attractions .... French.

4 Write questions using the correct past forms of *to be*.

1 you/at school at 6 am?
2 your parents/home at 10 pm last night?
3 your family/on holiday last July?
4 your friend/at school yesterday?
6 you/in your house in 2008?

5 SPEAKING Work with a partner. Ask and answer the questions in 4. Then tell the class two of your partner's answers.

Were you at school at 6 am? *No, I wasn't!*

GRAMMAR GUIDE

Past simple of *can*

6 Look at the sentences and answer the questions.

a Customers **could** buy guide books in the shop.
b Poor people **couldn't** go on holidays.
c **Could** they go by plane in 1860? No, they **couldn't**.

1 What part of the verb comes after **could** or **couldn't**?
2 What happens in questions? Where does **could** go?

GRAMMAR REFERENCE ▸ page 88

7 Look at the activities. Write sentences saying if people *could* or *couldn't* do these things in 1872.

1 travel around the world in a week
They couldn't travel around the world in a week.
2 sail from Britain to the USA
3 travel by car at 160 kph
4 fly from Britain to Japan
5 stay in hotels
6 go on holiday
7 buy travel tickets online

8 SPEAKING Find out at what age your partner could do these things for the first time.

1 swim
2 count to ten in English
3 walk
4 ride a bike
5 read
6 write your name
7 have a simple conversation in English

When could you swim?

I could swim when I was five. Could you?

No, I could swim when I was seven.

Transport

a

b

c

d

e

f

g

1 Match the photos with some of these words. Check that you understand the other words. Use your dictionary if necessary.

boat bus car coach helicopter lorry motorbike scooter ship taxi tram underground van

2 Complete the table with the words in 1.

Land	Air	Sea
train	*plane*	*boat*

3 SPEAKING Work in small groups. Say how often you travel by the different types of transport in 1. Ask other questions to find out more information.

I never travel by plane.
I sometimes travel by coach.

Where do you go when you travel by coach?

I usually go to see my cousin. She lives about fifty kilometres from here.

Tourist guides

Cross-curricular – Business
Starting a business

1 Work with a partner. Take it in turns to describe the photos. What do you think is the connection between the two photos? Guess and give details.

2 Read the text and check your ideas in 1.

Lonely Planet is a company which produces modern, dynamic guide books. It also produces TV programmes, a magazine and lots of useful digital material on the web. In 2008 there were 500 Lonely Planet books in eight languages, with annual sales of more than six million guide books.

The start of this global company was unusual. Maureen and Tony Wheeler were the two creators of Lonely Planet. Their first meeting was in Regent's Park in London in 1970. Maureen was just twenty. A year later, they were married. Their idea of the perfect honeymoon was to travel across Europe and Asia all the way to Australia.

Maureen and Tony's nine-month trip was a success. When they arrived in Australia, their friends asked how it was possible to make such a long trip with no money. Their answers to these questions were the basis of their first guidebook – *Across Asia on the Cheap*. The first edition of the book was the product of long nights writing at their kitchen table. After just one week, they were able to sell 1,500 books. It was the only guide book in the world written *by* adventurous young travellers *for* adventurous young travellers. And it was the first guide book for people travelling 'on the cheap'.

Lonely Planet was born. Two years later, there was another book by the Wheelers, and then another, and another. In 2007, the BBC bought 75% of the Lonely Planet company. The Wheelers continue to have the other 25%. There are now 300 people writing for Lonely Planet. And now, the Wheelers have more time to do what they enjoy – travel!

WORD BOOSTER

Match the words and definitions.

1 magazine
2 annual sales
3 honeymoon
4 basis
5 bought
6 on the cheap

a a holiday that two people have after they get married
b doing something without spending a lot of money
c a big, thin book with a paper cover, usually published once a month or once a week
d the number of things that a company sells in a year
e the reason why something is done
f the past simple of *buy*

3 Read the text again. Are these sentences true (T), false (F) or is the information not mentioned (NM)?

1 Maureen and Tony's friends were interested in the story of their trip to Australia. T/F/NM
2 Maureen and Tony's parents were rich. T/F/NM
3 Maureen and Tony were quite young when they started Lonely Planet. T/F/NM
4 Maureen and Tony write all the Lonely Planet books now. T/F/NM
5 Maureen and Tony don't like travelling now. T/F/NM
6 Maureen and Tony's favourite travel destination is Australia. T/F/NM

PROJECT

4 Work in groups. Each group is a business. Invent a product or service that you think can be popular.

1 Decide how to sell your product. Make an advertisement for it.
2 'Sell' your product to the rest of the class.
3 Decide which product is the best.

International cultural knowledge

A travel podcast

a

b

c

d

INSIDE INFORMATION

- Brighton is a town on the south coast of England.
- Eight million tourists visit Brighton each year.
- Brighton is famous for its cultural activities and for its nightlife.

5 LISTENING 2.04 **Listen to the podcast about Brighton – a popular place for tourists in England. Then put the photos in the order that you hear about them.**

1 .... 2 .... 3 .... 4 ....

6 **Listen again and complete the notes.**

Brighton is only an (**a**) .... from London by train. About (**b**) .... metres from the train station are some lovely (**c**) .... The next place you need to visit is the Royal Pavilion. On the outside the Pavilion appears to be like an (**d**) .... building, but inside it has a (**e**) .... style. After that, go to the milkshake shop where they have (**f**) .... different milkshakes. Then go to the beach. The only problem is that the water is sometimes (**h**) .... If the weather's bad you can go to a café or (**i**) .... near the beach.

7 SPEAKING **What about *you*?**

1 Would you like to visit Brighton?
2 What is a popular place for tourists in your country?

PROJECT

8 **Work in groups. Make notes to help visitors to your town or city.**

1 Think about these areas: sightseeing, shopping, things to do, places to eat and drink.
2 Each person in the group chooses one of the areas and finds out more information about it. Look for illustrations too.
3 In your group, decide how to present your information to the rest of the class. Prepare it and present it.

1 **Work with a partner. Look at the photo and make a list of things you think you can do on holiday in Paris.**

visit the Eiffel Tower
go on the river in a boat

2 LISTENING 2.05 **Listen to a girl talking about a trip to Paris. Tick (✓) any of the things in your list that she says.**

EXAM SUCCESS

In the next exercise, you listen and say if the statements are true or false. When should you read the statements – before listening or after listening? Why?

EXAM SUCCESS ▸ page 159

3 **Listen again. Are these sentences true (T) or false (F), or is the information not mentioned (NM)?**

1 Katie went to Paris with her family. T/F/NM
2 Katie didn't like travelling by boat. T/F/NM
3 Katie couldn't speak a word of French the first time she went. T/F/NM
4 Katie bought some *Asterix* comics. T/F/NM
5 Katie's friends weren't happy eating fast food. T/F/NM
6 Katie saw an adventure film on her trip. T/F/NM
7 It was impossible for Katie to understand the film she saw. T/F/NM

4 SPEAKING **What about *you*?**

Which city do you want to visit? Why?

I want to visit Madrid.

Why?

Because I love Spanish food.

GRAMMAR GUIDE

Past simple affirmative – regular and irregular verbs

1a Look at the sentences and put the verbs in the correct place in the table.

a I **loved** it.
b We **stayed** in a really nice hotel.
c They **hated** it.
d We **watched** a French film.
e I **listened** carefully.
f We **went** to Paris.
g We **took** a boat to Calais.
h I **spoke** to people there.
i I **bought** some things there.
j I **read** them again and again.
k I **ate** lots of French food.

Column A:		Column B:	
Infinitive	Past form	Infinitive	Past form
hate		buy	
listen		eat	
love	*loved*	go	
stay		read	
watch		speak	
		take	

1b Now decide which column is *Regular* and which is *Irregular*.

GRAMMAR REFERENCE ▸ page 88

1c Match the spelling rules for regular simple past forms (1–4) with the examples below (a–d).

1 Most verbs: Add *-ed* to most verbs. *b*
2 Verbs that end in *-e*: Add *-d*.
3 Verbs that end in a consonant + *y*: take away the *-y* and add *-ied*.
4 Verbs that end in one vowel + one consonant: double the consonant and add *-ed*.

a study – studied, cry – cried, try – tried
b walk – walked, want – wanted, need – needed
c stop – stopped, chat – chatted, jog – jogged
d decide – decided, phone – phoned, like – liked

STUDY SKILLS

What can you do to learn the spelling of new words?

STUDY SKILLS ▸ page 157

2a PRONUNCIATION 2.06 **Listen to the words in the table. What is the difference between the pronunciation of the *-ed* endings?**

/t/	/d/	/ɪd/
liked	listened	hated

2b 2.07 **Listen to these past simple verbs and write them in the correct column above.**

decided loved needed played started
stayed wanted washed watched worked

2c 2.08 **Listen, check and repeat.**

3 Complete the sentences with the past form of these verbs.

buy eat go read see speak take understand

Last year, I (**a**) .... to Italy with my family. I (**b**) .... a guide book with me and I (**c**) .... it to find out useful information. In Rome, we (**d**) .... the Colosseum and we (**e**) .... lots of really good pasta. I (**f**) .... some presents for my friends in a big shopping centre in Rome. My mum (**g**) .... Italian all the time because her Italian is very good. She (**h**) .... everything that people said to her.

4 Complete the sentences with the correct past form of the verbs given. Use the word list on page 166 to help you with irregular past forms. What are the underlined words?

1 Yesterday afternoon I .... (have) a lot of homework.
2 Last night my brother and I .... (make) the dinner.
3 The day before yesterday my parents .... (catch) a taxi to go to the airport.
4 Two days ago we .... (do) a history project at school.
5 Last week my friends and I .... (swim) in the sea.
6 Last month our English teacher .... (teach) us different parts of the body.
7 Last year I .... (come) to school by bus.
8 Three years ago my parents .... (buy) me a pet for my birthday.

5a SPEAKING **Write true sentences about you and your family. Begin the sentences with the underlined words in 4. Use any of the verbs on this page.**

Yesterday I bought a magazine.

Yesterday afternoon I played computer games with my friend.

5b Tell your partner the things that you did, but don't say when you did them. Can your partner guess when you did the different things?

I went to London.

I think it was last year.

No, it was three years ago.

1 **Look at Jenny's holiday photos. Match each photo (a–e) with one of the topics (1–8).**

a ..*1*.. b .... c .... d .... e ....

1 Where you went
2 Who you went with
3 How you went
4 Where you stayed
5 What you did
6 What you saw
7 What you ate
8 What you bought

2 SPEAKING **Work with a partner. Take it in turns to talk about Jenny's holiday using the photos.**

I think she went to Rio de Janeiro, in Brazil.

3a LISTENING 2.09 **Listen to Jenny talking about her holiday. What does she say about the topics in 1? Make notes.**

2 *Went with mum and two brothers*

3b SPEAKING **Compare your answers in 3a with your partner. Help each other to complete all the answers.**

4 **Complete the useful expressions in the Speaking Bank with *at, to, with* or *by*. Check that you understand all the words in the Speaking Bank. Use your dictionary if necessary.**

▶ **Speaking Bank**

Useful expressions to talk about a holiday

- I went (**a**) .... (Rio/Tokyo/Cairo)/(**b**) .... (car/plane/coach/train)/(**c**) .... (my family/my brother/my friends/my school).
- It took (20 minutes/two hours/a day) to get there.
- We stayed (**d**) .... (the Ritz Hotel/a campsite/a youth hostel/a bed and breakfast).
- We went (**e**) .... the beach.
- We did some sightseeing./We went sightseeing.
- We saw (a monument/bridge/tower).
- We bought (souvenirs/a shirt/a CD).
- We ate (tropical fruit/typical food).
- It was great/brilliant/spectacular/delicious.
- I had a great time./I loved it.

5 SPEAKING **Work with a partner. These are photos of your last holiday. Take it in turns to talk about a photo and say what you did.**

I went to Cairo.

I visited the pyramids.

Practice makes perfect

6a **Work with a partner. Take it in turns to do the task. You can help your partner by saying:**

Tell me about what you did/saw/ate.

Talk about a holiday that you really liked.
Include this information:

- when, where and how you went, and who you went with
- where you stayed and what you did and saw
- what you ate and bought

6b **Tell the class about your partner's holiday.**

▶ **EXAM SUCCESS**

How can you prepare for a speaking exam where you need to talk about past events? EXAM SUCCESS ▶ page 159

1a SPEAKING **Work with a partner. Which of these things are important for you to have a great holiday? Decide together and put them in order of importance.**

- the food you eat
- shopping
- sightseeing
- relaxing
- activities
- the hotel and area where you are staying
- the weather

The important thing for me is sightseeing. I like visiting interesting places.

I agree. But I think relaxing is important too, because holidays are for relaxing.

OK. So number 1 on our list is sightseeing and number two is relaxing.

1b Tell the class the top and bottom things on your list. Do people generally agree?

2a Read this postcard. Which of the things in 1 does Megan write about? Tick (✓) them.

Hi Alex,
Here we are in the Big Apple and we're having a brilliant time. We're sitting in a café, having a burger and a milkshake and thinking about you!
Yesterday we did some sightseeing and we went to the top of the Empire State Building! We also saw the Statue of Liberty and Times Square.
This morning we did some shopping. I bought some cool T-shirts, and a little present for you.
Wish you were here!
Love
Megan

2b Read the postcard again and underline any information about the things in 1.

3 Look at the postcard again and complete the useful advice in the Writing Bank.

▸ Writing Bank

Useful advice for writing a postcard

- We usually begin a postcard with (a) .... or *Dear* and the person's name.
- Then we talk about where we are and what we are doing. We use the (b) .... continuous to do this.
- When we talk about things we did before writing the postcard, we use the (c) .... simple.
- We usually end a postcard with *Wish you were* (d) ...., (e) ...., *Bye for now* or *See you soon.*

Practice makes perfect

4a Look at the task. Choose a city. Plan what you are going to write. Think about the order of the information.

You are on holiday. Write a postcard to an English friend. Say what you are doing now and what you did yesterday and this morning. You can talk about sightseeing, shopping, food and drink, your hotel …

4b Individually, write your postcard and then 'send' it to your partner.

▸ STUDY SKILLS

Do you usually make a plan before you write in English? Why is it a good idea?

STUDY SKILLS ▸ page 157

Language reference and revision

Grammar reference

Past simple of to be

Form

Affirmative	I/He/She/It **was** in Scotland last year. You/We/They **were** in Scotland last year.
Negative	I/He/She/It **wasn't (was not)** in Brazil last year. You/We/They **weren't (were not)** in Brazil last year.
Question	**Was** I/he/she/it in Italy last year? **Were** you/we/they in Italy last year?
Short answers	Yes, I/he/she/it **was**. No, I/he/she/it **wasn't**. Yes, you/we/they **were**. No, you/we/they **weren't**.

Past simple of can

Form

Affirmative	I/You/He/She/It/We/They **could** + verb. *He could swim when he was five.*
Negative	I/You/He/She/It/We/They **couldn't (could not)** + verb. *She couldn't ski when she was seven.*
Question	**Could** I/you/he/she/it/we/they + verb. *Could they speak French?*
Short answers	Yes, I/you/he/she/it/we/they **could**. No, I/you/he/she/it/we/they **couldn't**. *Yes, they could!* *No, he couldn't.*

- After **could/couldn't** we use the infinitive form of the verb without ***to***.

  She could use a computer.
  We couldn't write.

Past simple affirmative

Form

Affirmative	I/You/He/She/It/We/They **visited** India. I/You/He/She/It/We/They **went** to India.

Spelling

- Spelling of regular past forms
  - Most verbs: add *-ed.*
    walk – walked, want – wanted, need – needed.
  - Verbs that end in *-e*: add *-d.*
    decide – decided, phone – phoned, arrive – arrived.
  - Verbs that end in a consonant +*y*: take away *-y* and add *-ied.*
    study – studied, cry – cried, try – tried.
  - Verbs that end in one vowel + one consonant: double the consonant and add -ed.
    stop – stopped, chat – chatted, jog – jogged
- Many common verbs are irregular. See the list of irregular verbs on page 166.

Use

- We use the past simple to describe finished actions or situations in the past.
  I saw Red Square in Moscow in 2005.
- With the past simple we often use time expressions like **yesterday**, **yesterday morning/afternoon/evening**, **last night**, **the day before yesterday**, **two/three/four days/weeks/months/years ago**, **last week/month/year**.

Vocabulary

1 Countries and nationalities

Argentina/Argentinian
Brazil/Brazilian
Czech Republic/Czech
Egypt/Egyptian France/French
Germany/German Ireland/Irish
Italy/Italian Japan/Japanese
Poland/Polish Russia/Russian
Slovakia/Slovakian
South Africa/South African
Spain/Spanish Switzerland/Swiss
Turkey/Turkish the USA/American

2 Words connected with tourism

boat guide book hotel
luggage package holiday
passport plane sightseeing
tickets train trip/excursion

3 Transport

boat bus car coach
helicopter lorry motorbike
plane scooter ship taxi
train tram underground van

4 Other words and phrases ▸ page 151

Grammar revision

Past simple of *to be* and *can*

1 Complete the sentences with *was, were, wasn't, weren't, could* or *couldn't*.

1 Mozart .... very famous because he .... play the piano at the age of five.
2 Shakespeare .... American. He .... English.
3 We .... vote in the general election last year because we .... only 15 years old.
4 Nefertiti and Cleopatra .... Indian.

WORKBOOK ▸ page 56 — /7 points

Past simple affirmative – regular verbs

2 Complete the sentences with the past simple form of the verbs given.

1 Last night I .... (dance) at the party.
2 My brother .... (study) German last year.
3 My father .... (stop) smoking two years ago.
4 Last summer we .... (want) to go to Scotland for our holidays.
5 Last night I .... (decide) to go to bed early.
6 My mum .... (hate) the film on TV last night.

WORKBOOK ▸ page 59 — /6 points

Past simple affirmative – irregular verbs

3 Change the sentences from the present simple to the past simple.

1 She sees her grandparents at the weekend.
She saw her grandparents at the weekend.
2 He buys CDs and books.
3 I take a pen to the class.
4 We do a lot of sport on Friday.
5 Mrs Jones teaches maths.
6 My friend comes to school by bus.
7 My dad catches the train to work.
8 They get back home late on Saturday.

WORKBOOK ▸ page 59 — /7 points

Vocabulary revision

Countries and nationalities

1 Complete the table.

Country	Nationality
France	1 ....
Egypt	2 ....
3	Polish
4	Turkish
Scotland	5 ....
6	Swiss
Brazil	7 ....

WORKBOOK ▸ page 54 — /7 points

Words connected with tourism

2 Complete the sentences with these words.

guidebook luggage package holiday passport sightseeing ticket trip

1 Pass me the .... I want to read about the museum we visited this morning.
2 Is this all your .... – just these two bags?
3 I love .... When I went to New York I saw the Statue of Liberty, Times Square, the Empire State Building …
4 I bought a .... for the train; travelling from London to Scotland is really expensive!
5 Have you got your .... ? They can't let you into the country if you haven't got it.
6 When I was 12 we went on a .... to Oxford, just for the day.
7 I don't want to go on a .... , I want to explore and find my own places to stay when we get there.

WORKBOOK ▸ page 54 — /7 points

Transport

3 Complete the words for transport with vowels and mark Land, Sea or Air after each one.

1 l ... r r y Land/Sea/Air
2 s h ... p Land/Sea/Air
3 v ... n Land/Sea/Air
4 s c ... t ... r Land/Sea/Air
5 ... n d ... r g r ... n d Land/Sea/Air
6 c ... c h Land/Sea/Air

WORKBOOK ▸ page 57 — /6 points

Total /40 points

Gateway to exams Units 5–6

Reading

Tip For Reading Exams

In activities where you must put sentences in a dialogue, remember …

First, read the complete dialogue. This helps you to understand the general situation.

EXAM SUCCESS ▸ page 159

1 What does Helen say to Daniel? Complete the dialogue by putting sentences (**A**–**G**) in the gaps. There is one extra sentence.

DANIEL: Where did you go for your holidays last year?

HELEN: 0 *My family and I went to the south of Spain*

DANIEL: Did you go by plane?

HELEN: 1 ....

DANIEL: What did you do when you got there?

HELEN: 2 ....

DANIEL: Granada must be great. I'd love to go there!

HELEN: 3 ....

DANIEL: I also want to go to Italy one year.

HELEN: 4 ....

DANIEL: That's a good idea. My brother went last year and he had a great time.

HELEN: 5 ....

DANIEL: Yes, hotels are very expensive. But first we have to speak to our parents!

A Why don't we go there next year with some friends?
B No, my dad hates flying.
C We can stay at youth hostels.
D No, we didn't go to the beach.
E Mostly sightseeing because there are some beautiful cities there like Seville, Cordoba and Granada.
F My family and I went to the south of Spain.
G You should. There are a lot of things to see and do.

2 Work with a partner. Practise the completed dialogue in 1.

Listening

Tip For Listening Exams

In *True/False/Not mentioned* activities, remember …

Read the statements before you listen. They give you an idea of what you are listening for. EXAM SUCCESS ▸ page 159

3 Work with a partner. Look at the list. Which things are typical of good restaurants? Which are typical of bad ones?

1 The waiters give fast service. *good*
2 They don't give you much food.
3 The food is cold when it comes to your table.
4 They have a lot of things on the menu.
5 The kitchen isn't clean.
6 They don't give you what you ordered.

4 2.10 Listen to Philip asking Karen about a restaurant. Are the sentences true (T) or false (F) or are they not mentioned (NM)?

1 Karen's family ate out because it was her birthday. T/F/NM
2 They went to a Chinese restaurant. T/F/NM
3 The service in the restaurant was very slow. T/F/NM
4 There was no cheese on Karen's pizza. T/F/NM
5 Karen's brother didn't have any chips with his burger. T/F/NM
6 Karen's mum never eats meat. T/F/NM
7 The tomato salad was good. T/F/NM
8 Karen's parents didn't speak to the waiter about their bad experience in the restaurant. T/F/NM

Speaking

Tip For Speaking Exams

In activities where you have to talk about past events, remember …

Prepare by learning as many regular and irregular past forms as possible. Learn and use expressions of time (*then, after that …*) to explain when things happened.

EXAM SUCCESS ▸ page 159

5 Work with a partner. What are the past forms of these verbs? Some are regular, some are irregular.

buy eat get go hate like love make order read see speak stay take understand want

6 Work with a partner. Look at the situation below and role-play the dialogue. When you finish, change roles.

Talk about a restaurant that you went to and really liked or really hated. Include this information:

- where the restaurant was
- what type of restaurant it was
- when you went
- who you went with
- what you ate
- what was good or bad
- should people go to this restaurant? Why/Why not?

Writing

Tip For Writing Exams

In writing exams, remember …

When you write to a friend, you should use contractions and short, direct sentences. In informal invitations, use informal expressions like *Hi Pete, Can you come?, Let me know if you can make it.*, etc.

EXAM SUCCESS ▸ page 159

7 Read this invitation and answer the questions.

1 Who makes the invitation?
2 Why do they make the invitation?
3 What is the invitation for?
4 Where is the event?
5 What day/time is it?
6 What should they bring?

Dear Mr Franklin,

On Saturday morning a friend is arriving from the United States of America. To celebrate this, my parents and are having a barbecue in our garden. We are inviting you to come to this barbecue. Would you like to come? The barbecue starts at 6 o'clock in the evening. It is very important to bring something to drink. But it is not necessary to bring food because we have got burgers, chicken and also food for vegetarians.

Please inform me if you can come to this barbecue.

Jonathan Smith

8 Is the invitation in 7 informal? Why/Why not?

9 Use the information in the invitation in 7 to write an INFORMAL invitation to a friend.

'Can Do' Progress Check

CEF

1 How well can you do these things in English now? Give yourself a mark from 1 to 4.

1 = I can do it very well.
2 = I can do it quite well.
3 = I have some problems.
4 = I can't do it.

a I can talk about quantities with *some, any, a/an, a lot of, much, many.* ☐
b I can talk about good or bad ideas using *should* and *shouldn't.* ☐
c I can name different food and drink. ☐
d I can order food in a café or restaurant. ☐
e I can write a short invitation to a celebration. ☐
f I can talk about the past using the past simple affirmative. ☐
g I can name different countries and nationalities. ☐
h I can understand written and spoken texts about travel and tourism. ☐
i I can talk about a holiday. ☐
j I can write a postcard. ☐

2 Now decide what you need to do to improve.

1 Look again at my book/notes.
2 Do more practice exercises. ⇨ WORKBOOK page 62–63
3 Ask for help.
4 Other: ....

7 Famous works

Grammar ▸ Past simple – negative ▸ Past simple – questions and short answers
Vocabulary ▸ Places of work ▸ Jobs and work ▸ Culture and entertainment
Speaking ▸ An anecdote about a special weekend
Writing ▸ A biography

▸ Vocabulary

Places of work

1a Work with a partner. Match the pictures with some of these words.

clinic factory garage hospital office
outdoors restaurant shop studio

1b 2.11 Listen and repeat.

Jobs and work

2 Look again at the words in 1. Where do you find these people?

businessman/woman doctor engineer farmer
mechanic nurse secretary shop assistant
singer waiter/waitress

3 Match the definitions (1–8) with these words. Which two words do not have definitions?

actor/actress artist builder bus/taxi/lorry driver
cleaner cook dentist footballer hairdresser
journalist

1 Someone who reports the news for a newspaper, a magazine, a TV show or a radio show.
2 Someone whose job is to build or repair houses.
3 Someone whose job is to look after your teeth.
4 Someone whose job is to clean the rooms in a building.
5 Someone who works in films or in a theatre.
6 Someone who paints pictures.
7 Someone whose job is to cut people's hair.
8 Someone whose job is to prepare food in a restaurant.

4a PRONUNCIATION **Each of these words has three syllables. Put each word in the correct column.**

bus driver businessman engineer footballer
hairdresser journalist mechanic secretary

Ooo	oOo	ooO

4b 2.12 Listen, check and repeat.

5 SPEAKING **Work with a partner. Say where the people in 2 and 3 usually work.**

A dentist usually works in a clinic.

6 LISTENING **2.13 Listen to the people talk about their jobs. What are their jobs?**

1 .... 3 ....
2 .... 4 ....

7 SPEAKING **Choose a job from 2 or 3. Don't tell anybody what the job is. Work in groups and take it in turns to ask questions to discover the jobs. You can only answer *yes* or *no*. People can ask a maximum of 20 questions.**

Do you work in an office?

Yes, I do.

Do you have to make telephone calls?

No, I don't.

Do you make a lot of money?

No, I don't.

Do you sit all day?

No, I don't.

Are you a cleaner?

Yes, I am.

1 **Work with a partner. What jobs do you think actors and singers do before they become famous? Make a list.**

2 **Read this magazine article. Do any of the jobs in your list appear in the text?**

Before they were famous (and after!)

Jennifer Hudson – a life of ups and downs

Jennifer Hudson's life is like a film. Her father was a bus driver. He died when she was a teenager. At 16, Jennifer had to work as a cook at a fast-food restaurant. She needed money to pay for her studies. In the end, she didn't study at university. She became a singer on a cruise ship.

Next, she went on the TV programme *American Idol*. She was a finalist but didn't win. Then she made a film, *Dreamgirls*, and won an Oscar. At the ceremony, she talked about her first job. To thank her, the fast-food restaurant said she could eat for free at the restaurant for the rest of her life!

Sadly, in 2008, three members of Jennifer's family died. It was the same year that she went into the studio and made her first record. The next year, her record was Number 1 and she sang for the US president.

Brad Pitt – his many jobs

Success didn't come easily for Brad Pitt. He studied to be a journalist at the University of Missouri but he didn't finish the course. He left just two weeks before the end. He already knew he wanted to be an actor.

He went to live in Los Angeles in 1985. He became a student again, this time studying acting. He didn't have much money so he started to take other jobs to pay for his classes. At one time, he was a limousine driver. He also had a job taking fridges from the factory to people's homes.

Then he had an unusual job, dressing up as a chicken to get people to eat in a Mexican restaurant! Now, Brad is not only an actor but also a businessman with his own Hollywood production company.

EXAM SUCCESS

In the next activity, you match the person and the information. First, you should read the text to get a general understanding. What should you do next? **EXAM SUCCESS ▸ page 159**

3a Read the text again. Is this information about Brad Pitt (BP), Jennifer Hudson (JH) or both(B)?

1 They spent some time studying at university. BP/JH/B
2 They used a type of transport for a job before they became famous. BP/JH/B
3 It wasn't fast or easy for them to become successful. BP/JH/B
4 They prepared food at a restaurant. BP/JH/B
5 They had to do physical work before becoming famous. BP/JH/B
6 Something very sad happened to them after they became famous. BP/JH/B
7 They worked because they needed money to do some type of course. BP/JH/B
8 They received an important prize. BP/JH/B

3b Write details for each answer.

Brad Pitt studied to be a journalist before he became famous.

4 **Match the underlined words in the text with these definitions.**

1 without paying
2 a public event, often to give prizes for doing something well
3 wearing special clothes
4 a company that makes films
5 a big, expensive, comfortable car
6 a long trip by sea, visiting places for holidays
7 a person who takes part in a final of a competition

5 **SPEAKING What about *you*?**

1 Does any of the information in the texts surprise you? What and why?
2 Do you know about the early life of another famous person?

I didn't know Brad Pitt dressed as a chicken!

Jennifer Aniston was a waitress before she was famous.

GRAMMAR GUIDE

Past simple – negative

1 Look at the sentences and answer the questions.

a He **didn't finish** his course.
b He **wanted** to be an actor.
c They **didn't have** much money.
d She **didn't win** the competition.
e She **won** the Oscar.

1 Which sentences are negative?
2 What comes before the main verb in past simple negative sentences?

GRAMMAR REFERENCE ▶ page 102

2 Make the sentences negative.

1 She wanted to be a waitress.
2 They had a lot of money.
3 I did two different jobs.
4 He spoke three languages.
5 We made ten films.
6 I swam in the Olympics.
7 He ate in a Mexican restaurant.
8 You went to Hollywood.

3 Write about what these people did or didn't do before they were famous.

1 Gwen Stefani/not clean offices. She/work in a fast-food restaurant.
2 Johnny Depp/not act in films. He/play the guitar in a rock band.
3 Julia Roberts/not make ice-cream. She/be a shop assistant.
4 Kirsten Dunst/not do any other jobs. She/start acting at the age of eight.
5 J K Rowling, the creator of Harry Potter/not teach French. She/teach English.

4 Complete the text with the correct form of the verbs given.

Life (**a**) .... (be) hard for Noel Gallagher before his success with the group Oasis. He (**b**) .... (not like) school. When he (**c**) .... (leave) school, he (**d**) .... (work) as a builder for his dad. But he and his dad (**e**) .... (not have) a good relationship. In the end, he (**f**) .... (go) to work as a builder in another company but he (**g**) .... (have) an accident. After the accident he (**h**) .... (write) his first songs. A Manchester band (**i**) .... (need) a singer but they (**j**) .... (give) Noel a job helping to carry their guitars and instruments. Three years later, his young brother, Liam, (**k**) .... (ask) Noel to join his group as guitarist. In 2009, after many arguments with his brother he (**l**) .... (leave) Oasis.

5 Are these sentences true for you? If not, change them to make them true.

1 I liked coffee when I was eleven.
2 I played with toy cars when I was five.
3 I went to another country last summer.
4 I won a prize before the age of twelve.
5 I did sport last weekend.
6 I went out last night.
7 I had a party at my house for my last birthday.

6 SPEAKING **Work in groups of three. Compare sentences. How many sentences do you have the same? Tell the class which sentences they are.**

We didn't like coffee when we were eleven.

7a **Guess if the sentences are affirmative or negative and write the complete sentences.**

1 Neil Armstrong/walk on the moon in 1970.

2 Van Gogh/paint the *Mona Lisa*.

3 Brazil/win the World Cup in 2006.

4 Shakespeare/write *Hamlet*.

5 Michael Jackson/ sing *Thriller*.

6 Alexander Graham Bell/ invent the television.

7 Marie Curie/win two Nobel prizes.

8 The Wright Brothers/ build the world's first successful plane.

9 Ada Lovelace/write the world's first computer program.

10 Louis Pasteur/discover penicillin.

7b 2.14 **Listen and check. How many of your answers are correct?**

Developing vocabulary

Culture and entertainment

1a **Match the pictures with some of these words. Check that you understand the meaning of the other words. Use your dictionary if necessary.**

art ballet film literature opera poetry theatre

a

b

c

d

1b 2.15 **Listen and repeat.**

2 SPEAKING **Work with a partner. Find out which of the things in 1 your partner is interested in.**

Are you interested in ballet?

No, not really. What about you?

3 **Match the words in 1 with these people.**

actor composer dancer director musician novelist painter poet singer writer

dancer – ballet, actor – theatre, film

4 SPEAKING **Work with a partner. Try to think of a famous person from your country for each word in 3. They can be living or dead.**

Anna Pavlova was a famous dancer.

Famous musical works

Cross-curricular – Music
Important periods in classical music

1 2.16 **Listen to three short pieces of classical music. Do any of the pieces make you think of:**

1 babies or young children? 1/2/3/None
2 a horror film? 1/2/3/None
3 death? 1/2/3/None

2 Can you match each piece of music in 1 with its composer and picture?

1 Wolfgang Amadeus Mozart 1/2/3 (picture ....)
2 Frédéric Chopin 1/2/3 (picture ....)
3 Johann Sabastian Bach 1/2/3 (picture ....)

3 Read the text and match the composers in 2 with the correct period.

1
The Baroque Period
1600–1750

The name comes from a style of architecture. This style had lots of decoration. The music of this period was similar. Opera began in this period. Claudio Monteverdi wrote the first big opera in 1607. The idea of opera was to bring theatre, poetry and music together.

Important composers from this period were (a) ...., Antonio Vivaldi and George Friederich Handel.

2
The Classical Period
1750–1820

The name comes from an interest in the art of classical Greece. At the end of the Baroque period, composers started doing new things. Most composers worked for royal families. They wrote concertos, sonatas, symphonies and quartets. Each type of composition had its special rules.

Important composers from this period were Joseph Haydn, (b) .... and Ludwig van Beethoven.

3
The Romantic Period
1810–1900

The name comes from the popularity of old, medieval romance. Composers were interested in love, beauty and mystery. Composers didn't want to follow rules. They wanted to express personal emotions and feelings. Many composers also wrote works about their country. They put traditional folk music, poetry and dance into their compositions.

Important composers from this period were (c) ...., Giuseppe Verdi, Peter Tchaikovsky, Richard Wagner and Franz Liszt.

4 Read the text again. Write the correct period for each statement.

1 Composers were interested in using their own feelings to write music.
....
2 Composers wanted to express things about their nation.
....
3 Rules were important when writing music.
....
4 It took its name from a style of building.
....
5 They created a new form of musical entertainment, mixing different arts.
....

▸ WORD BOOSTER

Match the types of composition with their definitions. Use a dictionary if necessary.

1 concerto
2 sonata
3 symphony
4 quartet

a a piece of music for four musicians
b a piece of music for a piano or a piano and another instrument
c a piece of music for an instrument and an orchestra
d a long piece of music for an orchestra

5 What about *you*?

Do you like classical music? Why/Why not?

Out on your own
Cold and alone again
Can this be what you really wanted, baby?

Blame it on me
Set your guilt free
Nothing can hold you back now

Now that you're gone
I feel like myself again
Grieving the things I can't repair and willing ...

To let you blame it on me
And set your guilt free
Nothing can hold you back now love

I can't change who I am
Not this time, I won't lie to keep you near me
And in this short life, there's no time to waste on giving up
My love wasn't enough

And you can blame it on me
Just set your guilt free, honey
I don't want to hold you back now love

Popular culture
Lacrymosa by Evanescence

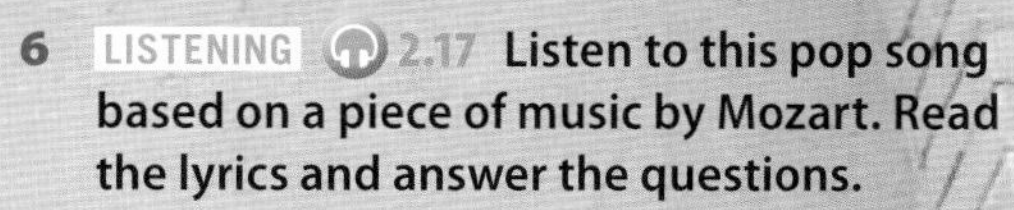

6 LISTENING 2.17 **Listen to this pop song based on a piece of music by Mozart. Read the lyrics and answer the questions.**

1 What do you think the song is about?
2 How do you think the singer feels?

7 **Listen again.**

1 Which part of the song is the chorus?
2 How many times do you hear the chorus?

8 SPEAKING **What about *you*?**

1 Do you like this song?
2 How does this song make you feel?
3 What are your favourite types of music?

WORD BOOSTER

on your own *alone, with nobody*
blame (v) *say that somebody did something bad*
guilt *the feeling that you did something bad*
grieving *feeling very sad about something*
willing *wanting*
waste *use in a bad way*
giving up *stopping*

PROJECT

9 **Work in groups. Choose a famous composer, singer, or group from your country. Prepare a presentation about them. Include information about their life and work.**

INSIDE INFORMATION

- *Evanescence* are an American band. People call their style 'gothic rock'.
- This song is from their 2006 album *The Open Door*. The music comes from part of Mozart's 'Requiem'.
- Amy Lee, the singer in the band, says this is her favourite piece of music ever. She heard it for the first time when she saw a film about Mozart called *Amadeus*.

1a **Look at the photo of Hollywood superstar Marilyn Monroe. Work with a partner. Make notes of any information that you know about her.**

She was popular in the 1950s.

1b LISTENING 2.18 **Listen to a TV quiz and check your ideas.**

EXAM SUCCESS

In this activity, you complete notes by writing a word or a few words in the spaces. How important do you think it is to spell the words correctly?

EXAM SUCCESS ▸ page 159

2 **Listen again and complete the notes.**

Marilyn Monroe trivia

- Marilyn Monroe once sang (a) .... for the American president John F Kennedy.
- Before she became famous, she worked in (b) ....
- She made the famous film *Gentlemen Prefer Blondes* in (c) ....
- One of her popular songs was *Diamonds are* (d) ....
- She studied (e) .... at the University of California, Los Angeles.
- She was (f) .... years old when she died.

3 **Listen again and complete the timeline for Marilyn Monroe.**

....	*She was born.*
1942–46:	....
1951:	....
1953:	....
1954:	....
1956:	....
1962:	....
....	*She died.*

4 SPEAKING **What about *you*?**

Who is your favourite film star? What do you know about their life?

My favourite actor is Matt Damon. He was born in the USA. I think he started university but he didn't finish ...

STUDY SKILLS

If you want to improve your listening, what can you listen to in English outside the classroom?

STUDY SKILLS ▸ page 157

GRAMMAR GUIDE

Past simple – questions and short answers

1 **Look at the sentences and choose the correct alternative in the rules.**

a When **did** Marilyn **make** that film?
b What **did** she **study** at university?
c **Did** Marilyn **win** an Oscar?
d Yes, she **did**./No, she **didn't**.

1 To make questions we use **did** + subject + the *infinitive/past* form of the verb.
2 In short answers we *repeat/don't repeat* the main verb (e.g. *go, finish, work*).

GRAMMAR REFERENCE ▶ page 102

2a **Complete the questions with the correct form of the verbs given.**

1 What film .... Johnny Depp .... (star) in as Jack Sparrow?
2 Which famous trilogy .... JRR Tolkien .... (write)?
3 Which cartoon family .... Matt Groening .... (create)?
4 What dance .... Michael Jackson .... (make) famous?
5 Which sport .... Martina Hingis .... (play)?
6 Which statue .... the French .... (give) to the USA in 1886?

2b **Work with a partner. Ask and answer the questions.**

3 **Write complete questions and write true short answers.**

1 you/go to school yesterday?
Did you go to school yesterday? Yes, I did.
2 you/pass your last English exam?
3 a friend/go to your house last weekend?
4 you and your family/watch TV last night?
5 you/have a big breakfast this morning?
6 you/walk to school today?
7 your class/go on an excursion last year?

4a **SPEAKING** **Look at the phrases. Add time expressions and write them as questions.**

1 win a competition
Did you win a competition last year?
2 take 100 photos or more
3 read more than 20 books
4 meet a famous person
5 travel somewhere by boat
6 go to three or more concerts
7 buy a new TV or computer
8 see a ballet, an opera, or a play at the theatre

4b **Now find one person who did each activity and write their name next to each question. You can only write a person's name once.**

5a **SPEAKING** **Write eight questions to find out about what your partner did last weekend. Use these words and expressions to help you.**

chat online dance do sport go out
go to the park/the cinema listen to music
play computer games/football/a musical instrument
ride your bike skate surf the Net take photos
watch a film

5b **Work with a partner. Ask your questions.**

Did you surf the Net?
Yes, I did.

5c **Work in groups. Tell the group about your partner's weekend. Say what they did and what they didn't do.**

Clara didn't go out. She watched a film. She also …

6 **Write questions for the underlined part of the answer.**

1 Lewis Carroll wrote *Alice in Wonderland*.
What did Lewis Carroll write?
2 Michael Jordan played basketball.
3 Sandra Bullock won an Oscar in 2009.
4 James Cameron directed the film *Avatar* in 2009.
5 Gustave Eiffel built the Eiffel Tower.
6 John Coltrane played the saxophone.
7 Claude Monet painted his garden.
8 Mark Zuckerberg created Facebook.

1 SPEAKING **Work with a partner. Look at the photos and talk about what you can see.**

In picture a there's a band.

Yes, with a singer and two musicians.

They're playing at a concert.

a

b

c

2 LISTENING 2.19 **Listen to Mark telling Sandra about his perfect weekend and then answer the questions.**

1 Which photo in 1 is similar to the event in the conversation?
2 How did Mark find out about the event?
3 What time did the event happen?

3 **Listen to the conversation again and tick (✓) the words and expressions in the Speaking Bank that you hear.**

Speaking Bank

Useful expressions to show interest in what someone says

- Did you?/Is he?/Have they?
- Really?
- I see.
- That's interesting.
- That's incredible!
- Then what happened?
- Why?

4a SPEAKING 2.20 **Listen to the useful expressions in the Speaking Bank.**

4b **Work with a partner. Practise saying the expressions with the correct intonation.**

5 **Put the questions in the order that Sandra asks them. Listen again if necessary.**

1 .... 3 .... 5 .... 7 ....
2 .... 4 .... 6 ....

a Where did you meet her?
b What time did you go?
c What did you do?
d What time did she arrive?
e Did you have a good weekend?
f Did you take a photo of her?
g How did you find out about that?

Practice makes perfect

6a SPEAKING **Look at the task and prepare notes about a perfect weekend. It can be real or invented. Maybe you went to a concert, met a famous person, saw a sports event ….**

> Tell a friend about a perfect weekend. Give details – say what you did, where it was, when it was, etc. …

6b **Work with a partner. Take it in turns to ask your partner about their weekend. Ask questions beginning with *What, Who, Why, When* and *Where* like the ones in 5. Use expressions from the Speaking Bank to show your interest.**

Did you have a good weekend?

Yes, it was brilliant. It was the perfect weekend!

Why? What did you do?

1 **Work with a partner. Do you know anything about the actor Heath Ledger?**

2 **Read the text and put the paragraphs in order.**

1 .... 3 ....
2 .... 4 ....

A At the age of 16, Heath left school to become an actor. In 1997 he made his first film, but he didn't have an important part in it. The following year he went to America. Two years later he made one of his first big films, *The Patriot*.

B Heath was only 28 when he died. He was a great actor who could make any type of film. Because of his incredible work, he is already thought of by some people as a Hollywood legend.

C After that, Heath became famous. They nominated him for an Oscar for the film *Brokeback Mountain* but he didn't win. Then, in 2007, he started work as The Joker in a Batman film. He died on 22 January 2008, before the film came out. In 2008 he got an Oscar for his work.

D Heath Ledger was born on 4 April 1979 in Australia. His mother was a French teacher and his father was an engineer. Heath acted for the first time at the age of ten. When he was 11, his parents got divorced.

3 **Look at the biography again. Which paragraph talks about …**

1 Heath's death and why he is famous now? ....
2 the start of his career? ....
3 when he was born and his life as a child? ....
4 the important part of his career? ....

STUDY SKILLS

What are paragraphs, and how do they help you to write good texts in English?

STUDY SKILLS ▸ page 157

4 **Words and expressions of time are useful in biographies. Tick (✓) the words and expressions in the Writing Bank which appear in the biography of Heath Ledger.**

Writing Bank

Words and expressions of time

- After that
- At the age of 16
- In 1997
- Next
- The following year
- Then
- Two years later
- When he was 11

5 **Complete the text with these words.**

after at following in in later when

Aaliyah was a famous American singer and actress. She was born (a) .... 1979. (b) .... she was twelve, she signed her first record contract. (c) .... the age of 15, her first CD appeared. Two years (d) ...., her second CD came out. It sold 8 million copies worldwide. (e) .... 2000 she made a film called *Romeo Must Die*. (f) .... that, she started making another film, about vampires. The (g) .... year, she died in a plane crash. One week after her death, her third CD went to number one. She continues to influence soul and hip-hop music today.

Practice makes perfect

6a **Look at the task and choose a person to write about. Find information and make notes.**

Write a short biography about an actor, singer, writer, artist or musician who is dead. Write about:

- when they were born and their life as a child
- their career
- their death and why they are important now

6b **Organise the information in your notes into three paragraphs and then write the biography. Use the texts and words and expressions in the Writing Bank to help you.**

Language reference and revision

Grammar reference

Past simple negative

Form

Negative	I/You/He/She/It/We/They **didn't (did not)** + verb. *He didn't dance.* *We didn't see a film.*

- After ***did/didn't*** we use the infinitive form of the verb.

Use

We use the past simple negative to talk about things that didn't happen in the past.

Past simple – questions and short answers

Form

Question	**Did** I/you/he/she/it/we/they + verb? *Did they dance?* *Did you see a film?*
Short answers	Yes, I/you/he/she/it/we/they **did**. No, I/you/he/she/it/we/they **didn't**. *Yes, I did.* *No, I didn't.*

- After **did/didn't** and the subject we use the infinitive form of the verb.
- In short answers we do not repeat the main verb.

Use

We use past simple questions to ask about things that happened in the past.

Vocabulary

1 Places of work

clinic factory garage hospital office outdoors restaurant shop studio

2 Jobs and work

actor/actress artist builder bus/taxi/lorry driver businessman/woman cleaner cook dentist doctor engineer farmer footballer hairdresser journalist mechanic nurse secretary shop assistant singer waiter/waitress

3 Culture and entertainment

art ballet composer dancer director film literature musician novelist opera painter poet poetry singer theatre writer

4 Other words and phrases ▶ page 153

Grammar revision

Past simple – negative

1 Look at the affirmative sentences and write negative sentences.

1 He went by train. He .... by plane.
2 They finished at 7 pm. They .... at 5 pm.
3 We had lunch at home. We .... lunch at school.
4 I read a book. I .... a magazine.
5 She swam in the sea. She .... in a swimming pool.
6 He wrote a novel. He .... a poem.
7 My mum bought a new bag. She .... new shoes.

WORKBOOK ▶ page 66 — / 7 points

Past simple – question forms

2 Put the words in order to make questions.

1 time get you did What up yesterday?
2 Why teacher class stop did your the?
3 you go night Who did last out with?
4 family What do your summer last did?
5 When Beethoven compose symphony fifth his did?
6 they eat How did hamburgers many?
7 Egyptians did build How pyramids ancient the the?

WORKBOOK ▶ page 69 — / 7 points

Past simple – question forms and short answers

3 Make questions and write true short answers.

1 you/go to school last Monday?
Q: ....
A: ....

2 Mozart/play the piano?
Q: ....
A: ....

3 Elvis Presley/sing opera?
Q: ....
A: ....

4 you and your family/go on holiday last summer?
Q: ....
A: ....

5 Picasso/draw cartoons?
Q: ....
A: ....

6 Marilyn Monroe/make films?
Q: ....
A: ....

WORKBOOK ▶ page 69 — / 6 points

Vocabulary revision

Places of work

1 Where do these people work?

1 a mechanic: ....
2 a waiter: ....
3 a secretary: ....
4 a farmer: ....
5 a nurse: ....

WORKBOOK ▶ page 64 — / 5 points

Jobs and work

2 Put the letters in order to make jobs.

1 tenistd
2 realnec
3 redbuli
4 ratewi
5 greenine
6 rantojusil
7 redreshrisa
8 submenswainos

WORKBOOK ▶ page 64 — / 8 points

Culture and entertainment

3 Complete the sentences with these words.

actor art ballets dancers director literature novelists operas painters poet poetry theatre

1 *Swan Lake* and *Sleeping Beauty* are famous ....
2 *Rigoletto* and *La Traviata* are .... by Verdi.
3 Poems and novels are different types of ....
4 'Roses are red, Violets are blue, Sugar is sweet, And so are you' is a bad example of ....
5 Van Gogh and Da Vinci were two famous ....
6 Steven Spielberg is a famous film .... His job is to make the film and tell people what they have to do.
7 Shakespeare wrote works for the ....

WORKBOOK ▶ page 67 — / 7points

Total / 40 points

8 Me and the world around me

Grammar ▸ Comparative adjectives ▸ Superlative adjectives
Vocabulary ▸ Feelings ▸ Personality ▸ Social problems
Speaking ▸ Describing a photo
Writing ▸ A formal letter of opinion

▸ Vocabulary

Feelings

1a **Work with a partner. Match the pictures with some of these words.**

angry bored excited happy interested relaxed sad surprised tired worried

1b 2.21 **Listen and repeat.**

1c **Draw faces for the other five words. Can your partner guess the words?**

2 LISTENING 2.21 **Listen to four conversations. How do the people feel? Write one adjective from 1 for each person.**

1 ....
2 ....
3 ....
4 ....

3a **SPEAKING** **Think about when you have the feelings in 1 and write sentences.**

I feel happy when my football team wins.

3b **Read your sentences to your partner in a different order, but don't say the adjective. Can your partner guess it?**

I feel ________ when I swim.

Tired?

No.

Relaxed?

Yes!

Personality

4 **Complete the sentences with these adjectives.**

cheerful hard-working intelligent kind lazy quiet responsible serious

1 A .... person helps other people and is good to them.
2 An .... person understands and learns things quickly.
3 A .... person doesn't like working or making an effort.
4 A .... person is usually happy and friendly.
5 A .... person is reliable and can be trusted to do all the things that they should do.
6 A .... person doesn't talk much.
7 A .... person thinks carefully about things and does not laugh much.
8 A .... person puts a lot of effort in their work.

5a **Write three sentences about yourself using adjectives in 4.**

I think I'm a cheerful person because I'm usually happy.
I can be lazy sometimes because I like sleeping and relaxing.
I'm not quiet because I talk a lot.

5b **Give your piece of paper to your teacher. Your teacher will read out sentences. Can you guess which person wrote the sentences?**

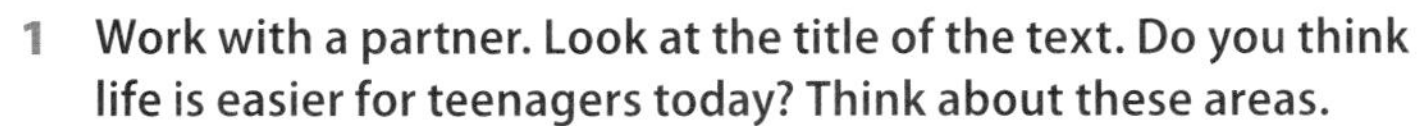

1 **Work with a partner. Look at the title of the text. Do you think life is easier for teenagers today? Think about these areas.**

fashion   jobs around the house   money   school   technology

2 **Read the text. Which of the four people think that life is easier for teenagers today?**

Do you think life is easier for teenagers today than for teenagers in the past?

Katie82

When I was a teenager, I was more responsible than today's teenagers. After school, I had to do a lot of jobs at home. My parents were really angry when I didn't do my chores. Today's teenagers are lazier. They come home from school and then play computer games for the rest of the day.

Sarah45

Young people nowadays aren't better or worse than young people in the past. Teenagers today have the same problems that we did. They're worried about finding their own identity and their own place in the world. I once read this quotation: 'Children nowadays just love the easy life. They're bad mannered, have no respect for authority or for older people, and they make their teachers mad.' Do you know who said that? It was Socrates. He lived about 2,400 years ago!

Patty52

In the media, they always say that teenagers have an easy life. They say they're lazy and irresponsible. But I work with young people and lots of them are responsible and hard-working. I also meet teenagers who are the opposite. Isn't it the same with adults?! Perhaps teenagers have more money now. And they have lots of modern gadgets like MP3 players. But those things don't always make life easier or make you happier.

Ned23

Who says teenagers have an easy life? Exams are harder now than in the past. It's more difficult to get a job so your marks need to be higher. The media make us worry about our appearance nowadays too; so a lot of teenagers aren't happy. They think they should be taller or thinner, like the people they see on TV. Maybe the problems are different from the past. But that doesn't make life easier. It's probably the opposite!

3 **Read the text again. Who says that …**

1 there are good and bad teenagers?
2 teenagers and adults aren't very different?
3 teenagers in the present and past are really the same?
4 life is probably more difficult for teenagers today?
5 they did more work than modern teenagers?
6 the main problems for teenagers are how they think they look?
7 school was easier before?
8 they don't believe what the newspapers and TV say?

STUDY SKILLS

What can you do when there are new words in a text and you don't have a dictionary?

STUDY SKILLS ▸ page 157

4 **Look at the underlined words in the text. Guess the meaning of the words and write a simple definition or similar word.**

chores – jobs you have to do at home

5 **Write one or two sentences to summarise what each person in the text thinks about teenagers today.**

Katie82 thinks that life is easier for teenagers today because they don't work at home. They are lazy and play all day.

6 **SPEAKING** **What about *you*?**

1 Do you agree with the opinions of the people in the text? Which one(s), and why?
2 How easy do you think your life is?

I agree with Sarah45. I think teenagers today are similar to teenagers in the past.

I don't agree. I agree with Ned23. Teenagers today have more to worry about.

GRAMMAR GUIDE

Comparative adjectives

1a Look at the sentences and complete the table with the words in bold.

1 Today's teenagers are **lazier** than teenagers in the past.
2 Young people nowadays aren't **better** or **worse** than young people in the past.
3 Exams are **harder** now than in the past.
4 They think they should be **thinner.**
5 I was **more responsible** than today's teenagers.

Adjective	Comparative adjective	Rule
hard	(a)	One-syllable adjectives – add *-er*
thin	(b)	One-syllable adjectives ending in one vowel and one consonant – double the consonant and add *-er*
lazy	(c)	Two-syllable adjectives ending in *-y* – omit *-y* and add *-ier*
responsible	(d)	Adjectives with two syllables or more – put *more* before the adjective
good **bad** **far**	(e) .... (f) .... farther, further	Irregular

1b Look at sentences *1, 2, 3* and *5*. Which word do we use after the comparative adjective when we compare two things?

GRAMMAR REFERENCE ▸ page 114

2 Look at the adjectives. Think about the rules in the table in 1 and write the comparative form.

1 easy *easier*
2 beautiful
3 high
4 kind
5 hard-working
6 pretty
7 friendly
8 fat

3a PRONUNCIATION 2.23 **Look at the sentences and listen.**

1 Mike is older than John.
2 Steve and Paul are lazier than Chris.
3 Your sister is better at maths than Helen.
4 Learning Japanese is harder than learning English.
5 Jenny is friendlier than Sarah.

3b Listen again and repeat each sentence. Put more stress on the words in red.

4a Do you know these facts? Choose the correct adjective and write the comparative form to complete the sentence.

1 China is .... (big/small) than Russia.
2 Istanbul is .... (near/far) from London than Athens.
3 K2 is .... (high/low) than Aconcagua.
4 In the summer, it is .... (hot/cool) in Madrid than in Paris.
5 The Eiffel Tower is .... (tall/short) than the Great Pyramid of Giza.
6 Elephants walk .... (fast/slow) than penguins.
7 Platinum is .... (cheap/expensive) than gold.

4b 2.24 **Listen and check. How many did you get right?**

5a Make the two sentences into one using the comparative form of the adjective.

1 Charlotte is angry. Sophie is very angry.
Sophie is angrier than Charlotte.
2 Jake is worried. Luke is very worried.
3 Amy is happy. Holly is very happy.
4 Max is bored. Ben is very bored.
5 Emma is intelligent. Isabelle is very intelligent.
6 Adam is bad at French. Charlie is very bad at French.

5b Now practise saying the sentences with the correct stress.

6a **SPEAKING** **Put the adjectives given in the comparative form. Then write sentences that are true for you.**

1 I think *ice hockey* is *better* (good) than *football*.

2 .... is .... (difficult) than ....

3 In my opinion, ... is .... (bad) than ....

4 .... is .... (big) than ....

5 I think .... is .... (easy) than ....

6 .... is .... (funny) than ....

6b **Work in small groups. Compare your sentences. Do you agree or disagree with other people's ideas?**

7a **SPEAKING** **Work with a partner. Write sentences comparing life now to one hundred years ago. Look at these topics for ideas. Use adjectives that you have learnt.**

fashion and hair   life in general   school   technology
transport   TV

7b **Read some of your sentences to the class. Do you have similar ideas?**

Social problems

1a **Work with a partner. Match the photos with some of these words.**

crime   homelessness   hunger   pollution
poverty   unemployment   violence

1b 2.25 **Listen and repeat.**

2 **SPEAKING** **Work with a partner. Choose three problems which you think are really important now. Say why you think they are more important than the other problems.**

I think unemployment is more important than pollution at the moment.

I agree. A lot of people haven't got jobs.

Peace

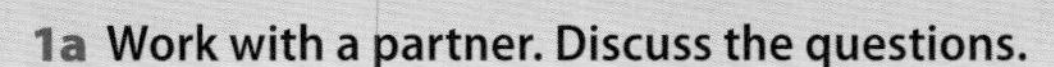

Cross-curricular – Citizenship
Peace One Day

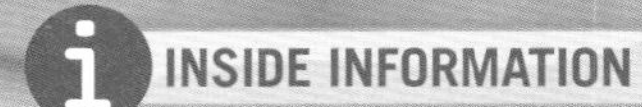

INSIDE INFORMATION

- Citizenship became a school subject in England and Wales in 2002.
- The idea was to help young people to become responsible citizens who can make a positive contribution to society.
- One area of study in citizenship is peace.

1a Work with a partner. Discuss the questions.

1. Who are the people in the photo? Why are they famous?
2. Do you know when international Peace Day is?
3. What happens on international Peace Day?
4. Does your school or town/city do anything to celebrate international Peace Day?

1b LISTENING 2.26 **Listen to a radio programme about an organisation called Peace One Day and Jeremy Gilley, the man who started it. Answer the questions.**

1. When is international Peace Day?
2. What is the main idea of international Peace Day?
3. Does the man who is speaking think that international Peace Day is a good idea or not?

2 Listen again. Are these sentences *true* (T) or *false* (F)?

1. The first international Peace Day was in 1999. T/F
2. Jeremy Gilley is an English film actor. T/F
3. Gilley made a film of the process of starting international Peace Day. T/F
4. The United Nations didn't help Gilley with his idea. T/F
5. The actor Jude Law worked on a film about Peace One Day with Gilley. T/F
6. International Peace Day gave a lot of medical help to children in 2007 and 2008. T/F

PROJECT

3 Work in groups. Prepare something for an international Peace Day exhibition. Here are some ideas:

- texts about famous peacemakers like Ghandi or Martin Luther King
- texts about organisations that work for peace
- pictures or photographs
- songs in English about peace
- reviews of films or books about peace
- quotations and poems about peace

1. Each person in the group chooses one of the ideas and finds information and/or illustrations. Make notes about the information.
2. In your group, decide how to present your material to the rest of the class. Prepare it and present it.

Literature
The Freedom Writers

4 **Look at the photo. It shows some people who were in a group called *the Freedom Writers*. Who do you think these people were? How and why do you think they became famous?**

5 **Read this text about the Freedom Writers and see if your ideas in 4 were correct.**

In 1994, Erin Gruwell began teaching in a high school in Long Beach, California. She was a new teacher and teaching in Long Beach was not easy for Erin. That's because life was not easy for her 14-year-old students. These students lived in a very poor area of Long Beach. The students all hated school; they all hated the teacher; and they all hated each other.

But Erin introduced her students to books written by teenagers – books like *The Diary of Anne Frank*. The students learnt to have more respect for each other. They called themselves the 'Freedom Writers' and started to write an anonymous diary. In the diary they talked about their difficult experiences in life. Writing about all the bad things in their lives helped them. They learned to accept the past and go forward. They learnt to not let other people limit their dreams.

The students' dreams came true when the diary became a real book, *The Freedom Writers Diary*, and the book became famous. Erin and her students appeared on TV, in newspapers and magazines. In 2006, they made a Hollywood film of their story with young actors playing the parts of the students. In real life, many of the students went to university. Some of them are now teachers and they want to help new students to follow their own dreams.

WORD BOOSTER

Match the words and definitions.

1 anonymous
2 poor
3 limit
4 experience
5 respect
6 introduce
7 dream

a something that happened to you
b to treat someone like they are important
c to provide someone with a new experience
d to control or reduce
e having little money and not owning a lot of things
f written by someone whose name is not known
g something you hope to achieve in the future

6 **Read this summary of the text about The Freedom Writers. Find five mistakes and correct them.**

Erin Gruwell was a teacher with a lot of experience. Her fifteen-year-old students loved school. Erin helped them. She started to write a diary about them. A lot of people bought the book, called *The Freedom Writers Diary*. In 2006, the students appeared in a film about their lives. Today, some of the students continue doing the good work they learned from their teacher Erin.

7 SPEAKING **What about *you*?**

1 Would you like to read *The Freedom Writers Diary*? Why/Why not?
2 Do you think that books can change the world? Why/Why not?

I'd like to read it because I'd like to know some of the students' problems.

▶ Listening

1 **Work with a partner. Did you read, see or hear the news yesterday? Talk about any news stories you remember.**

2 LISTENING 2.27 **Listen to three news stories. What is the topic of each story? Choose from these topics.**

homelessness hunger pollution poverty unemployment violence

1 ……

2 ……

3 ……

3 **Listen again and choose the correct answers.**

1 The situation for homeless people this month is
   a more difficult than usual.
   b the same as usual.
   c better than usual.
2 They say that …… of every thousand people are without a home.
   a 4
   b 14
   c 40
3 The number of knife attacks this year is probably
   a more than 277.
   b 277.
   c under 277.
4 The public thinks the situation with knife crime today is
   a serious.
   b not very serious.
   c better than before.
5 Many …… are losing their jobs.
   a men between 25 and 50
   b men between 35 and 50
   c women between 25 and 50
6 The financial crisis is …… for people who work in construction or car factories.
   a only bad
   b especially bad
   c not bad

▶ Grammar in context

GRAMMAR GUIDE

Superlative adjectives

1a Look at the sentences and complete the table with the words in bold.

1 It is one of **the most important** problems in the country today.
2 This is **the coldest** month.
3 This is **the worst** month for many people.
4 They are **the best** people in the world to solve the problem.
5 This is **the biggest** group affected by the economic recession.

Adjective	Superlative adjective	Rule
cold	(**a**) ……	One-syllable adjectives – add *-est*
big	(**b**) ……	One-syllable adjectives ending in one vowel and one consonant – double the consonant and add *-est*
lazy	the laziest	Two-syllable adjectives ending in *-y* – omit *-y* and add *-iest*
important	(**c**) ……	Adjectives with two syllables or more – put *most* before the adjective
good **bad** **far**	(**d**) …… (**e**) …… the farthest, the furthest	Irregular

1b Complete the sentence with the correct words.

He's …… best singer …… the world.

GRAMMAR REFERENCE ▶ page 114

2 Complete the sentences with the superlative form of the adjectives given.

1 Vatican City is .... (small) country in the world.
2 The cheetah is .... (fast) land animal in the world.
3 In 2009, Cristiano Ronaldo was .... (expensive) football player in the world.
4 Monkeys or dolphins are probably .... (intelligent) animals in the world.
5 William McGonagall is sometimes called .... (bad) poet in the world.
6 *The Burning of the Red Lotus Temple* is .... (long) film in history – it lasts 27 hours!
7 *The Hurt Locker* won the Oscar for .... (good) film in 2009.

3 Look at this table with information on three films about teenagers and school. Complete the sentences with the comparative or superlative form of the adjectives.

	Dead Poets Society	*Dangerous Minds*	*High School Musical 3*
year	1989	1995	2008
length	128 minutes	99 minutes	100 minutes
prizes	one Oscar and 13 other prizes	five prizes	two prizes
critics' opinion	****	***	**

1 *Dead Poets Society* is .... (long) than *High School Musical 3*.
2 *Dead Poets Society* is .... (long) film.
3 The critics think that *Dangerous Minds* is .... (good) than *High School Musical 3*.
4 The critics think that *Dead Poets Society* is .... (good).
5 *Dead Poets Society* is .... (old) than *Dangerous Minds*.
6 *High School Musical 3* is .... (new).
7 *Dangerous Minds* is .... (short).
8 *Dead Poets Society* is .... (successful) and won the most prizes.

4 Write sentences giving your opinion about these things. Use the superlative form of the adjectives.

1 good/band in the world
I think Arctic Monkeys is the best band in the world.
2 famous/singer in this country
3 funny/actor in the world
4 difficult/subject at school
5 bad/programme on TV
6 good/place in the world

5 SPEAKING Work with a partner. Interview them to find out their answers in 4.

Who do you think is the best band in the world?

I think it's Arctic Monkeys.

EXAM SUCCESS

The next activity is a cloze activity. You have a text with gaps, but you do not have words to fill in the gaps. What type of words do you think go in the gaps – prepositions, articles, nouns, verbs, auxiliary verbs, pronouns?

EXAM SUCCESS ▸ page 159

6 Complete the text. Write one word in each gap.

Last night I saw (**a**) .... very interesting programme on TV. It was about an orchestra from Venezuela. A composer called José Antonio Abreu started the orchestra (**b**) .... 1975 with just eleven poor children. Some of the young musicians were always in and out of trouble. (**c**) .... orchestra helped them. Now the project is bigger and (**d**) .... important than before. It now helps 250,000 children and (**e**) .... are over 200 local orchestras. Today they play in some of the (**f**) .... important concert halls in America and Europe. Some experts think they are better (**g**) .... a lot of other professional orchestras. The famous Placido Domingo, one of the best opera singers (**h**) .... the world, cried when he heard them play! More countries are starting similar projects to help young people escape.

1 SPEAKING Work with a partner. Look at the photos. Are there any similarities between the two photos? Give reasons for your answer.

2 LISTENING 2.28 Listen to a student describing one of the photos. Which photo is it?

3 Complete the description with the missing words. Listen again if necessary. Don't worry about the different colours.

This is a picture of people at home. I can see (**a**) .... people. I think it's a (**b**) .... and her (**c**) .... They're probably in the boy's (**d**) .... I think the boy is eleven or twelve. Perhaps he's doing (**e**) .... because he's at a desk and he's got books, pens and paper on the desk in front of him. On the right, I can see shelves and there are lots of (**f**) .... on the shelves. On the left we can see the boy. He's sitting down but his mother is (**g**) .... I think that the mother is (**h**) .... the boy to do his homework. I think she's asking the boy a question or explaining something. There's a (**i**) .... on the table but they aren't using it.

a

b

4 Look at the description again and answer the questions.

1. What expressions are used to begin the description?
2. What type of words are the words in blue? Why are they important in a description of a photo?
3. Look at the verbs in green. What tense are they?
4. Look at the words and expressions in red. Do we use them when we are 100% sure of something or when we are making a guess?

5 Read the information in the Speaking Bank and check your answers to the questions in 4.

Speaking Bank

Useful expressions to describe photos

- We often begin with expressions like: *This is a picture of . . . / I can see . . .*
- We use *On the right/left, In the middle* and prepositions (*on, at, in front of, behind . . .*) to say where people and things are.
- We usually use the present continuous to say what people are doing (*He's sitting down, She's asking the boy a question*).
- To make guesses, we use words and expressions like *I think, maybe, perhaps, she* looks *relaxed*.

6 SPEAKING Work with a partner. Look at photo a. Say where these things are. Use the expressions from the Speaking Bank.

1. the people
2. the boy
3. the father
4. the cupboard
5. the sink

Practice makes perfect

7a Work with a partner. Look at photo a. Think of things to say about the photo. Use the expressions in the Speaking Bank to help you.

7b Take it in turns to describe the photo.

This is a picture of a kitchen, maybe an English kitchen. I can see two people in the kitchen.

EXAM SUCCESS

When you describe a photo, what should you do when you don't know the word for something in the photo?

EXAM SUCCESS ▸ page 159

1 Look at this short article and editorial from a newspaper. What problem do they talk about? What is the possible cause of it?

Results of recent IQ tests of British fourteen-year-olds are going down, not up. Professor James Flynn thinks the explanation is probably that teenagers spend so much time on the Internet and playing video games.

The editor says

I am worried about teenagers today. When I was a child, I played outside with my friends after school. There were no computers and no games consoles. We had television but we could only watch at the weekend. But we were happy, healthy and we had a lot of imagination. Now results of IQ tests show that teenagers in the past were more intelligent than now. Today's teenagers need to change fast, or the future looks very dark.

2 Work with a partner. Do you agree with the editorial? Why/Why not?

3 Read this letter to the editor. Does the writer agree or disagree with the editorial? Why?

Dear Sir/Madam,

I am writing about your editorial from last Thursday's newspaper. I agree completely with what you say in this editorial.

In my opinion, teenagers today are not learning anything. They sit in front of a computer all day. This does not make you intelligent. It stops you from thinking, and from doing other things like playing sport and making friends.

Personally, I think that the real problem is that teenagers today never read. In my view, reading helps you to learn new words, it helps you to be more creative, and it helps your thinking. Spending three hours reading makes you more intelligent than playing a computer game for three hours.

I feel very strongly about this subject. I am very interested in hearing other readers' opinions.

Yours faithfully

Robert Dean

4 Look at the letter again. Which paragraph …

1 asks for other people's opinions?
2 gives an explanation of why you are writing and a quick statement of opinion?
3 gives a second opinion and explanation?
4 gives a first opinion and explanation?

STUDY SKILLS

Why is it important to know who we are writing to when we write a text in English?

STUDY SKILLS ▸ page 157

5 Look at the letter again and complete the useful expressions in the Writing Bank.

Writing Bank

Useful expressions in formal letters of opinion

- We write *Dear* .... when we do not know the name of the person we are writing to.
- We do not use contractions. For example, we write ...., not *I'm writing about your editorial.*
- To express our opinions, we use words and phrases like *I agree, I disagree, I think, Personally, In my* .... or *In my* ....
- When we do not know the name of the person we are writing to, we end the letter *Yours* ....

Practice makes perfect

6a What do *you* think about the editorial in 1? Do you agree with it or not? Make notes about your ideas.

6b Write your letter to the editor. Use the information in the Writing Bank and follow the paragraph plan in the model letter in 3.

Language reference and revision

Grammar reference

Comparative adjectives

Form

	Adjective	Comparative
One syllable	kind cold	kinder colder
One syllable ending in one vowel and one consonant	big sad	bigger sadder
Two syllables ending in -*y*	lazy happy	lazier happier
Two or more syllables	serious boring	more serious more boring
Irregular	bad good far	worse better farther/further

Use

- We use comparative adjectives to compare two people, places or things.
  London is bigger than Manchester.
- We use **than** in sentences that compare two people, places or things.
  Jack is taller than Tim.

Superlative adjectives

Form

	Adjective	Superlative
One syllable	kind cold	the kindest the coldest
One syllable ending in one vowel and one consonant	big sad	the biggest the saddest
Two syllables ending in -*y*	lazy happy	the laziest the happiest
Two or more syllables	serious boring	the most serious the most boring
Irregular	bad good far	the worst the best the farthest/furthest

Use

- We use superlative adjectives to compare more than two people, places or things.
  My sister is the tallest girl in her class.
- We use **the** before the superlative form of the adjective and we often use **in**.
  It's the most exciting city in the world.

Vocabulary

1 Feelings

angry bored excited happy interested relaxed sad surprised tired worried

2 Personality

cheerful hard-working intelligent kind lazy quiet responsible serious

3 Social problems

crime homelessness hunger pollution poverty unemployment violence

4 Other words and phrases page 153

Grammar revision

Comparative adjectives

1 Write the comparative form of the adjectives.

1 hot ....
2 silly ....
3 beautiful ....
4 good ....
5 long ....
6 angry ....
7 modern ....
8 bad ....
9 lazy ....

WORKBOOK ▶ page 74

/9 points

Superlative adjectives

2 Look at the information about three people and write sentences using the superlative forms of the adjectives.

Name	Tom	Richard	Harry
Age	13	15	18
Height	1 metre 80	1 metre 65	1 metre 70
IQ	100	120	140

1 Tom/tall
2 Richard/short
3 Harry/old
4 Tom/young
5 Harry/intelligent
6 Tom/intelligent

WORKBOOK ▶ page 77

/6 points

Comparative and superlative adjectives

3 Choose the correct alternative.

1 I'm *worse/worst* at biology than Mark.
2 I think she's *0/the* most famous singer in the world.
3 What's the *more/most* expensive food in the world?
4 In my opinion, tennis is more exciting *than/that* football.
5 Is she the most intelligent person *of/in* the class?
6 I think English is *0/more* easier than maths.

WORKBOOK ▶ page 77

/6 points

Vocabulary revision

Feelings

1 What are these feelings?

1 the opposite of happy: ....
2 when you want to know about something or learn about it: ....
3 when something happens, but you didn't think it was going to happen: ....
4 when you are calm because you have no problems: ....
5 after you finish working hard or doing a lot of sport: ....
6 when you are thinking about something bad that could happen: ....
7 when you are very happy because you think something good could happen: ....
8 when you have no interest in something: ....

WORKBOOK ▶ page 72

/8 points

Social problems

2 Use these words to say what problems the people have.

crime homelessness hunger pollution poverty unemployment

1 Barbara hasn't got enough money to buy things.
2 Daniel hasn't got a place to live.
3 Jessica hasn't got a job.
4 Somebody attacked Charlie and took his money.
5 Mary and her family haven't got anything to eat.
6 Because of smoke from the car factory, Martha has trouble breathing.

WORKBOOK ▶ page 75

/6 points

Personality

3 Match these words with the pictures.

cheerful hard-working intelligent kind lazy

1

....

2

....

3

....

4

....

5

....

WORKBOOK ▶ page 72

/5 points

Total /40 points

Gateway to exams *Units 7–8*

Reading

Tip For Reading Exams

In matching activities, remember …

First, read all parts of the text. Then read the pieces of information you need to find. Try to find the places in the text where the information is. Read them again slowly.

EXAM SUCCESS ▸ page 159

1 Work with a partner. Look at the two people in the photos. Do you know who they are? What do you think they have in common? Make a list of ideas.

2 Read the text. Does it talk about any of your ideas in 1?

They're rich and famous. Oprah Winfrey and Angelina Jolie also give money to help others.

Oprah Winfrey is one of the most famous TV presenters in the world. Now, she's also an important and successful businesswoman. She became the first ever African-American billionaire. But her life as a child was difficult and she knew all about poverty. Perhaps that's why she helps people with her money. For example, she gave money to help the victims of Hurricane Katrina in New Orleans. And she went there and helped them in person. In 2007, she also began a school in South Africa to help poor girls to get a good education. She even has her own charity organisation, Oprah's Angel Network.

Angelina Jolie is one of the most famous actresses in the world. And she uses her money and fame to help other people. For example, she does a lot of work for an organisation called UNHCR. This organisation helps refugees – people who have to leave their homes and live in camps. She often visits these places to help the people. But she uses her own money to pay for her trips and she doesn't sleep in five-star hotels. She works and lives in the same conditions as the people who work for UNHCR. Angelina helps other charities too, such as the charity Yele Haiti. This was started by her friend, hip-hop musician Wyclef Jean. It helps poor people in Haiti. Thanks to all her charity work, Jolie was the first person to win the Citizen of the World Award.

3 Read the text again. Are the sentences about Oprah Winfrey (OW), Angelina Jolie (AJ) or both (B)?

1. She received an award for her charity work. OW/AJ/B
2. She started her own organisation to help others. OW/AJ/B
3. She does two or three different jobs. OW/AJ/B
4. She visits people who need help. OW/AJ/B
5. She had problems when she was young. OW/AJ/B
6. She doesn't want special conditions when she goes to help other people. OW/AJ/B
7. She went from having no money to having a lot of money. OW/AJ/B

Listening

Tip For Listening Exams

In activities where you complete notes, remember …

Be careful with the spelling of simple words. If not, you could lose marks.

EXAM SUCCESS ▸ page 159

4 Read the notes about Gandhi. Do you know any of the missing information?

Gandhi was (a) .... in India on 2nd October 1869. He went to (b) .... to study law. After that he went to South Africa. He went back to India in 1915. At that time India was part of the (c) .... Empire. Gandhi wanted India to be free. Many people were poor. Life was difficult for people (d) .... in factories. Gandhi didn't want to use (e) .... because he thought it was a bad thing.

In 1930 Gandhi walked (f) .... kilometres to the sea. A lot of people went with him. He wanted to (g) ...., but in a peaceful way.

People started to respect Gandhi because he was kind, intelligent, and (h) .... He won independence for India in (i) ....

5 LISTENING 2.29 Now listen to a history programme about Gandhi and complete the text.

Use of English

Tip For Use Of English Exams

In cloze activities, remember …

The words that you need are usually prepositions, articles, auxiliary verbs, pronouns or linking words.

EXAM SUCCESS ▸ page 159

6 Read this text and answer the questions. Don't worry about the gaps at the moment.

1 Where did Sue go last Saturday?
2 Why did she like it?
3 What didn't she like?

Hi Joe,

Last Saturday, I went to (1) .... concert. It was great! A lot (2) .... my favourite groups and singers were there. (3) .... concert was to get money to help poor people in Africa. I think it's important that the richest countries (4) .... the world help some of (5) .... poorest countries.

Anyway, the concert was really exciting. I always think that listening to live music is better (6) .... listening to a CD. However, I hated one new singer. I can't remember (7) .... name but she was really bad! The other problem was that I couldn't always see very well because there were a group of tall boys just in (8) .... of me. Apart from that, I had a great time.

What about you? What (9) .... you do last Saturday? Write back and tell me.

All the best

Sue

7 Read the text again. Write one word in each gap.

Speaking

Tip For Speaking Exams

In activities where you describe a photo, remember …

If you don't know a word for something in the photo, explain it with other, simple words. You don't have to describe every detail in the photo.

EXAM SUCCESS ▸ page 159

8 Work with a partner. Look at the two lists of words. How do we use these words to describe a photo?

List A:
perhaps, I think, he/she/it looks, he/she/it doesn't look, maybe …

List B:
in front of, on the right, on the left, in the middle, at, on, in, behind …

9 Work with a partner. Take turns to describe the photo.

'Can Do' Progress Check

CEF

1 How well can you do these things in English now? Give yourself a mark from 1 to 4.

1 = I can do it very well.
2 = I can do it quite well.
3 = I have some problems.
4 = I can't do it.

a I can talk about the past using the past simple. ☐
b I can talk about different jobs and places of work. ☐
c I can understand simple written and spoken texts about culture and entertainment. ☐
d I can tell an anecdote about a special weekend. ☐
e I can write a short biography of a famous person. ☐
f I can compare people and things using comparative and superlative adjectives. ☐
g I can talk about feelings and different personalities. ☐
h I can understand simple written and spoken texts about social problems. ☐
i I can describe photos. ☐
j I can write a basic formal letter of opinion. ☐

2 Now decide what you need to do next to improve.

1 Look again at my book/notes.
2 Do more practice exercises. ⇨ WORKBOOK page 80–81
3 Ask for help.
4 Other: ....

9 Wild world

Grammar ▸ *Be going to* ▸ *Will/Won't*
Vocabulary ▸ Wild animals and insects ▸ The natural world ▸ The weather
Speaking ▸ Making plans
Writing ▸ Taking phone messages

▸ Vocabulary

Wild animals and insects

1a **Work with a partner. Match the photos with some of these words. Check that you understand the other words. Use your dictionary if necessary.**

alligator bear bee eagle jellyfish lizard scorpion
shark snake spider tiger wolf

1b 2.30 **Listen and repeat.**

2 **Put the words from 1 in the correct column(s).**

Land	Water	Air

3 SPEAKING **Some wild animals or insects *bite* (sharks). Others *sting* (bees). Work with a partner. Which animals and insects in 1 bite? Which sting?**

The natural world

4a **Match the features in the picture (a–l) with these words.**

field flowers forest grass
hill island lake mountain
river sky valley waterfall

4b 2.31 **Listen and repeat.**

5 2.32 **Listen. What can you hear? Write a word from 1 or 4 for each sound.**

1 .... 5 ....
2 .... 6 ....
3 .... 7 ....
4 ....

6 SPEAKING **Work with a partner. Take it in turns to ask and answer the questions.**

1 Are there any mountains or hills near your home? What are they called?
2 Do you live near a forest?
3 Is there a lake near where you live?
4 What is the name of the nearest river?
5 Are there any big waterfalls in your country? Where are they and what are they called?

Reading

1 **Work with a partner. What can you see in the photo? Do you know anything about this man, Bear Grylls? If so, what?**

2 **Read three texts about Bear Grylls. Match the texts and the text types.**

1 Text 1: ....
2 Text 2: ....
3 Text 3: ....

a an Internet review of a Bear Grylls DVD
b part of the biography of Bear Grylls
c an advert for a novel by Bear Grylls

1

Bear Grylls was born in 1974. In the 1990s, he was in the British SAS (Special Air Service), but he had a bad accident. He jumped from a plane and his parachute didn't work. He broke his back in
5 three places and was in hospital for a long time. But, after that, he became the youngest British man to climb Everest! He was just 23. Later, he started making a TV series about how to survive in extreme conditions. 1.2 billion people
10 worldwide watched the series, *Man vs. Wild*.

File Edit View Favorites Tools Help Links

2 This must be Bear's best programme yet! He fights an alligator in Louisiana and wins! And he comes face to face with a bear in the forests of Transylvania.
5 But his biggest problem comes from a simple bee in Mexico. The bee stings him on his face and he can't see anything because he can't open his eyes! Later, he
10 jumps down waterfalls. I hope Bear isn't going to stop making brilliant programmes like this one!

3

In this incredible story, Beck Granger and his friend, Peter, join Uncle Al for a holiday in Africa. They have no idea that they are going to find
5 themselves in the middle of an adventure in the Sahara Desert. They discover a secret criminal organisation and have to jump out of a plane over the desert. It isn't going to be easy to survive. They must find their way back, but first they have to survive snakes, scorpions and the hot sun! This
10 is a great African adventure which includes real survival details. What are Beck and Peter going to do? Read it or miss all the excitement.

3 **Read the texts again. Are the sentences true (T) or false (F)? Write the number of the line(s) where you find the answer.**

1 Bear Grylls had a bad accident in an aeroplane. T/F
2 Bear Grylls was 20 when he climbed the highest mountain in the world. T/F
3 In one of his TV programmes, an insect creates more problems for him than a bear. T/F
4 Beck Granger and his friend go to Africa because they want an adventure. T/F
5 In the novel, there are ideas for how to live through difficult situations in real life. T/F

4 **Match the underlined words in the text with these definitions.**

1 hits and kicks
2 an exciting, unusual and sometimes dangerous trip
3 very unusual and difficult
4 continue living in difficult conditions
5 large piece of cloth that is used by someone jumping out of a plane
6 fail to take advantage of a chance

5 **SPEAKING What about *you*?**

Would you like to do dangerous or unusual things like Bear Grylls? Why/Why not?

I wouldn't like to do dangerous things like him.

Why not?

I'm afraid!

GRAMMAR GUIDE

Be going to

1 Look at the sentences and answer the question.

a He**'s going to climb** a mountain in the Antarctic.
b He **isn't going to stop** making TV series.
c What **are** you **going to do**?

- We use **be going to** to talk about future plans and intentions. What form of the verb comes after **be going to**?

GRAMMAR REFERENCE ▸ page 128

2a PRONUNCIATION 2.33 **Listen to the dialogue. How is *going to* pronounced?**

A: What are you going to do tomorrow?
B: I'm going to meet my friends.
A: Are you going to go out?
B: No, we're going to watch TV.

2b Listen again and repeat the dialogue. Practise saying *going to*.

3 Write about the future plans of these adventurers. Use *be going to*.

1 Holly *isn't going to fly* (not/fly) across the Sahara Desert. She .... (ride) a motorbike across it!
2 Tom and Evan .... (ski) down Everest.
3 Andy .... (not/sail) across the Atlantic. He .... (sail) around the world.
4 Hannah .... (walk) from New York to Los Angeles.
5 Emma .... (travel) in space.
6 Lucy .... (make) a film about alligators.
7 Luke .... (live) alone on a desert island.

4 Match the people with their plans for the future. Write sentences with *be going to*.

Katie's going to buy a pet spider.

5a SPEAKING **Write questions with *be going to*.**

1 Rose and Tyler/live on an island?
Are Rose and Tyler going to live on an island?
2 What/Jacob/do?
3 Brandon and Sam/jump down a waterfall?
4 Zak/buy a pet spider?
5 What/Lily/do?
6 Katie/make a TV series about wildlife?
7 Who/build a house in the country?

5b Work with a partner. Take it in turns to ask and answer the questions.

Are Rose and Tyler going to live on an island?

No, they aren't. They're going to make a TV series about wildlife.

6 **SPEAKING** **Work with a partner. Find out about your partner's plans for the weekend. Ask questions about these activities.**

1 do homework
2 surf the Internet
3 stay at home on Sunday
4 go out on Saturday night
5 meet friends
6 go to bed late
7 get up early on Sunday morning
8 do sport

Are you going to do homework?

Yes, I am. On Saturday morning.

7 **Think of two big plans you have for the future and write them down. Give your sentences to your teacher.**

I'm going to be a famous adventurer.
My brother and I are going to start a band.

8 **Listen to your teacher read out some of your sentences. Who do you think wrote each sentence?**

The weather

1a **Work with a partner. Match the pictures to some of these adjectives.**

cloudy cold dry foggy hot icy snowy stormy sunny warm wet/rainy windy

1b **Now match the adjectives to these nouns.**

cloud fog ice rain snow sun storm wind

2 **Complete the sentences with the correct forms of the words given.**

1 At the moment it's .... (rain).
2 It's very .... (sun) here in August.
3 Yesterday it was .... (wind).
4 There is usually .... (snow) here in January.
5 Here we never have big .... (storm).
6 We don't have much .... (fog) here.
7 It's .... (cloud) here in July.
8 We don't have a lot of .... (rain) here.

3 **SPEAKING** **Work with a partner. Are the sentences in 2 true or false for where you live? Correct the false sentences.**

At the moment it isn't rainy. It's sunny.

Click onto... Wild Canada

Cross-curricular – Geography
Canada's geography and climate

1 Work with a partner. Can you answer the questions? If you don't know, guess.

1 Where is Canada?
2 Is Canada bigger than China?
3 How many people live in Canada?
4 What is the capital of Canada?
5 What language(s) do people speak in Canada?
6 What is the weather like in the winter?

2 Read the text and check your answers in 1.

3a Look at the map. Label as many of the cities as you can.

- Canada is part of North America. To its south is the USA. To its north-east is Greenland.
- Canada goes from the Atlantic Ocean in the east to the Pacific Ocean in the west.
- Canada has more lakes than any other country in the world.
- Canada is the world's second largest country. Russia is first.
- Canada has got a population of 33,487,208. That's only 3.5 people per square kilometre. This is one of the lowest numbers in the world.
- Most people live in the big cities of Toronto and Montreal. The capital is Ottawa. Vancouver, Calgary and Quebec City are other important cities.
- In the province of Quebec, French is the official language. But, in the rest of Canada, English and French are both official languages.
- Temperatures can change a lot in Canada. In many parts of Canada, it can be -40°C and very windy in the winter. In the north, it is very cold, with lots of snow and ice. Summer temperatures are generally warm (20°C) but can be hot (40°C) in some areas.

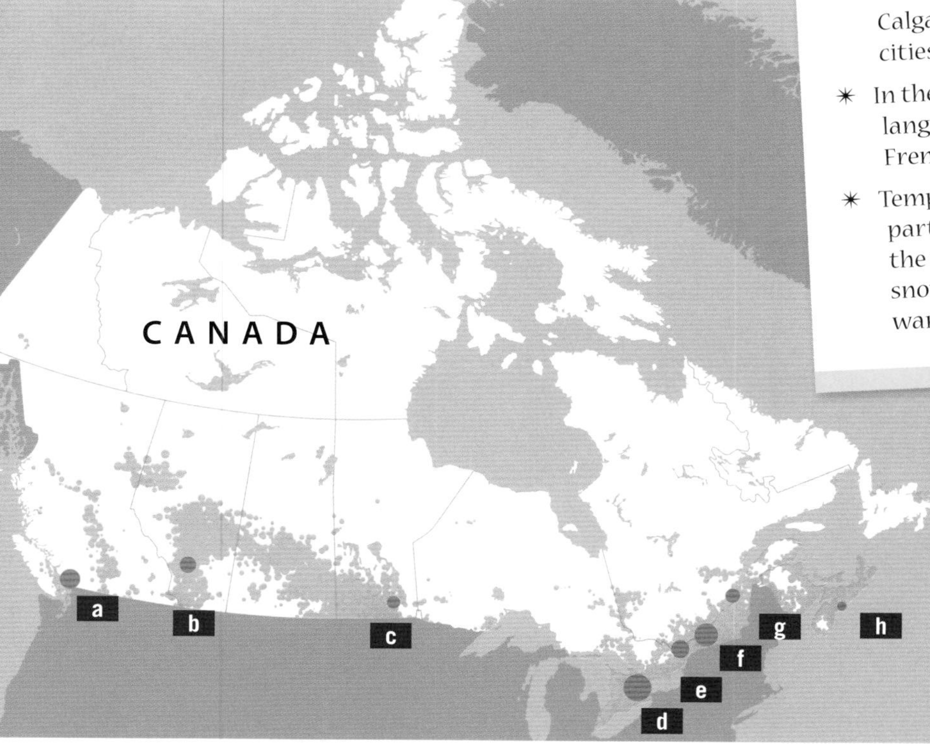

a ....
b ....
c ....
d ....
e ....
f ....
g ....
h ....

3b This map is a demographic map of Canada – it shows the distribution of the population, or where people live. What do you think explains this distribution? Think about the text and these topics: the weather, transport, history, the economy.

3c LISTENING 2.34 **Listen to a geography teacher talking about where people live in Canada and answer the questions.**

1 What are two reasons why more people live in the south than in the north?
2 What are two reasons why more people live in the east than in the west?
3 Why is Toronto in a good position?

4 What about *you*?

Where is the population biggest in your country and why?

Literature
White Fang by Jack London

INSIDE INFORMATION

- Jack London (1876 –1916) was an American writer. Before he started writing he went to look for gold in the Yukon.The Yukon is a wild area with lots of mountains, forests and rivers in the north-west of Canada.
- The story of White Fang takes place mostly in the Yukon. White Fang is the name of a wolf that was born there, in the wild.
- In the text White Fang is still a cub – a young wolf.

The cub had many things to learn. The world was full of surprises for him. But he loved to feel the life inside himself. Running after meat made him feel excited and he enjoyed fighting. And after a hunt, he loved to lie in the sun, full of food. He was very much alive, very happy, and very proud of himself.

One day, however, life suddenly changed. The cub ran down to the river to drink early one morning. He was still sleepy, so at first he did not notice anything. Then, suddenly, he saw and smelled something strange. Five strange animals were sitting in front of him. The cub had never seen men before, and suddenly he felt very small.

The cub knew nothing about men. But his parents and grandparents knew about men. They knew men were more powerful than any other living thing. And somehow the cub could feel that, too.

The men were Indians. One of them walked over to him. Then slowly the man reached down to pick him up. The cub's hair stood up on his back, and he showed his little teeth.

'Look at his white fangs!' the man laughed. The man's hand came closer and closer. Then the cub suddenly bit the man's hand. At once, the man hit him on the head, and the cub fell onto his side. Suddenly the cub forgot all about fighting. He sat up and cried.

5 Read the Inside Information about White Fang. Do you know the story?

6 Read the text. It describes an important moment in White Fang's life. What is this important moment?

7 Read the text again and answer the questions.

1. How does White Fang enjoy passing the time?
2. What are the 'five strange animals' in the text?
3. What does White Fang's family think about humans?
4. What is White Fang's reaction when the man goes to pick him up?
5. Where does the name White Fang come from? What does it mean?
6. What does the man do to White Fang?

▸ WORD BOOSTER

Match the words and definitions.

a	proud of himself	1	past tense of *bite*; to use your teeth to cut something
b	smelled	2	strong, able to control others
c	powerful	3	feeling happy with the things he did
d	reached down	4	moved a hand down towards something
e	bit	5	noticed something with his nose

8 What do you think happens next to White Fang? Work with a partner and write a paragraph.

▸ STUDY SKILLS

Make a list of different things that we read, e.g. novels, textbooks, poems, telephone directories . . . Do we read them all in the same way? STUDY SKILLS ▸ page 157

Listening

1 Work with a partner. Ask and answer the questions.

1 Do you like visiting zoos, safari parks or wildlife centres? Why/Why not?
2 When was the last time that you went to one of these places?
3 What can you usually do in a place like this?
4 Do you think the animals in the photos are in danger?

2 LISTENING 2.35 **Listen to a radio advert for a wildlife centre. Tick (✓) the animals that they name in the advert.**

monkey ☐	tiger ☐	eagle ☐	elephant ☐
camel ☐	zebra ☐	giraffe ☐	polar bear ☐
penguin ☐	wolf ☐	snake ☐	giant panda ☐
brown bear ☐	lion ☐		

3 Listen again. Are these sentences true (T) or false (F)?

1 There is a safari area where you can drive, and another where you can walk. T/F
2 There are five restaurants and four shops at the Wildlife Centre. T/F
3 You can travel on a special bus. T/F
4 You can see polar bears at the Wildlife Centre. T/F
5 The Centre is open every day of the week. T/F
6 If you are 14, the price is £17. T/F

Grammar in context

GRAMMAR GUIDE

Will/Won't

1 We use *will* and *won't* to talk about the future and future predictions. Look at the sentences and answer the questions.

a These animals **will** need our help in the future.
b You'**ll** have a great time!
c Come for a wild day out that you **won't** forget.
d **Will** tigers disappear one day? Yes, they **will**./No, they **won't**.
e What **will** happen to these animals in the future?

1 What are the contractions for **will** and **will not**?
2 What form of the verb comes after **will** and **will not**?

GRAMMAR REFERENCE ▸ page 128

2 Complete the sentences with *will* or *won't* and the verb given.

1 Don't worry. The lions *won't attack* (not attack).
2 We .... (not have) time to go to the Wildlife Centre next weekend.
3 Jack and I .... (see) the crocodiles.
4 It .... (not rain) tomorrow.
5 I think she .... (eat) in that restaurant.
6 We .... (not buy) anything in the shops.
7 The door's open. The monkeys .... (escape).
8 Do you think it .... (snow) this winter?

3a SPEAKING **What's your opinion? Complete the predictions with *will* or *won't* and the verb given.**

1 Polar bears .... (disappear) soon.
2 The weather .... (change) a lot in the future.
3 Next summer .... (be) very hot.
4 People .... (drive) electric cars in 20 years.
5 There .... (be) food for everybody in the future.
6 The ice at the North Pole .... (disappear) in the next 25 years.
7 People .... (eat) meat in the future.

3b Work with a partner. Compare your sentences.

Polar bears won't disappear soon.

I disagree. I think they will disappear!

4 SPEAKING **Work with a partner. Take it in turns to ask and answer the questions. Use short answers to reply.**

1 Will it be sunny tomorrow?
2 Will Argentina win the next football World Cup?
3 Will fashions change much in the next five years?
4 Will an actor from your country win an Oscar this year?
5 Will people live on the moon one day?
6 Will this class finish late today?
7 Will school be open on Sunday?
8 Will scientists find a cure for cancer?
9 Will humans go to Mars?

Will it be sunny tomorrow?

Yes, it will!

5a Look at these questions about your future. Write *Yes* or *No* for each question.

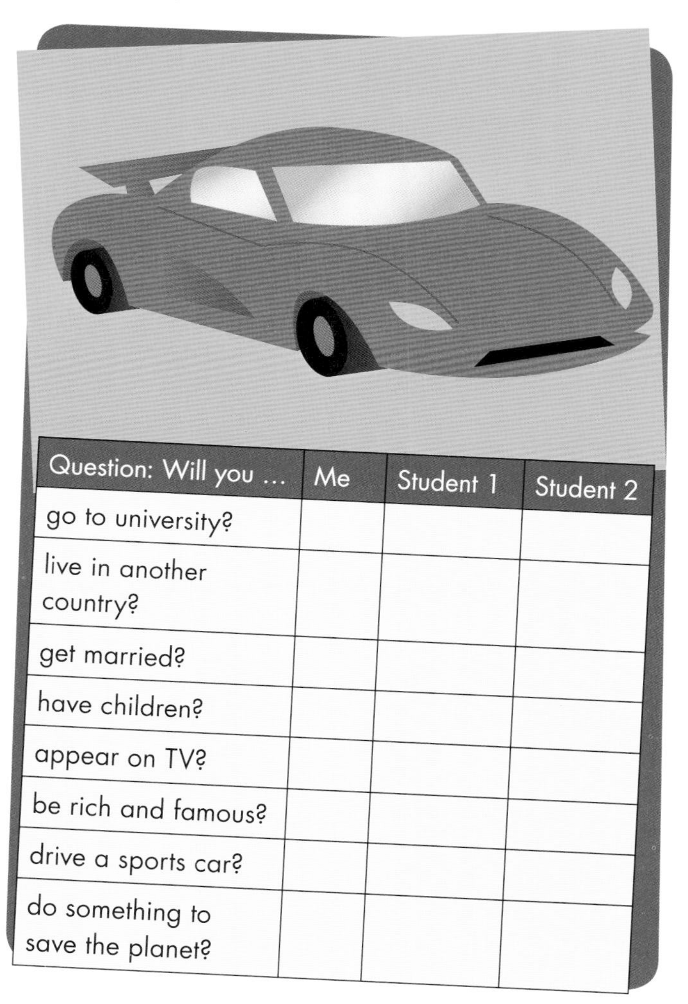

Question: Will you ...	Me	Student 1	Student 2
go to university?			
live in another country?			
get married?			
have children?			
appear on TV?			
be rich and famous?			
drive a sports car?			
do something to save the planet?			

5b SPEAKING **Work in groups of three. Use the questions to interview the other students in your group.**

Will you go to university?

Yes, I will.

6 Write five more questions about the future. Use your questions to interview two other students.

1a SPEAKING **Work with a partner. Name the places you can see in the photos. What other places can you go to at the weekend or in the holidays?**

a

b

c

1b **What can you do at each different place?**

At the cinema you can see films.

You can meet your friends there.

And you can eat popcorn!

2 LISTENING 2.36 **Listen to two people talking about next week. Answer the questions.**

1 Where do they decide to go?
2 When do they decide to go?
3 Where do they decide to meet?
4 What time do they decide to meet?

3 **Listen again and complete the dialogue.**

EMMA: Next week we're on holiday. Do you want to go out one day?
PAUL: Yes, sure.
EMMA: Why don't we go and (**a**) ....?
PAUL: OK. Let's go on (**b**) ....
EMMA: Sorry, I'm busy on (**c**) .... I'm taking my little sister to the (**d**) .... with her friends.
PAUL: What about (**e**) ....? Are you free then?
EMMA: Yes, that's fine.
PAUL: Let's meet (**f**) .... at (**g**) ....
EMMA: OK. See you there!

4 **Look at the useful expressions in the Speaking Bank. Which two expressions do not appear in the dialogue in 3?**

Speaking Bank

Useful expressions to make plans

Asking about somebody's plans
- Do you want to (*verb in the infinitive*)?
- Are you free (*on + day/at + time*)?

Making suggestions
- Why don't we (*verb in the infinitive*)?
- Let's (*verb in the infinitive*).
- What about (*noun/verb + ing*)?

Accepting suggestions
- Yes, sure.
- Yes, that's fine.
- OK.
- Great.

Rejecting suggestions
- Sorry, I can't.
- Sorry, I'm busy.

5 SPEAKING **Work with a partner. Practise the dialogue in 3 but use different words and expressions from the Speaking Bank to fill in the gaps.**

EXAM SUCCESS

When you do a speaking exam in pairs, is it important to listen to what your partner says? Why/Why not?

EXAM SUCCESS ▸ page 160

Practice makes perfect

6 **Work with a partner. Do this role-play using the dialogue in 3 and the Speaking bank to help you.**

Student A: Begin the activity. Look at page 167.
Student B: Look at page 160.

Next week you and your partner are on holiday. You want to go out together one day. Decide where to go and on which day. Agree where and when to meet.

STUDY SKILLS

What do you need to do now? Work on speaking faster, or work on mistakes?

STUDY SKILLS ▸ page 157

1 LISTENING 2.37 **Listen to a telephone conversation. What does Robert want?**

2 **Listen again and read Samantha's message to Mike. One piece of information in the message is incorrect. What is it?**

Mike,

Robert phoned. He wants to use your biology textbook because he's got an exam tomorrow. He thinks it's the same book that you had last year. He's at school now but he'll come here to get it. His telephone number is 549 0023.

I'm going to go the shops now. Call me on my mobile if you need anything.

Samantha

3a **Read this phone message and answer the questions.**

Bob,

Headmaster phoned. Wants to know why you didn't go on school excursion to wildlife centre today. Not very happy! Wants to see you 9am tomorrow.

Going to pool now. See you tonight.

Claire

1 Who is the message for?
2 Who is the person who made the phone call?
3 What does this person want?
4 Who wrote the message?
5 Is the message formal or informal?

3b **Put these words in the phone message. What types of words are they?**

the he the the he is he at
I'm the I'll

4 **Read the information in the Writing Bank. What types of words can we leave out of informal messages?**

Writing Bank

Leaving out words in informal messages

We can sometimes leave out:
- articles (*a, an, the*)
- subject pronouns (*I, he*)
- prepositions (*at, in*)
- auxiliary verbs (*am, is, does, will*)

We cannot leave out:
- nouns
- main verbs
- adjectives

BUT if you are not sure if you can leave a word out it is better to include it.

5 **Read the message. Put a line through any words you can leave out.**

Linda,

The computer is not working. I called a friend who can fix it. He will come at 5pm. His name is Pete.

Mum called in the morning. She needs to speak to you. It's urgent. She's going to be in the office all afternoon, so call her there.

Dad

Practice makes perfect

6a **Read this phone dialogue and underline the most important information.**

ZAC: Hello, 873 0980.
LIZ: Hi. Is that Patrick Dawson?
ZAC: No, sorry, he isn't here at the moment. Can I take a message?
LIZ: Yes, please. Can you tell him that we'd like to interview him for a summer job at Barton Safari Park? He should ring me to arrange a time for the interview.
ZAC: OK. What's your telephone number?
LIZ: It's 332 5487. My name is Liz. He can call me between 10 and 5 o'clock.
ZAC: Fine.
LIZ: Oh, and he should also bring a letter saying why he thinks he should get the job.
ZAC: Right. Should he bring photos or anything?
LIZ: No, that won't be necessary.
ZAC: When does the job start?
LIZ: On 3rd July. And it finishes on 29th August.
ZAC: OK. Anything else?
LIZ: No, I think that's everything. Thanks! Bye.

6b **Look at the task and write your message using the phone conversation in 6a.**

Write a phone message. Include this information:
- who the message is for
- who wants to send the message
- where that person is
- what the person wants

EXAM SUCCESS

Look at your message. Is it easy to read your handwriting? Show it to other students. Do they agree? How important is good handwriting in an exam?

EXAM SUCCESS ▸ page 160

Language reference and revision

Grammar reference

Be going to

Form

Affirmative	I/You/He/She/We/They + **am/are/is** + **going to** + verb *I'm going to swim.*
Negative	I/You/He/She/We/They + **am not/aren't/isn't** + **going to** + verb *She isn't going to dance.*
Question	**Am/Are/Is** + I/you/he/she/we/they + **going to** + verb? *Are we going to eat?*
Short answers	Yes, I/you/he/she/we/they + **am/are/is**. No, I/you/he/she/we/they + **am not/aren't/isn't**. *Yes, I am.* *No, he isn't.*

Use

- We use **be going to** to talk about plans and intentions for the future.
  We're going to go out at the weekend.
  I'm going to buy a new computer.
- After **be going to** we use the verb in the infinitive.
  She's going to have a holiday.
  They're going to see the film.

Will/Won't

Form

Affirmative	I/You/He/She/We/They + **will ('ll)** + verb. *I will go.*
Negative	I/You/He/She/We/They + **will not (won't)** + verb. *They won't win.*
Question	**Will** + I/you/he/she/we/they + verb? *Will he pass?*
Short answers	Yes, I/you/he/she/we/they + **will**. No, I/you/he/she/we/they + **won't**. *Yes, she will.* *No, she won't.*

Use

- We use **will** and **won't** to talk about the future and make predictions.
  We'll pass our exams.
  It'll be sunny tomorrow.
- The contraction of **will** is **'ll**. The contraction of **will not** is **won't**.
  He'll pass his exams.
  I won't pass because I didn't study.
- After **will** and **won't** we use the verb in the infinitive.
  They won't win the competition.
  I'll write a book one day.

Vocabulary

1 Wild animals and insects

alligator bear bee eagle
jellyfish lizard scorpion shark
snake spider tiger wolf
sting bite

2 The natural world

field flowers forest grass
hill island lake mountain
river sky valley waterfall

3 The weather

cloud/cloudy cold dry
fog/foggy hot ice/icy
snow/snowy storm/stormy
sun/sunny warm wet/rainy/rain
wind/windy

4 Other words and phrases ▸ page 154

Grammar revision

Be going to

1 Look at Daniel's plans and write sentences with the correct form of *be going to*.

Mon	*visit a friend in hospital*
Tue	*do the shopping*
Wed	*have dinner with Alex*
Thur	*play tennis*
Fri	*have a party*

1 On Monday/visit his mum in hospital
On Monday he's not going to visit his mum in hospital.
2 On Tuesday/do his homework
3 On Tuesday/do the shopping
4 On Wednesday/have lunch with Alex?
5 No. (*Write a short answer for the question in 4*)
6 On Thursday/play tennis
7 What/do on Friday?
8 On Friday/have a party

WORKBOOK ▸ page 84 /7 points

Will/Won't

2 Complete the dialogue with the correct form of *will*.

JOURNALIST: Professor, in your opinion, what (**a**) .... happen to polar bears in the future? (**b**) .... they disappear completely?

PROFESSOR: No, they (**c**) .... But the future (**d**) .... be good for them because thousands of polar bears (**e**) .... disappear.

JOURNALIST: Why?

PROFESSOR: It (**f**) .... be easy for polar bears to survive because experts say that it (**g**) .... be warmer in the future. The icy regions where polar bears live (**h**) .... disappear.

WORKBOOK ▸ page 87 /8 points

Vocabulary revision

Wild animals and insects

1 Complete the words with vowels.

1 w...lf
2 j...llyf...sh
3 sp...d...r
4 b......
5 sn...k...
6 ...ll...g...t...r
7 l...z...rd
8 sh...rk
9 sc...rp......n

WORKBOOK ▸ page 82 /9 points

The weather

2 Choose the correct alternative.

1 At the top of Mount Everest it's very *ice/icy*.
2 It was *sun/sunny* today, but with some white *clouds/cloudy*.
3 In the Sahara, it's very *dry/wet*.
4 They couldn't see anything because it was really *windy/foggy*.
5 Last night there was a terrible *storm/stormy*.
6 It *rains/rainy* a lot in Britain in the winter.
7 40ºC is really *warm/hot*.

WORKBOOK ▸ page 85 /8 points

The natural world

3 Label the pictures.

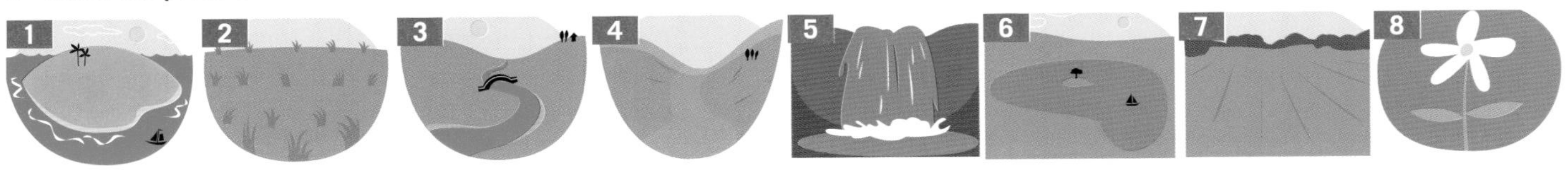

WORKBOOK ▸ page 82 /8 points

Total /40 points

10 Good buy

Grammar ▸ Present perfect – affirmative ▸ Present perfect with *just* ▸ Present perfect – negative, questions and short answers ▸ Present perfect with *already* and *yet*
Vocabulary ▸ Clothes ▸ Accessories ▸ Shops
Speaking ▸ Shopping
Writing ▸ A job application form

▸ Vocabulary

Clothes

1a Work with a partner. Match the photos with some of these words. Check that you understand the other words. Use your dictionary if necessary.

blouse boots coat dress jacket jeans jumper shirt shoes
shorts skirt socks suit tie tights top trainers trousers T-shirt

1b 2.38 Listen and repeat.

2 LISTENING **2.39 Listen to Joe talking about clothes and answer these questions.**

1. What does he usually wear at the weekend?
2. What is he wearing now?
3. What is his favourite item of clothing and why?

Accessories

3a Where on the body do you wear these items? Put the words in the correct part of the table. You can use the same word more than once.

belt cap glasses hat jewellery
scarf sunglasses watch

Head	
Eyes	
Neck	
Body	*belt*
Arm	

3b 2.40 Listen, check and repeat.

4a How often do you wear the accessories in 3? Write sentences.

I sometimes wear a belt.
I never wear a hat.

4b SPEAKING **Work with a partner. Ask and answer the questions.**

1. What is your favourite item of clothing? Why?
2. How often do you wear it?

Reading

1 SPEAKING Work with a partner. Ask and answer the questions.

1 How often do you go shopping for clothes?
2 Do you shop for clothes alone, with friends, or with a member of your family?
3 Which of these things are most important when you are deciding what clothes to buy?

- They're comfortable.
- They're made by a famous fashion designer.
- They look good.
- Your friends wear similar clothes.

2 Read the online magazine article. Which of the teenagers do you think are 'fashion-mad'?

3 Read the text again. Which person …

1 has somebody who buys their clothes? Chloe/Joe/Max
2 loves buying clothes? Chloe/Joe/Max
3 thinks wearing the right clothes is important to keep your friends? Chloe/Joe/Max
4 only buys clothes if it's necessary? Chloe/Joe/Max
5 thinks clothes make you happy? Chloe/Joe/Max
6 thinks that designer clothes are essential now? Chloe/Joe/Max

4a SPEAKING Which person is most similar to you and your opinion of clothes and fashion? Write three or four sentences explaining why.

I'm similar to Chloe because I love clothes. New clothes make me feel good. But I always look at the price and I always wear the clothes I buy.

4b Now tell your partner which person you are most similar to and why.

5 What do the underlined words in the text mean? Look at the words in context and then use your dictionary to check your ideas.

6 SPEAKING What about *you*?

1 Describe the last time you went to a clothes shop.
2 Describe the last item of clothing you bought.

I went to a clothes shop in a shopping centre near my house.

Who did you go with?

With my sister and her friends.

File Edit View Favorites Tools Help Links

Are British teenagers fashion-mad?

Recently a company asked young people in the UK some questions about money and shopping. They discovered that British teenagers can't live without buying new clothes, even when they don't have much money. We've interviewed some British teenagers to see if they really are mad about fashion.

Chloe Broderick, 15

I go shopping for clothes with my friends every Saturday. I always buy something. Today I bought some jeans but I've bought things that I don't really need too. But a new dress or top can make you feel really good. So it's worth the money even if you only wear it once. To be honest, I don't really look at the price. When I like something, I just buy it. I've written articles about fashion in our school magazine and I've drawn some designs for clothes. Maybe one day I'll be a fashion designer myself.

Joe Clark, 16

Me? Mad about fashion? No way! For a start, I hate shopping for clothes. My mum usually buys my stuff. She knows what I like. The things I wear aren't usually very expensive. Personally, I think that people spend too much money on clothes. They buy things that they don't wear later. The most expensive thing I've ever bought is my leather jacket. I bought it two years ago and I've worn it hundreds of times. It looks good, so why should I buy a new one?

Max Dawson, 17

You can't just buy jeans or trainers nowadays. They have to be Calvin Klein jeans or Dolce and Gabbana trainers. My friends all wear designer clothes so I've started doing the same. I've just spent a hundred pounds on one shirt! Sometimes I've found that later I don't even like what I've bought. Or what I've bought is really uncomfortable so I don't wear it again. But it's important for me to wear the same clothes as my friends. If not, I'm not part of the group.

GRAMMAR GUIDE

Present perfect – affirmative

1 Look at the sentences and complete the rules with the correct word.

a We've **interviewed** some British teenagers.
b I've **written** articles about fashion in our school magazine.
c I've **bought** things that I don't really need.
d I've **started** buying designer clothes.

1 We can use the present perfect to talk about the past, but only when we don't say *when* the action happened.
2 We make the present perfect with the present simple of (**a**)........................ + the past participle of the main verb.
3 Regular past participles end in (**b**) .... but there are many irregular past participles. See the third column of the verb list on page 166 and exercise 2 below.

GRAMMAR REFERENCE ▶ page 140

2 Match the irregular verbs with their past participle forms.

Verb	Past participle
1 be	a made
2 break	b seen
3 buy	c taken
4 do	d bought
5 draw	e broken
6 drink	f done
7 eat	g been
8 give	h given
9 go	i written
10 have	j gone/been*
11 make	k had
12 see	l drawn
13 take	m drunk
14 wear	n won
15 win	o eaten
16 write	p worn

* I've **been** to the shops. = I went and came back.
He's **gone** to the shops. = He went and is at the shops now.

3 Complete the sentences about the model Elle Macpherson. Use the present perfect and the verbs given.

1 She .... (make) films.
2 She .... (appear) in magazines.
3 She .... (work) on TV.
4 She .... (create) a company that makes clothes and beauty products.
5 They .... (make) a statue of her in Madame Tussaud's in London.
6 She .... (do) a lot of work for charity.
7 She .... (have) two children.
8 She .... (be) married once.

4 Complete the sentences with the present perfect form of these verbs. Use each verb once only.

break buy go make read see wear win write

1 I .... a chocolate cake.
2 I .... the book *The Lord of the Rings*.
3 I .... the film *Pirates of the Caribbean*.
4 My mum .... a competition.
5 I .... more than fifty emails.
6 I .... a glass.
7 My friends and I .... on holiday together.
8 I .... a present for my parents with my own money.
9 I .... a suit.

5 SPEAKING **Work in small groups. Say which sentences in 4 are true for you.**

I've worn a suit.

I've worn a suit too. It was at a wedding.

6a SPEAKING **Write three sentences about interesting experiences you have had. Write two true sentences and one false sentence.**

6b **Tell people your sentences. Do they know which are true and which is false?**

I've been on TV. I've won three swimming competitions. I've ridden a horse.

I don't think you've been on TV. I think that's false.

No, it's true!

GRAMMAR GUIDE

Present perfect with just

7 **We use the present perfect with *just* to talk about very recent events. Look at the sentences. Does *just* usually go before or after the past participle?**

a Look! I've **just** bought these jeans.

b I've **just** spent a hundred pounds on this shirt.

GRAMMAR REFERENCE ▸ page 140

8 **Write replies to the questions using the present perfect form of the verbs given and *just*.**

1 **A:** Is your dad at home?
B: No, I'm sorry. He *'s just gone* (go) out.

2 **A:** What are you looking for?
B: My keys. I .... (lose) them.

3 **A:** Am I late?
B: Yes, the class .... (start).

4 **A:** Why is everybody leaving the cinema?
B: The film .... (finish).

5 **A:** Are you hungry?
B: No, we .... (eat).

6 **A:** Why is Matt at the hospital?
B: He .... (break) his leg.

7 **A:** Is the computer on?
B: No, I .... (switch) it off.

9a SPEAKING **Work with a partner. A friend looks really happy. Think of reasons why. Use the present perfect with *just*.**

She's just passed an exam.

She's just won a competition.

9b **Compare answers with other students. Who has the most sentences?**

Shops

1 **Match these shops with the examples of things you can find in them (1–16).**

bakery bank bookshop butcher's chemist's clothes shop department store electrical goods shop greengrocer's jeweller's newsagent's post office shoe shop sports shop stationery shop supermarket

1 tennis rackets and balls
2 boots
3 medicine
4 paper and pens
5 food, drink and other products
6 money
7 stamps
8 bread and cakes
9 meat
10 fruit and vegetables
11 novels and dictionaries
12 gold watches and rings
13 newspapers and magazines
14 fridges and washing machines
15 shirts, tops and jeans
16 almost anything!

2 **Play this memory game. One student begins by saying what shop they've been to and what they've bought there. The next student has to repeat what the first person said and add another example. Continue. How many can you remember?**

I've been to the bakery and I've bought a doughnut.

I've been to the bakery and I've bought a doughnut. And I've been to the butcher's and I've bought some chicken.

I've been to the bakery and I've bought a doughnut. I've been to the butcher's and I've bought some chicken. And I've been …

A famous shop

International cultural knowledge
A world-famous department store

1 **Work with a partner. Look at the products in the photos. Can you usually buy these things in a department store?**

2 LISTENING 2.41 **Listen to Cath and Jim talking about a famous department store called Harrods. They mention all the things in the photos. What else do they mention that can be bought at Harrods?**

a dogs
b snow
c cake

3 **Listen again. Are these sentences true (T) or false (F)?**

1 The pot of honey wasn't expensive. T/F
2 The watch cost £650. T/F
3 They had clothes, jewellery and beds for cats. T/F
4 You could buy real snow at Harrods. T/F
5 When you buy a gold bar, you have to take it home. T/F
6 Jim doesn't want a chocolate bar. T/F

4 SPEAKING **What about *you*?**

1 What do you think of Harrods based on the information in the listening?
2 What are the good and bad things about shopping in a big department store?

I think Harrods is unusual. It sells strange things like clothes for cats.

I agree.

INSIDE INFORMATION

- Harrods is one of the largest department stores in the world. It has 330 different departments.
- Harrods opened in 1834, but at first it only sold food and tea.
- In 2007 Harrods had a cobra to protect a pair of sandals that cost £62,000!

Cross-curricular – Literature
The department store lion

5 **Work with a partner. Look at the photo. Describe what you can see. What is your opinion of having a lion as a pet?**

6 **Read this true story about a lion. Where does the lion live …**

1 at the start of the story?
2 later?
3 at the end of the story?

There was a time in the past when you could buy anything in Harrods. For example, there was a department which even sold wild animals. In 1969, two Australians, John Rendall and Anthony Bourke, went to visit this department to see the animals, not planning to buy anything. But they saw a small lion cub there that looked sad and alone. Rendall and Bourke decided to buy him. They took the lion to their home in Chelsea and named it Christian.

Christian lived like a normal pet in the house. He went for walks with Rendall and Bourke and loved playing games. He was never violent. But he went from weighing 16 kilos to weighing 84 kilos in just one year! Because he was so big, John and Anthony knew that Christian couldn't stay in a house in London for ever.

One day, they heard about a man in Africa who helped domesticated lions to live in the wild. They contacted him and decided to take Christian to Kenya. At first, Christian found Africa hot and uncomfortable. But he slowly adapted to his new life in the wild. Rendall and Bourke went back to Britain.

One year later, the two Australians wanted to see Christian again. Nobody knew exactly where he was. But Rendall and Bourke went back to the place in Kenya where they left him. As if by magic, Christian appeared the day before their arrival. The next day, when the lion saw them, he walked up slowly, then jumped up and played with them, exactly the same as when he was a little cub.

Somebody filmed the emotional reunion for a TV documentary. More than 30 years later, this clip has become famous on the Internet, with more than 44 million hits. Rendall and Bourke only saw Christian one more time. They have written a book about their incredible life with the lion from Harrods.

7 **Read the text again. Are these sentences true (T) or false (F)?**

1 John Rendall and Anthony Bourke went to Harrods because they wanted to buy a lion. T/F
2 Christian had the normal life of a lion. T/F
3 Christian couldn't stay in the house in Chelsea because he was really big. T/F
4 Christian immediately liked living in Africa. T/F
5 Rendall and Bourke went back to Kenya because they wanted to bring Christian back to London. T/F
6 Christian remembered Rendall and Bourke. T/F
7 The two Australians see Christian from time to time. T/F
8 There is a book about Rendall and Bourke's experiences with Christian. T/F

▸ WORD BOOSTER

Match the words and definitions.

1 alone	a when people meet again after a long time apart
2 domesticated	b the number of times people look at a page on the Internet
3 adapted	c a TV programme or film about something real
4 by magic	d made changes to accept a new situation
5 reunion	e no one else is with you
6 documentary	f trained to live with humans
7 hits	g in a surprising way that can't be explained

8 **What about *you*?**

1 What do you think of this story?
2 What is the most unusual thing you have bought in a shop?

I think it's a beautiful story because the lion really loved the two men.

1 **Work with a partner. Talk about what you can see in the picture.**

2 LISTENING 2.42 **Listen to a phone conversation between Luke and his mum. What does Luke's mum need to buy? What has she bought?**

EXAM SUCCESS

You are going to do a multiple-choice listening activity. In this type of activity you have three or four answers and you choose the best answer. Why is it a bad idea to write your answers quickly? EXAM SUCCESS ▸ page 160

3 **Listen again and choose the correct answer.**

1 Luke's mum …
 a is already at the sports shop.
 b is going to go to the sports shop.
 c has already been to the sports shop.

2 Luke wants new tennis balls because …
 a he hasn't got any.
 b he doesn't know where his old ones are.
 c he can't play well with the ones he has got.

3 The sports shop at Park Road has got …
 a good tennis balls.
 b good service.
 c cheap tennis balls.

4 Luke's mum will spend about …
 a £8 on tennis balls.
 b £16 on tennis balls.
 c £28 on tennis balls.

5 Luke is worried about dinner because he …
 a hasn't eaten anything all day.
 b can't find anything to eat.
 c hasn't finished his homework yet.

6 Today the sports shop closes at …
 a half past five.
 b six o'clock.
 c half past six.

GRAMMAR GUIDE

Present perfect – negative, questions and short answers

1 **Look at the sentences and choose the correct alternative.**

 a I **haven't been** to the clothes shop.
 b We **haven't bought** anything for dinner.
 c What **have** you **bought**?
 d **Have** you **been** to the sports shop?
 e Yes, I **have**./No, I **haven't**.

1 We make the negative form of the present perfect by adding **not** or **n't** to *have/the past participle*.
2 In questions, *have/the past participle* goes before the subject.
3 In short answers, we *use/don't use* the past participle.

GRAMMAR REFERENCE ▸ page 140

2a SPEAKING **Write true sentences about your life experiences. Use the affirmative or negative present perfect form of the verb.**

1 My friends and I/appear on TV.
 My friends and I haven't appeared on TV.
2 I/travel by plane.
3 I/eat sushi.
4 My parents and I/go to Ireland.
5 I/write a song.
6 I/see my favourite group in concert.
7 I/buy jewellery for my pet.

2b Work with a partner. Tell them your negative sentences. How many are the same?

My friends and I haven't appeared on TV.

Me neither./I have.

3a Write questions in the present perfect.

1 you/do/sport this week?
2 How many books/you/read this week?
3 you/have/any exams this week?
4 you/buy/any clothes this week?
5 you/write/a text in English this week?
6 you/eat/out this week?
7 What/you/watch/on TV this week?
8 you/send/any emails this week?

3b Think of some more, similar questions to ask.

3c SPEAKING **Use the questions to ask your partner about what they have or haven't done this week.**

Have you done sport this week?

Yes, I have. I've played basketball and I've done judo.

4 Complete the dialogue with the present perfect form of the verbs given.

LILY: Where (**a**) .... you .... (be)?

OLIVER: I (**b**) .... (be) shopping.

LILY: (**c**) .... you .... (buy) anything?

OLIVER: Yes, I (**d**) ....

LILY: (**e**) .... you .... (spend) a lot of money?

OLIVER: No, I (**f**) .... I (**g**) .... (not buy) anything expensive.

LILY: Why (**h**) .... you (**i**) .... (come) back?

OLIVER: Because all the shops (**j**) .... (close)!

GRAMMAR GUIDE

Present perfect with already *and* yet

5 Look at the sentences and decide if the statements below are *true* (T) or *false* (F).

a She's **already** been to the supermarket.
b You've **already** done your homework.
c Have you bought any food **yet**?
d I haven't been there **yet**.

1 We use **already** to talk about something that has happened. T/F
2 We use **yet** to talk about something that has not happened but we think it is going to happen soon. T/F
3 **Already** usually goes after the past participle. T/F
4 **Yet** usually goes at the end of the sentence. T/F

GRAMMAR REFERENCE ▸ page 140

6 Look at the list of jobs that Emily has to do today. Write sentences with *already* and *yet* to say what she has or hasn't done.

She's already bought the bread.

buy the bread ✓
write an email to Lisa ✓
send a birthday card to Sarah ✗
run 5 K ✓
phone Jack ✗
take the dog for a walk ✗
have my piano lesson ✓
make a cake for party ✗

7 SPEAKING Test your partner's memory. Ask them to close their book. Then ask them questions.

Has Emily bought the bread yet?

Yes, she has.

Correct!

8a Write down the name of a …

- new film
- new book/magazine
- new computer game
- new singer/song/group/CD
- new TV programme

8b Prepare questions using the present perfect and *yet*.

Have you read 'Breaking Dawn' yet?

8c Work in small groups. Ask and answer the questions.

▸ STUDY SKILLS

Think about what you have studied this year. What areas of English (grammar, vocabulary, speaking, writing, reading, listening …) have you made most progress in?

STUDY SKILLS ▸ page 157

1 SPEAKING **Work with a partner. Describe the picture.**

2 LISTENING 2.43 **Listen to two dialogues and answer the questions.**

1 Which dialogue, 1 or 2, goes with the photo?
2 What does the first customer buy?
3 What does the second customer want to buy?

3 Put the expressions (1–5) in the gaps (a–e) in the dialogue.

1 We don't have any large ones at the moment.
2 How much are they?
3 Do you sell rugby shirts?
4 What size are they?
5 You're welcome.

CUSTOMER: Excuse me. (**a**) ....
SHOP ASSISTANT: Yes, we've got these white England shirts and we've also got these red ones.
CUSTOMER: (**b**) ....
SHOP ASSISTANT: The white ones are £45 and the red ones are £40.
CUSTOMER: (**c**) ....
SHOP ASSISTANT: They're both medium.
CUSTOMER: Oh, I need large.
SHOP ASSISTANT: I'm sorry. (**d**) ....
CUSTOMER: OK. Thanks anyway.
SHOP ASSISTANT: (**e**) ....

4a PRONUNCIATION 2.44 **Listen to four expressions from the conversations. Do you think they sound polite?**

4b **Listen again and repeat with the correct intonation.**

STUDY SKILLS

It's important to think about WHAT we say in a conversation. Is HOW we say it important? STUDY SKILLS ▸ page 157

5 SPEAKING **Work with a partner. Practise the dialogue in 3 using the correct intonation.**

6 Look at the useful expressions in the Speaking Bank. Who says them – the Customer (C) or the Shop Assistant (SA)?

Speaking Bank

Useful expressions in a shop

- Can I help you? *SA*
- I'll take it/them.
- Excuse me. How much is this?
- Anything else?
- That's (£5).
- Here's your change.
- I'd like this.
- Would you like a bag?
- Do you sell (pencils)?
- You're welcome.
- Sorry. We don't have any at the moment.

EXAM SUCCESS

In this multiple-choice activity, you read five short dialogues. You choose the right answer to complete each one. Look at the activity. Do you know where the people are? Do you know who is speaking on each side of the dialogue?

EXAM SUCCESS ▸ page 160

7 Complete the five dialogues. Choose the correct responses.

1 Can I help you?
  a You're welcome.
  b That's £10.
  c Yes, I'd like two of those cakes, please.
2 That's £6.20, please.
  a Here you are.
  b I'm sorry. We don't have any.
  c You're welcome.
3 Thanks for your help.
  a Do you sell bread here?
  b You're welcome.
  c Can I help you?
4 How much is this?
  a It's large.
  b That's all right.
  c It's £10.
5 Would you like a bag?
  a Yes, here you are.
  b Yes, please. I need one.
  c Yes, here's your change.

Practice makes perfect

8a Work with a partner. Choose a shop and a product that you want to buy there. Prepare a dialogue. You must use at least five expressions from the Speaking Bank.

8b Act out your dialogue for the class. They must write down the correct shop and the product.

1 **SPEAKING** **Work with a partner. Ask and answer the questions.**

1 Would you like to work in a supermarket? Why/Why not?
2 What is your ideal job?

2 **Look at the application form for a part-time job in a supermarket. Say where each piece of information should go on the application form.**

- [*f*] 1 Home – 0453 7632/Mobile – 653 923936
- [ ] 2 M
- [ ] 3 Johnson
- [ ] 4 Brookside School, York
- [ ] 5 James
- [ ] 6 20/12/1993
- [ ] 7 I have a good working knowledge of most computer programs. I can speak French. I am learning to drive at the moment. I'm very hard-working and responsible.
- [ ] 8 (James Johnson's signature)
- [ ] 9 25 Orchid Avenue, Blackpool
- [ ] 10 I have worked as a monitor on a summer camp and as a waiter in a fast-food restaurant.
- [ ] 11 Mornings
- [ ] 12 Gary's Greengrocer

3 **Look at the Writing Bank. Find a word, expression or letters that say or ask …**

1 if you are a boy or girl: ....
2 when you were born: ....
3 for your signature: ....
4 what things you can do: ....
5 for your family name: ....
6 where you have worked before: ....

JOB APPLICATION

Please fill in this application form carefully. When we have read your application form, if you have the skills and experience we need, we will contact you for an interview.

One week after the interview we will contact you to tell you if we can offer you a job.

Good luck!

PERSONAL INFORMATION

Surname:	(a)
First name(s):	(b)
Date of birth:	(c)
Gender:	(d) M/F
Address:	(e)
Phone no.:	(f)
Best time to contact to arrange an interview:	(g)

EDUCATION, EXPERIENCE AND SKILLS

Education:	(h)
Current employment:	(i)
Previous employment:	(j)
Skills:	(k)

Signed: (l) ____________________

▶ Writing Bank

Useful words or expressions in an application form

You need to be able to understand these words or expressions to be able to fill in a job application form.

- Surname
- Date of birth
- Gender: M/F
- Current employment
- Previous employment
- Skills
- Signed

Practice makes perfect

4a **Complete the application form with information about you. Make up information if you need to.**

4b **Prepare questions to interview your partner for the supermarket job.**

What's your name?
What's your date of birth?

4c **Interview your partner. They must use the information on their application form.**

Should they get the job?

Hello. What's your name?

Helen Carson.

What is your date of birth?

Language reference and revision

Grammar reference

Present perfect

Form

Affirmative	I/You/He/She/We/They + **have/has** + past participle *She has met a famous person.*
Negative	I/You/He/She/We/They + **haven't/hasn't** + past participle *We haven't seen that new film.*
Question	**Have/Has** + I/You/He/She/We/They + past participle *Have you bought anything?*
Short answers	Yes, I/You/He/She/We/They + **has/have**. No, I/You/He/She/We/They + **hasn't/haven't**. *Yes, I have. No, they haven't.*

Use

- We can use the present perfect to talk about an experience in someone's lifetime, without saying the exact time when the event occurred. When it happened is not important.
  I've been to Australia.
  She hasn't read 'War and Peace'.
  Have they eaten all the cake?
  Yes, they have!

Just

Use

- We use **just** with the present perfect to emphasise the fact that something happened very recently.
- **Just** goes before the past participle.
  I have just washed my hair. (= I washed my hair only a few moments ago)
  Have you just taken the rubbish out?

Already, yet

Use

- We use **already** to talk about something that has happened earlier than we expected.
- **Already** usually goes before the past participle.
  Don't buy any bread. I've already bought some.
- We use **yet** to ask if something we expect has happened, or to say that it hasn't. It is used in questions or negative sentences.
- **Yet** usually goes at the end of a sentence or clause.
  Have you spoken to the teacher yet?
  I haven't read the book yet.

Vocabulary

1 Clothes

blouse boots coat dress jacket jeans jumper shirt shoes shorts skirt socks suit tie tights top trainers trousers T-shirt

2 Accessories

belt cap glasses hat jewellery scarf sunglasses watch

3 Shops

bakery bank bookshop butcher's chemist's clothes shop department store electrical goods shop greengrocer's jeweller's newsagent's post office shoe shop sports shop stationery shop supermarket

4 Other words and phrases ▸ page 155

Grammar revision

Present perfect affirmative

1 Complete the text with the verbs given in the correct form of the present perfect.

My sister is a famous fashion designer.
She (**a**) .... (do) lots of interesting things in her life. She (**b**) .... (make) dresses for the Queen. She (**c**) .... (meet) lots of famous actors. She (**d**) .... (win) some important prizes too. Sometimes I (**e**) .... (help) her. For example, we (**f**) .... (write) articles together for fashion magazines.

WORKBOOK ▶ page 92

/ 6 points

Present perfect with *just*

2 Complete the sentences with the present perfect form of the verb given and *just*.

1 Her hair is wet because she .... (have) a shower.
2 She's sad because her favourite tennis player .... (lose).
3 They're cold because they .... (be) outside in the snow.
4 I'm happy because I .... (hear) my favourite song on the radio.

WORKBOOK ▶ page 92

/ 4 points

Present perfect negative and question forms

3a Put the words in order to make questions.

1 film the Have seen you *Avatar*?
2 cities in many How you have lived?
3 people week have Which famous met you this?

3b Answer question 1 with a short answer and write complete sentences for questions 2 and 3. Your answers must be true.

1 ....
2 ....
3 ....

WORKBOOK ▶ page 95

/ 6 points

Present perfect with *already* and *yet*

4 Complete the sentences with *already* or *yet*.

1 I haven't spoken to my mum ....
2 I'm bored. I've .... seen this programme.
3 You're fast! You've .... finished this exercise!
4 Has the teacher arrived ....?
5 Have they been shopping ....?
6 She hasn't visited the museum ....

WORKBOOK ▶ page 95

/ 6 points

Vocabulary revision

Clothes

1 Write the names of the clothes.

1 
....

2 
....

3 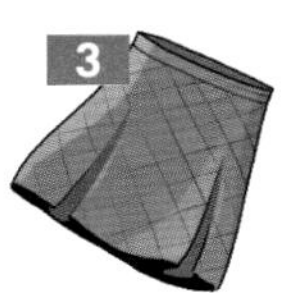
....

4 
....

5 
....

6 
....

WORKBOOK ▶ page 90

/ 6 points

Accessories

2 What are these accessories?

1 You wear it to tell the time. ....
2 You wear it to keep your neck warm in the winter. ....
3 You wear it to keep your trousers up. ....
4 You wear it on your head. It can stop the sun going in your eyes. ....
5 You wear them to see better. ....

WORKBOOK ▶ page 90

/ 5 points

Shops

3 Write an example of something you can buy in these shops.

1 stationery shop ....
2 department store ....
3 chemist's ....
4 butcher's ....
5 bakery ....
6 newsagent's ....
7 post office ....

WORKBOOK ▶ page 93

/ 7 points

Total */ 40 points*

Gateway to exams *Units 9–10*

Listening

Tip For Listening Exams

In multiple choice activities, remember …

Don't answer the questions too quickly. Sometimes the speaker says one thing and then changes what they say or adds new information. EXAM SUCCESS ▸ page 160

1 Work with a partner. Talk about the clothes you usually wear at school. If you wear a school uniform, describe it.

2 2.45 Listen to Josh and Sarah talking about a friend who goes to school in the USA. Choose the correct answer **A**, **B** or **C** for each question.

1 When did Emma start school in the USA?
- **A** Last year.
- **B** Last week.
- **C** Very recently.

2 At her school, Emma
- **A** has to wear school uniform.
- **B** isn't totally free to decide what to wear.
- **C** can wear what she likes.

3 At Emma's school, you can
- **A** never wear T-shirts.
- **B** only wear T-shirts for one subject.
- **C** always wear T-shirts.

4 Emma
- **A** has already bought some new clothes for school.
- **B** will buy new clothes on Saturday or Sunday.
- **C** is going to buy new jeans and T-shirts.

5 Why does Josh think school uniforms are OK?
- **A** You don't spend time deciding what to wear.
- **B** It's easy to wear.
- **C** He doesn't like his weekend clothes.

3 What about *you*?

Do you think school uniform is a good idea? Why/Why not?

Speaking

Tip For Speaking Exams

In pair activities, remember …

It is important to listen to what your partner says. In a conversation, we listen to the other person and then respond to what they say to us. EXAM SUCCESS ▸ page 160

4 Work with a partner. Match the expressions (1–7) to the situations (a–j).

1 Hello. Can I help you? *a*
2 Here's three pounds change. Would you like a bag?
3 You're welcome.
4 How much is it?
5 Yes, please. What size is this shirt?
6 We've got small, medium, large and extra large.
7 I'll take it. Here's ten pounds.

Shop assistant	Customer
a Ask the customer if they need help.	b Accept the offer of help. You can't see the size on a shirt that you like.
c Say the size.	d Say you need a different size. Ask if they have that size.
e Explain all the different sizes you have.	f Ask the price.
g Say the price.	h Say you want it. Give the money.
i Give the change. Ask if they need a bag.	j Say you want a bag. Say thank you.
k Accept the thanks and say goodbye.	

5 Work with a partner. Look at the situation below and act out the conversation. When you finish, change roles.

You want to buy a friend a T-shirt. Go to the shop and ask the shop assistant about the T-shirt and then buy it.

Use of English

Tip For Use Of English Exams

In activities where you have to choose the right answer to complete short dialogues, remember …

Think about the situation, place and people before you try to choose the correct answer. **EXAM SUCCESS ▸ page 160**

6 Look at the start of five short dialogues. For each dialogue, try to decide what the situation is, where the people are, and/or who the people are.

1 Excuse me, what size is this shirt?
2 Why don't we go to the shopping centre tomorrow?
3 Could I have a cheeseburger, please?
4 Can you tell me where the chemist's is?
5 Hello? Mrs Johnson? Is that you?

7 Complete the five dialogues in 6 by choosing **A**, **B** or **C**.

1 **A** I'm sorry. We don't have any.
B I think it's small.
C It's ten pounds.

2 **A** You're welcome.
B Sorry, I can't. I'm busy.
C Because I like shopping.

3 **A** Would you like chips with it?
B That's all right.
C Here's your change.

4 **A** Yes, thanks.
B That's all right.
C Go past the bank and it's on your left.

5 **A** No, she isn't.
B Yes, speaking.
C Sorry. Can I leave a message?

Writing

Tip For Writing Exams

In writing exams, remember …

Good handwriting and presentation are very important. You will probably lose marks if the examiner finds it difficult to read your work. EXAM SUCCESS ▸ page 160

8 Look at these different types of words. Write YES if we can sometimes leave them out when we write informal messages. Write NO if we can't.

1 articles (*a, the*)
2 nouns (*shops, trainers*)
3 auxiliary verbs (*be, do*)
4 main verbs (*go, buy*)
5 adjectives (*new, free*)
6 subject pronouns (*I, he*)
7 prepositions (*at, in*)

9 Use this information to write a phone message for Steve.

Who phoned? Robbie

Who did he want to speak to? Steve

What did he say? 'Can you tell Steve that I'm going to the city centre tomorrow? If he's free, he can meet me there. I'm going to go to buy some new trainers. Then I'll have lunch in one of the fast-food places there. Tell him to call me tonight and tell me his plans. I won't be at home. I'll be at Mark's house. Tell him to call me there or on my mobile. The number is 876 321986. Thanks!'

'Can Do' Progress Check

CEF

1 How well can you do these things in English now? Give yourself a mark from 1 to 4.

1 = I can do it very well.
2 = I can do it quite well.
3 = I have some problems.
4 = I can't do it.

a I can talk about the future using *be going to* or *will* ☐
b I can understand written and spoken texts about animals and the natural world. ☐
c I can talk about the weather. ☐
d I can make and accept suggestions. ☐
e I can take basic phone messages. ☐
f I can talk about actions or experiences in the past using the present perfect. ☐
g I can talk about recent activities using the present perfect with *just* and *already*. ☐
h I can understand written and spoken texts about clothes, fashion and shops. ☐
i I can have simple conversations in a shop. ☐
j I can write a basic job application form. ☐

2 Now decide what you need to do to improve.

1 Look again at my book/notes.
2 Do more practice exercises. ⇨ WORKBOOK page 98–99
3 Ask for help.
4 Other: ....

Wordlists

(adj) = adjective (adv) = adverb (conj) = conjunction (det) = determiner (n) = noun (phr) = phrase (prep) = preposition (pron) = pronoun (v) = verb	The most common and useful words in English are marked according to the Macmillan Dictionary 'star rating'. This is so that you can easily recognise the vocabulary you need to know especially well. ★★★ = very common words ★★ = common words ★ = fairly common words If there is no star next to the word, this means that it is not very common.

Starter unit

Classroom objects

board (n) ★★★	/bɔːd/
board rubber (n)	/'bɔːd ˌrʌbə/
CD player (n)	/siː 'di ˌpleɪə/
chair (n) ★★★	/tʃeə/
computer (n) ★★★	/kəm'pjuːtə/
desk (n) ★★★	/desk/
dictionary (n)	/'dɪkʃən(ə)ri/
notebook (n)	/'nəʊtˌbʊk/
pen (n) ★★	/pen/
pencil (n) ★★	/'pens(ə)l/
pencil sharpener (n)	/'pens(ə)l ˌʃɑː(r)p(ə)nə/
rubber (n)	/'rʌbə/
ruler (n) ★	/'ruːlə/
textbook (n)	/'teks(t)ˌbʊk/

Colours

black (adj) ★★★	/blæk/
blue (adj) ★★★	/bluː/
brown (adj) ★★★	/braʊn/
dark blue (adj)	/ˌdɑːk 'bluː/
green (adj) ★★★	/griːn/
grey (adj) ★	/greɪ/
orange (adj)	/'ɒrɪndʒ/
pink (adj)	/pɪŋk/
purple (adj)	/'pɜːp(ə)l/
red (adj) ★★★	/red/
white (adj) ★★★	/waɪt/
yellow (adj) ★★★	/'jeləʊ/

Some English-speaking countries and nationalities

Australia (n)	/ɒ'streɪliə/
Australian (adj)	/ɒ'streɪliən/
Canada (n)	/'kænədə/
Canadian (adj)	/kə'neɪdiən/
England (n)	/'ɪŋglənd/
English (adj)	/'ɪŋglɪʃ/
Ireland (n)	/'aɪələnd/
Irish (adj)	/'aɪrɪʃ/
Scotland (n)	/'skɒtlənd/
Scottish (adj)	/'skɒtɪʃ/
United States of America (n)	/juːˌnaɪtɪd steɪts əv ə'merɪkə/
American (adj)	/ə'merɪkən/

Days

Monday (n) ★★★	/'mʌndeɪ/
Tuesday (n) ★★★	/'tjuːzdeɪ/
Wednesday (n) ★★★	/'wenzdeɪ/
Thursday (n) ★★★	/'θɜːzdeɪ/
Friday (n) ★★★	/'fraɪdeɪ/
Saturday (n) ★★★	/'sætədeɪ/
Sunday (n) ★★★	/'sʌndeɪ/

Months

January (n) ★★★	/'dʒænjuəri/
February (n) ★★★	/'februəri/
March (n) ★★★	/mɑːtʃ/
April (n) ★★★	/'eɪprəl/
May (n) ★★★	/meɪ/
June (n) ★★★	/dʒuː(n)/
July (n) ★★★	/dʒʊ'laɪ/
August (n) ★★★	/'ɔːgəst/
September (n) ★★★	/sep'tembə/
October (n) ★★★	/ɒk'təʊbə/
November (n) ★★★	/nəʊ'vembə/
December (n) ★★★	/dɪ'sembə/

Ordinal numbers

first (1st) (number) ★★★	/fɜːst/
second (2nd) (number) ★★★	/'sekənd/
third (3rd) (number)	/θɜːd/
fourth (4th) (number)	/fɔːθ/
fifth (5th) (number)	/fɪfθ/
sixth (6th) (number)	/sɪksθ/
seventh (7th) (number)	/'sev(ə)nθ/
eighth (8th) (number)	/eɪtθ/
ninth (9th) (number)	/naɪnθ/
tenth (10th) (number)	/tenθ/
eleventh (11th) (number)	/ɪ'lev(ə)nθ/

twelfth (12th) (number)	/twelfθ/
thirteenth (13th) (number)	/ˌθɜː'tiːnθ/
fourteenth (14th) (number)	/ˌfɔː'tiːnθ/
fifteenth (15th) (number)	/ˌfɪf'tiːnθ/
sixteenth (16th) (number)	/ˌsɪks'tiːnθ/
seventeenth (17th) (number)	/ˌsev(ə)n'tiːnθ/
eighteenth (18th) (number)	/ˌeɪ'tiːnθ/
nineteenth (19th) (number)	/ˌnaɪn'tiːnθ/
twentieth (20th) (number)	/'twentiəθ/
twenty-first (21st) (number)	/ˌtwenti 'fɜːst/
thirty-first (31st) (number)	/ˌθɜːti 'fɜːst/

The family

aunt (n) ★★	/ɑːnt/
brother (n) ★★★	/'brʌðə/
cousin (n) ★★	/'kʌz(ə)n/
daughter (n) ★★★	/'dɔːtə/
father (n) ★★★	/'fɑːðə/
grandchildren (n)	/'grænd,tʃɪldrən/
granddaughter (n)	/'græn(d)ˌdɔːtə/
grandfather (n) ★	/'græn(d)ˌfɑːðə/
grandmother (n) ★	/'græn(d)ˌmʌðə/
grandparents (n)	/grænd,peərənts/
grandson (n)	/'græn(d)ˌsʌn/
husband (n) ★★★	/'hʌzbənd/
mother (n) ★★★	/'mʌðə/
nephew (n)	/'nefjuː, 'nevjuː/
niece (n)	/niːs/
parent (n) ★★★	/'peərənt/
sister (n) ★★★	/'sɪstə/
son (n) ★★★	/sʌn/
uncle (n) ★	/'ʌŋk(ə)l/
wife (n) ★★★	/waɪf/

Basic descriptions

beard (n)	/bɪəd/
black hair (n)	/ˌblæk 'heə/
blue eyes (n)	/'bluː ˌaɪz/
brown eyes (n)	/'braʊn ˌaɪz/
dark hair (n)	/'dɑːk ˌheə/
fair hair (n)	/'feə ˌheə/
glasses (n)	/'glɑːsɪz/
green eyes (n)	/'grin ˌaɪz/
long hair (n)	/'lɒŋ ˌheə/
moustache (n)	/mə'stɑːʃ/
red hair (n)	/'red ˌheə/
short (adj) ★★★	/ʃɔːt/
short hair (n)	/'ʃɔːt ˌheə/
tall (adj) ★★★	/tɔːl/
thin (adj) ★★★	/θɪn/

Words in classroom expressions and instructions in this book

act out (v)	/ˌækt 'aʊt/
add (v) ★★★	/æd/
alternative (n) ★★	/ɔːl'tɜːnətɪv/
answer (n & v) ★★★	/'ɑːnsə/
can (v)	/kæn/
change (v) ★★★	/tʃeɪndʒ/
check (v) ★★★	/tʃek/
choose (v) ★★★	/tʃuːz/
compare (v) ★★★	/kəm'peə/
complete (v) ★★★	/kəm'pliːt/
conversation (n) ★★★	/ˌkɒnvə'seɪʃ(ə)n/
correct (adj) ★★★	/kə'rekt/
description (n) ★★★	/dɪ'skrɪpʃ(ə)n/
dialogue (n) ★★	/'daɪəˌlɒg/
different (adj) ★★★	/'dɪfrənt/
discover (v) ★★★	/dɪ'skʌvə/
draw (v) ★★★	/drɔː/
false (adj) ★★	/fɔːls/
fill in (v)	/ˌfɪl 'ɪn/
gap (n) ★★	/gæp/
guess (v) ★★	/ges/
how (adv & conj) ★★★	/haʊ/
if necessary (adj)	/ˌɪf 'nesəseri/
language (n) ★★★	/'læŋgwɪdʒ/
letter (of alphabet) (n) ★★★	/'letə/
list (n) ★★★	/lɪst/
list (v) ★★	/lɪst/
listen (v) ★★★	/'lɪs(ə)n/
look (v) ★★★	/lʊk/
match (v) ★★	/mætʃ/
mean (v) ★★★	/miːn/
object (=thing) (n) ★★★	/'ɒbdʒɪkt/
partner (n) ★★★	/'pɑːtnə/
photo (n) ★★	/'fəʊtəʊ/
picture (n) ★★★	/'pɪktʃə/
practise (v) ★★	/'præktɪs/
question (n) ★★★	/'kwestʃ(ə)n/
read (v) ★★★	/riːd/
repeat (v) ★★★	/rɪ'piːt/
say (v) ★★★	/seɪ/
sorry (adj) ★★★	/'sɒri/
spell (v) ★	/spel/
table (=chart) (n) ★★★	/'teɪb(ə)l/
take it in turns (phr)	/ˌteɪk ɪt ɪn 'tɜːnz/
translate (v) ★	/træns'leɪt/
true (adj) ★★★	/truː/
understand (v) ★★★	/ˌʌndə'stænd/
what (det, pron) ★★★	/wɒt/
who (pron) ★★★	/huː/
word (n) ★★★	/wɜːd/
work (n & v) ★★★	/wɜːk/
write (v) ★★★	/raɪt/

Grammar words

adjective (n) ★	/'ædʒɪktɪv/
affirmative (adj)	/ə'fɜːmətɪv/
apostrophe (n)	/ə'pɒstrəfi/
contraction (n)	/kən'trækʃ(ə)n/
negative (adj) ★★	/'negətɪv/

noun (n) ★ /naʊn/
phrase (n) ★★★ /freɪz/
plural (adj) ★ /ˈplʊərəl/
possessive (adj) /pəˈzesɪv/
pronoun (n) /ˈprəʊnaʊn/
sentence (n) ★★★ /ˈsentəns/
short answer (n) /ˌʃɔːt ˈɑːnsə/
singular (adj) /ˈsɪŋgjʊlə/
subject (n) ★★★ /ˈsʌbdʒɪkt/
subject (adj) /ˈsʌbdʒɪkt/
verb (n) ★ /vɜːb/

Other words and phrases

again (adv) ★★★ /əˈgen/
birthday (n) ★★ /ˈbɜːθdeɪ/
date (n) ★★★ /deɪt/
end (n) ★★★ /end/
family tree (n)
favourite (adj) ★★ /ˈfeɪv(ə)rət/
friend (n) ★★★ /frend/
half past (phr) ★★★ /hɑːf/
how old (phr) /ˌhau ˈəʊld/
meet (v) ★★★ /miːt/
middle (n) ★★★ /ˈmɪd(ə)l/
name (n) ★★★ /neɪm/
new (adj) ★★★ /njuː/
nice (adj) ★★★ /naɪs/
o'clock (adv) ★★ /əˈklɒk/
other (det, pron) ★★★ /ˈʌðə/
quarter (n) ★★★ /ˈkwɔːtə/
similar (adj) ★★★ /ˈsɪmɪlə/
singer (n) /ˈsɪŋə/
start (n & v) ★★★ /stɑːt/
student (n) ★★★ /ˈstjuːd(ə)nt/
today (adv) ★★★ /təˈdeɪ/
tomorrow (adv) ★★★ /təˈmɒrəʊ/
win (v) ★★★ /wɪn/

Unit 1

School subjects

art (n) ★★★ /ɑːt/
biology (n) /baɪˈɒlədʒi/
chemistry (n) /ˈkemɪstri/
English (n) /ˈɪŋglɪʃ/
French (n) /frentʃ/
geography (n) /dʒiːˈɒgrəfi/
German (n) /ˈdʒɜː(r)mən/
history (n) ★★★ /ˈhɪst(ə)ri/
information and communication technology (ICT) (n) /ˌaɪ siː ˈtiː/
maths (n) /mæθs/
music (n) ★★★ /ˈmjuːzɪk/
physical education (P.E.) (n) /ˌfɪzɪkəl edjʊˈkeɪʃ(ə)n/ /ˌpiː ˈiː/
physics (n) ★ /ˈfɪzɪks/
Spanish (n) /ˈspænɪʃ/

School activities

ask/answer a question (v) /ˌɑːsk/ˌɑnsə ə ˈkwestʃən/
do homework (v) /ˌduː ˈhəʊmwɜːk/
finish (school/classes) (v) ★★★ /ˈfɪnɪʃ/
have a break (v) /ˌhæv ə ˈbreɪk/
have lunch (v) /ˌhæv ˈlʌntʃ/
sit (v) ★★★ /sɪt/
stand (v) ★★★ /stænd/
start (school/classes) (v) ★★★ /stɑːt/

Everyday activities

get (un)dressed (v) /get (ˌʌn)ˈdrest/
get up (v) /ˌget ˈʌp/
go to bed (v) /ˌgəʊ tə ˈbed/
go to school by bike/bus/car/train (v) /gəʊ tə ˌskuːl baɪ ˈbaɪk/ˈbʌs/ˈkɑː/ˈtreɪn/
have a shower (v) /ˌhæv ə ˈʃaʊə/
have breakfast/lunch/dinner (v) /hæv ˈbrekfəst/ˈlʌntʃ/ˈdɪnə/
make breakfast/lunch/dinner (v) /meɪk ˈbrekfəst/ˈlʌntʃ/ˈdɪnə/
play football/tennis/computer games (v) /pleɪ ˈfʊtbɔːl/ˈtenɪs/ˈkəmpjuːtə geɪmz/
walk to school (v) /ˌwɔːk tə ˈskuːl/

Other words and phrases

advanced (adj) ★ /ədˈvɑːnst/
all (det, pron) ★★★ /ɔːl/
and (conj) ★★★ /ən, ənd, ænd/
and so (conj) /ˌənd ˈsəʊ/
at home (adv) /ət ˈhəʊm/
bad (adj) ★★★ /bæd/
bad (adv) /bæd/
because (conj) ★★★ /bɪˈkɒz/
before (conj, prep) ★★★ /bɪˈfɔː/
but (conj) ★★★ /bət, bʌt/
cafeteria (n) /ˌkæfəˈtɪəriə/
can't stand (v) /ˌkɑːnt ˈstænd/
certificate (n) ★★ /səˈtɪfɪkət/
city (n) ★★★ /ˈsɪti/
clean (v) ★★★ /kliːn/
clothes (n) ★★★ /kləʊðz/
cold (adj) ★★★ /kəʊld/
compulsory (adj) ★ /kəmˈpʌlsəri/
design (n) ★★★ /dɪˈzaɪn/
different (adj) ★★★ /ˈdɪfrənt/
difficult (adj) ★★★ /ˈdɪfɪk(ə)lt/
each (det) ★★★ /iːtʃ/
education (n) ★★★ /ˌedjʊˈkeɪʃ(ə)n/
electronic (adj) ★★ /ˌelekˈtrɒnɪk/
email (n) ★★★ /ˈiːmeɪl/
encyclopaedia (n) /ɪnˌsaɪkləˈpiːdiə/
except (for) (prep) ★★★ /ɪkˈsept/
expensive (adj) ★★★ /ɪkˈspensɪv/
food (n) ★★★ /fuːd/
genius (n) /ˈdʒiːniəs/

good (adj) ★★★	/gʊd/
great (adj) ★★★	/greɪt/
hate (v) ★★★	/heɪt/
leave (v) ★★★	/liːv/
lesson (n) ★★★	/ˈles(ə)n/
level (n) ★★★	/ˈlev(ə)l/
like (v) ★★★	/laɪk/
love (v) ★★★	/lʌv/
made (v)	/meɪd/
material (n) ★★★	/məˈtɪəriəl/
mean (v) ★★★	/miːn/
next (det, adj) ★★★	/nekst/
OK/okay (phr)	/ˌəʊˈkeɪ/
open (adj) ★★★	/ˈəʊpən/
pay (v) ★★★	/peɪ/
practical (adj) ★★★	/ˈpræktɪk(ə)l/
private (adj) ★★★	/ˈpraɪvət/
product (n) ★★★	/ˈprɒdʌkt/
ready (adj) ★★★	/ˈredi/
relax (v) ★★	/rɪˈlæks/
same (adj) ★★★	/seɪm/
state (adj)	/steɪt/
take something out of (phr)	/ˌteɪk sʌmθɪŋ ˈaʊt əv/
technology (n) ★★★	/tekˈnɒlədʒi/
textile (n)	/ˈtekstaɪl/
timetable (n)	/ˈtaɪmˌteɪb(ə)l/
typical (adj) ★★★	/ˈtɪpɪk(ə)l/
university (n) ★★★	/ˌjuːnɪˈvɜːsəti/
unusual (adj) ★★	/ʌnˈjuːʒʊəl/

Unit 2

Free-time activities

chat online (v)	/ˌtʃæt ɒnˈlaɪn/
collect things (v)	/kəˈlekt ˌθɪŋz/
dance (v) ★★★	/dɑːns/
do sport (v)	/ˈduː ˌspɔːt/
draw (v) ★★★	/drɔː/
go out with friends (v)	/gəʊ aʊt wɪð frendz/
listen to music (v)	/ˌlɪsən tə ˈmjuːzɪk/
play a musical instrument (v)	/pleɪ ə mjuːzɪkəl ɪnstrəmənt/
read (v) ★★★	/riːd/
surf the Internet (v)	/sɜːf ði ɪntənet/
take photos (v)	/teɪk fəʊtəʊz/
watch films (v)	/wɒtʃ fɪlmz/

Places to go in a town

cinema (n) ★★	/ˈsɪnəmə/
fast-food restaurant (n)	/ˌfɑːst ˈfuːd rest(ə)rɒnt/
library (n) ★★★	/ˈlaɪbrəri/
museum (n) ★★★	/mjuːˈziːəm/
park (n) ★★	/pɑːk/
shopping centre (n)	/ˈʃɒpɪŋ ˌsentə(r)/
sports centre (n)	/ˈspɔː(r)ts sentə(r)/
stadium (n)	/ˈsteɪdiəm/
swimming pool (n)	/ˈswɪmɪŋ ˌpuːl/
theatre (n) ★★	/ˈθɪətə/

Other words and phrases

active (adj) ★★★	/ˈæktɪv/
announcement (n) ★	/əˈnaʊnsmənt/
appear (v) ★★★	/əˈpɪə/
Atlantic Ocean (n)	/ətˌlæntɪk ˈəʊʃən/
autograph (n)	/ˈɔːtəˌgrɑːf/
become ★★★	/bɪˈkʌm/
bungee jumping (n)	/ˈbʌndʒiː ˌdʒʌmpɪŋ/
camera (n) ★★★	/ˈkæm(ə)rə/
certainly (adv) ★★★ (=yes, of course)	/ˈsɜːt(ə)nli/
climber (n)	/ˈklaɪmə/
cloud (n) ★★★	/klaʊd/
collection (n) ★★★	/kəˈlekʃ(ə)n/
collector (n)	/kəˈlektə/
colony (n)	/ˈkɒləni/
comedy (n) ★	/ˈkɒmədi/
comic (n)	/ˈkɒmɪk/
compatible (adj)	/kəmˈpætəb(ə)l/
concert (n) ★★	/ˈkɒnsət/
defend (v) ★★	/dɪˈfend/
easy (adj) ★★★	/ˈiːzi/
event (n) ★★★	/ɪˈvent/
explorer (n)	/ɪkˈsplɔːrə/
extreme sport (n)	/ɪkˌstriːm ˈspɔː(r)t/
film director (n)	/ˈfɪlm dəˌrektə(r)/
first edition (n)	/ˌfɜː(r)st ɪˈdɪʃ(ə)n/
flower (n) ★★★	/ˈflaʊə/
funny (adj) ★★★	/ˈfʌni/
high (adj) ★★★	/haɪ/
how long (phr)	/ˌhaʊ ˈlɒŋ/
how much (phr)	/ˌhaʊ ˈmʌtʃ/
illustration (n) ★	/ˌɪləˈstreɪʃ(ə)n/
introduce (v) ★★★	/ˌɪntrəˈdjuːs/
island (n) ★★★	/ˈaɪlənd/
land (n) ★★★	/lænd/
length (n) ★★★	/leŋθ/
location (n) ★★	/ləʊˈkeɪʃ(ə)n/
magazine (n) ★★	/ˌmægəˈziːn/
match (=football) (n) ★★★	/mætʃ/
meet (v) ★★★	/miːt/
mountain (n) ★★★	/ˈmaʊntɪn/
music group (n)	/ˈmjuːzɪk ˌgruːp/
national anthem (n)	/ˌnæʃ(ə)nəl ˈænθəm/
native (adj) ★	/ˈneɪtɪv/
Netherlands (n)	/neðələndz/
officially (adv) ★	/əˈfɪʃəli/
original (adj) ★★★	/əˈrɪdʒ(ə)nəl/
painting (n) ★★	/ˈpeɪntɪŋ/
population (n) ★★★	/ˌpɒpjʊˈleɪʃ(ə)n/
price (n) ★★★	/praɪs/
publication (n) ★	/ˌpʌblɪˈkeɪʃ(ə)n/

radio station (n)	/'reɪdiəʊ ˌsteɪʃ(ə)n/
save (=save somebody) (v) ★★★	/seɪv/
shirt (n) ★★★	/ʃɜːt/
signature (n) ★	/'sɪgnətʃə/
simple (adj) ★★★	/'sɪmp(ə)l/
size (n) ★★★	/saɪz/
team (n) ★★★	/tiːm/
ticket (n) ★★★	/'tɪkɪt/
title (n) ★★★	/'taɪt(ə)l/
to be mad about (phr)	/tə bi 'mæd əˌbaʊt/
tree (n) ★★★	/triː/
under (adv & prep) ★★★	/'ʌndə/
volcano (n)	/vɒl'keɪnəʊ/
website (n)	/'webˌsaɪt/
wedding (n) ★★	/'wedɪŋ/
You're welcome. (phr)	/ˌjɔː 'welkəm/

Gateway to exams, Units 1–2

academy (n)	/ə'kædəmi/
energy bar (n)	/'enə(r)dʒi ˌbɑː(r)/
every (det) ★★★	/'evri/
session (n) ★★	/'seʃ(ə)n/
special (adj) ★★★	/'speʃ(ə)l/
special (n)	/'speʃ(ə)l/
summer (n) ★★★	/'sʌmə/
training (n) ★★★	/'treɪnɪŋ/

Unit 3

Rooms

bathroom (n) ★★	/'bɑːθˌruːm/
bedroom (n) ★★	/'bedruːm/
dining room (n)	/'daɪnɪŋ ˌruːm/
garage (n) ★	/'gærɑːʒ, 'gærɪdʒ/
garden (n) ★★★	/'gɑːd(ə)n/
hall (n) ★★★	/hɔːl/
kitchen (n) ★★★	/'kɪtʃən/
living room (n) ★★	/'lɪvɪŋ ˌruːm/

Household objects and furniture

armchair (n)	/'ɑːmˌtʃeə/
bath (n) ★★★	/bɑːθ/
bed (n) ★★★	/bed/
CD player (n)	/siː 'di ˌpleɪə/
chair (n) ★★★	/tʃeə/
clock (n) ★★★	/klɒk/
computer (n) ★★★	/kəm'pjuːtə/
cooker (n)	/'kʊkə/
cupboard (n) ★	/'kʌbəd/
desk (n) ★★★	/desk/
DVD player (n)	/ˌdiː viː 'diː pleɪə/
fridge (n) ★	/frɪdʒ/
games console (n)	/'geɪmz ˌkɒnsəʊl/
lamp (n) ★★	/læmp/
light (n) ★★★	/laɪt/
microwave (n)	/'maɪkrəˌweɪv/
phone (n) ★★★	/fəʊn/
poster (n)	/'pəʊstə/
radiator (n)	/'reɪdiˌeɪtə/
shelf (n) ★★	/ʃelf/
shower (n) ★	/'ʃaʊə/
sink (n)	/sɪŋk/
sofa (n)	/'səʊfə/
table (n) ★★★	/'teɪb(ə)l/
toilet (n) ★	/'tɔɪlət/
TV (n) ★★★	/ˌtiː 'viː/
washing machine (n) ★	/'wɒʃɪŋ məˌʃiːn/
window (n) ★★★	/'wɪndəʊ/

Jobs around the house

cook (v) ★★★	/kʊk/
do the ironing (v)	/ˌduː ði 'aɪənɪŋ/
do the shopping (v)	/ˌduː ðə 'ʃɒpɪŋ/
do the washing (v)	/ˌduː ðə 'wɒʃɪŋ/
lay the table (v)	/ˌleɪ ðə 'teɪb(ə)l/
make the bed (v)	/ˌmeɪk ðə 'bed/
take the rubbish out (v)	/ˌteɪk ðə 'rʌbɪʃ aʊt/
tidy up (v)	/ˌtaɪdi 'ʌp/
wash the dishes (v)	/ˌwɒʃ ðə 'dɪʃɪz/

Other words and phrases

access (n) ★★	/'ækses/
alien (n)	/'eɪliən/
basketball (n)	/'bɑːskɪtˌbɔːl/
best (adj) ★★★	/best/
block of flats (n)	/blɒk əv 'flæts/
bungalow (n)	/'bʌŋgəˌləʊ/
coffee cup (n)	/'kɒfi ˌkʌp/
cool (adj) ★★★	/kuːl/
cottage (n) ★	/'kɒtɪdʒ/
court (n) ★★★ (=basketball court)	/kɔːt/
detached (adj)	/dɪ'tætʃt/
energy (n) ★★★	/'enədʒi/
enormous (adj) ★★	/ɪ'nɔːməs/
flat (n) ★★	/flæt/
floor (=storey) (n) ★★★	/flɔː/
glass (n) ★★★	/glɑːs/
government (n) ★★★	/'gʌv(ə)nmənt/
grass (n) ★★★	/grɑːs/
hall of residence (n)	/ˌhɔːl əv 'rezɪd(ə)ns/
hang on (v)	/ˌhæŋ 'ɒn/
hot (adj) ★★★	/hɒt/
houseboat (n)	/'haʊsˌbəʊt/
ideal (adj) ★	/aɪ'dɪəl/
inside (adv) ★★★	/'ɪnˌsaɪd/
nature (n) ★★★	/'neɪtʃə/
plant (n) ★★★	/plɑːnt/
player (n) ★★★	/'pleɪə/

pollution (n) ★★	/pə'luːʃ(ə)n/
popcorn (n)	/'pɒpˌkɔːn/
semi-detached (adj)	/ˌsemidɪ'tætʃt/
shoe (n) ★★★	/ʃuː/
skate park (n)	/'skeɪt ˌpɑː(r)k/
skateboarding (n)	/'skeɪtˌbɔː(r)dɪŋ/
sleep (v) ★★★	/sliːp/
space (=empty space) (n) ★★★	/speɪs/
speaking(v) (=Mrs. Jones? Yes, speaking.)	/'spiːˌkɪŋ/
spectacular (adj)	/spek'tækjʊlə/
statue (n)	/'stætʃuː/
summer (n) ★★★	/'sʌmə/
sun (n) ★★★	/sʌn/
surprise (n) ★★★	/sə'praɪz/
tank (=water tank) (n) ★★	/tæŋk/
terraced (adj)	/'terəst/
top (adj) ★★★	/tɒp/
towel (n) ★	/'taʊəl/
ventilation (n)	/ˌventɪ'leɪʃ(ə)n/
village (n) ★★★	/'vɪlɪdʒ/
wall (n) ★★★	/wɔːl/
warm (adj) ★★★	/wɔːm/
winter (n) ★★★	/'wɪntə/
wrong (adj) ★★★	/rɒŋ/

Unit 4

Parts of the body

arm (n) ★★★	/ɑːm/
back (n) ★★★	/bæk/
chest (n) ★★★	/tʃest/
ear (n) ★★★	/ɪə/
eye (n) ★★★	/aɪ/
face (n) ★★★	/feɪs/
finger (n) ★★★	/'fɪŋgə/
foot (n) ★★★	/fʊt/
hand (n) ★★★	/hænd/
head (n) ★★★	/hed/
leg (n) ★★★	/leg/
mouth (n) ★★★	/maʊθ/
neck (n) ★★★	/nek/
nose (n) ★★★	/nəʊz/
shoulder (n) ★★★	/'ʃəʊldə/
stomach (n) ★★	/'stʌmək/
toe (n) ★	/təʊ/
tooth (n) ★★★	/tuːθ/

Basic physical activities

climb (v) ★★★	/klaɪm/
dive (v)	/daɪv/
fall (v) ★★★	/fɔːl/
hit (v) ★★★	/hɪt/
jump (v) ★★★	/dʒʌmp/
kick (v) ★★★	/kɪk/
rest (v) ★★★	/rest/
ride (a horse/bike) (v) ★★	/raɪd/
run (v) ★★★	/rʌn/
skate (v)	/skeɪt/
ski (v)	/skiː/
swim (v) ★★	/swɪm/

Sports

baseball (n)	/'beɪsˌbɔːl/
basketball (n)	/'bɑːskɪtˌbɔːl/
cycling (n)	/'saɪklɪŋ/
fishing (n)	/'fɪʃɪŋ/
football (n) ★★	/'fʊtbɔːl/
golf (n) ★	/gɒlf/
gymnastics (n)	/dʒɪm'næstɪks/
ice skating (n)	/'aɪs ˌskeɪtɪŋ/
judo (n)	/'dʒuːdəʊ/
netball (n)	/'netˌbɔːl/
rugby (n)	/'rʌgbi/
sailing (n)	/'seɪlɪŋ/
table tennis (n)	/'teɪb(ə)l ˌtenɪs /
tennis (n)	/'tenɪs/
volleyball (n)	/'vɒliˌbɔːl/

Other words and phrases

accident (n) ★★★	/'æksɪd(ə)nt/
advice (n) ★★★	/əd'vaɪs/
aerobic (adj)	/eə'rəʊbɪk/
air (n) ★★★	/eə/
along (prep) ★★★	/ə'lɒŋ/
anaerobic (adj)	/ˌænə'rəʊbɪk/
athletics (n)	/æθ'letɪks/
avalanche (n)	/'ævəˌlɑːntʃ/
beat (v) ★★★	/biːt/
beat (n)	/biːt/
between (prep) ★★★	/bɪ'twiːn/
break (v) ★★★	/breɪk/
breathe (v) ★★	/briːð/
by accident (phr)	/ˌbaɪ 'æksɪd(ə)nt/
calm (adj) ★★	/kɑːm/
close (v) ★★★	/kləʊz/
concentrate (v) ★★★	/'kɒns(ə)nˌtreɪt/
conclusion (n) ★★★	/kən'kluːʒ(ə)n/
cool down (v)	/ˌkuːl 'daʊn /
cover (v) ★★★	/'kʌvə/
cricket (n)	/'krɪkɪt/
diameter (n)	/daɪ'æmɪtə/
die (v) ★★★	/daɪ/
escape (v) ★★	/ɪ'skeɪp/
fast (adv) ★★★	/fɑːst/
fit (adj) ★	/fɪt/
flexible (adj) ★	/'fleksəb(ə)l/
gentle (adj) ★	/'dʒent(ə)l/
gradually (adv) ★★	/'grædʒuəli/
gym (n)	/dʒɪm/

gymnastics (n)	/dʒɪm'næstɪks/
heart (n) ★★★	/hɑːt/
heart rate (n)	/'hɑː(r)t ˌreɪt/
heavy (adj) ★★★	/'hevi/
holiday (n) ★★★	/'hɒlɪdeɪ/
how often (phr)	/ˌhaʊ 'ɒf(t)ən/
intense (adj) ★	/ɪn'tens/
interview (v) ★	/'ɪntəˌvjuː/
joint (n)	/dʒɔɪnt/
left (adv)	/left/
little by little (phr)	/ˌlɪt(ə)l baɪ 'lɪt(ə)l/
lose (v) ★★★	/luːz/
martial arts (n)	/ˌmɑːʃəl 'ɑts/
medium (adj) ★	/'miːdiəm/
mistake (n) ★★	/mɪ'steɪk/
motivate (v)	/'məʊtɪˌveɪt/
movement (n) ★★★	/'muːvmənt/
muscle (n) ★★	/'mʌs(ə)l/
must (v) ★★★	/məst, mʌst/
near (prep) ★★★	/nɪə/
necessary (adj) ★★★	/'nesəs(ə)ri/
need (v) ★★★	/niːd/
obligatory (adj)	/ə'blɪgət(ə)ri/
opposite (prep) ★	/'ɒpəzɪt/
panic (v)	/'pænɪk/
past (=go past) ★★★	/pɑːst/
patient (adj) ★★	/'peɪʃ(ə)nt/
period (n) ★★★	/'pɪəriəd/
permission (n) ★★	/pə'mɪʃ(ə)n/
positive (adj) ★★★	/'pɒzətɪv/
practice (n) ★★★	/'præktɪs/
reduce (v) ★★★	/rɪ'djuːs/
regulate (v)	/'regjʊˌleɪt/
relevant (adj) ★★★	/'reləv(ə)nt/
rescue (n) ★	/'reskjuː/
right (adv) ★★★	/raɪt/
shout (v) ★★★	/ʃaʊt/
show (v) ★★★	/ʃəʊ/
signal (n) ★★★	/'sɪgn(ə)l/
slow down (v)	/ˌsləʊ 'daʊn/
smoke (v) ★★	/sməʊk/
specific (adj) ★★★	/spə'sɪfɪk/
speed (n) ★★★	/spiːd/
stay (v) ★★★	/steɪ/
straight on (adv)	/streɪt ɒn/
stretch (v) ★★	/stretʃ/
survive (v) ★★★	/sə'vaɪv/
tall (adj) ★★★	/tɔːl/
tempo (n)	/'tempəʊ/
theory (n) ★★	/'θɪəri/
transmitter (n)	/trænz'mɪtə/
travel (v) ★★★	/'træv(ə)l/
triathlon (n)	/traɪ'æθlən/
turn (v) ★★★	/tɜː(n)/
uniform (n) ★★	/'juːnɪˌfɔːm/
wear (v) ★★★	/weə/
weather (n) ★★★	/'weðə/
weigh (v) ★★	/weɪ/
wind (n) ★★★	/wɪnd/
without (adv) ★★★	/wɪð'aʊt/

Gateway to exams, Units 3–4

bottom (adj) (=of the swimming pool)	/'bɒtəm/
goal (n) ★★★	/gəʊl/
salt (n) ★	/sɔːlt/
score (v) ★★	/skɔː/
substitute (n)	/'sʌbstɪˌtjuːt/
underwater (adj & adv)	/ˌʌndə'wɔːtə/

Unit 5

Food

apple (n) ★★★	/'æp(ə)l/
banana (n)	/bə'nɑːnə/
bean (n)	/biːn/
biscuit (n)	/'bɪskɪt/
bread (n) ★★★	/bred/
burger (n)	/'bɜːgə/
butter (n) ★★	/'bʌtə/
cake (n) ★★	/keɪk/
cheese (n) ★★	/tʃiːz/
chicken (n) ★★	/'tʃɪkɪn/
chips (n) ★★	/tʃɪps/
egg (n) ★★★	/eg/
fish (n) ★★★	/fɪʃ/
grape (n)	/greɪp/
ice cream (n) ★	/'aɪs ˌkriːm/
lemon (n)	/'lemən/
meat (n) ★★★	/miːt/
melon (n)	/'melən/
nuts (n) ★	/nʌts/
pizza (n)	/'piːtsə/
rice (n) ★	/raɪs/
salad (n) ★	/'sæləd/
salt (n) ★	/sɔːlt/
strawberry (n)	/'strɔːb(ə)ri/
sugar (n) ★★	/'ʃʊgə/
tomato (n)	/tə'mɑːtəʊ/

Drink

coffee (n) ★★★	/'kɒfi/
hot chocolate (n)	/ˌhɒt 'tʃɒklət/
lemonade (n)	/ˌlemə'neɪd/
milk (n) ★★★	/mɪlk/
milkshake (n)	/'mɪlkˌʃeɪk/
mineral water (n)	/'mɪn(ə)rəl ˌwɔːtə(r)/
orange juice (n)	/'ɒrɪndʒ ˌdʒuːs/
tea (n) ★★★	/tiː/

Containers

bottle (n) ★★★	/'bɒt(ə)l/
can (n) ★★	/kæn/
carton (n)	/'kɑːt(ə)n/
cup (n) ★★★	/kʌp/
glass (n) ★★★	/glɑːs/
packet (n) ★	/'pækɪt/
slice (n) ★	/slaɪs/

Other words and phrases

additive (n)	/'ædətɪv/
antioxidant (n)	/ˌænti'ɒksɪd(ə)nt/
at least (phr)	/ət 'liːst /
balanced (adj)	/'bælənst/
bill (=in restaurant) (n) ★★★	/bɪl/
blueberry (n)	/'bluːb(ə)ri/
both (det, pron) ★★★	/bəʊθ/
calcium (n)	/'kælsiəm/
cancer (n) ★	/'kænsə/
celebrate (v) ★★	/'seləˌbreɪt/
change (n) ★★★	/tʃeɪndʒ/
cheerful (adj)	/'tʃɪəf(ə)l/
chemical (adj)	/'kemɪk(ə)l/
choose (v) ★★★	/tʃuːz/
colourful (adj)	/'kʌləf(ə)l/
contentment (n)	/kən'tentmənt/
cost (v) ★★★	/kɒst/
customer (n) ★★★	/'kʌstəmə/
delicious (adj) ★	/dɪ'lɪʃəs/
dessert (n) ★	/dɪ'zɜːt/
enjoy (v) ★★★	/ɪn'dʒɔɪ/
evidence (n) ★★★	/'evɪd(ə)ns/
extremely (adv) ★★★	/ɪk'striːmli/
flavour (n) ★	/'fleɪvə/
glad (adj) ★★	/glæd/
healthy (adj) ★★	/'helθi/
home-made (adj)	/'həʊmeɪd/
hormone (n)	/'hɔːməʊn/
how many (phr)	/ˌhaʊ 'meni/
how much (phr)	/ˌhaʊ 'mʌtʃ/
huge (adj) ★★★	/hjuːdʒ/
include (v) ★★★	/ɪn'kluːd/
ingredient (n)	/ɪn'griːdiənt/
laboratory (n) ★	/lə'bɒrət(ə)ri, 'læbrəˌtɔːri/
large (adj) ★★★	/lɑːdʒ/
lately (adv)	/'leɪtli/
main (=main course) (n)	/meɪn/
oxygen (n)	/'ɒksɪdʒ(ə)n/
peel (v)	/piːl/
picnic (n)	/'pɪknɪk/
preservative (n)	/prɪ'zɜːvətɪv/
protect (v) ★★★	/prə'tekt/
regular (adj) ★★★ (=regular or large)	/'regjʊlə/
secret (adj) ★★	/'siːkrət/
share (v) ★★★	/ʃeə/
silly (adj) ★	/'sɪli/
starter (n)	/'stɑːtə/
stress (=pronunciation) (n) ★	/stres/
syllable (n)	/'sɪləb(ə)l/
throw (v) ★★★	/θrəʊ/
violent (adj) ★★★	/'vaɪələnt/
waiter (n)	/'weɪtə/

Unit 6

Countries and nationalities

Argentina (n)	/ɑːdʒən'tiːnə/
Argentinian (adj)	/ɑːdʒən'tɪniən/
Brazil (n)	/brə'zɪl/
Brazilian (adj)	/brə'zɪliən/
Czech (adj)	/tʃek/
Czech Republic (n)	/tʃek rɪ'pʌblɪk/
Egypt (n)	/'iːdʒɪpt/
Egyptian (adj)	/ɪ'dʒɪpʃən/
France (n)	/frɑːns/
French (adj)	/frentʃ/
Germany (n)	/'dʒɜːməni/
German (adj)	/'dʒɜː(r)mən/
Ireland (n)	/'aɪələnd/
Irish (adj)	/'aɪrɪʃ/
Italy (n)	/'ɪtəli/
Italian (adj)	/ɪ'tæljən/
Japan (n)	/dʒə'pæn/
Japanese (adj)	/ˌdʒæpə'niːz/
Poland (n)	/'pəʊlənd/
Polish (adj)	/'pəʊlɪʃ/
Russia (n)	/'rʌʃə/
Russian (adj)	/'rʌʃ(ə)n/
Slovakia (n)	/slə'vækiə/
Slovakian (adj)	/slə'vækiən/
South Africa (n)	/ˌsaʊθ 'æfrɪkə/
South African (adj)	/ˌsaʊθ 'æfrɪkən/
Spain (n)	/'speɪn/
Spanish (adj)	/'spænɪʃ/
Switzerland (n)	/'swɪtsələnd/
Swiss (adj)	/swɪs/
Turkey (n)	/'tɜːki/
Turkish (adj)	/'tɜː(r)kɪʃ/
the USA (n)	/ˌjuː es 'eɪ/
American (adj)	/ə'merɪkən/

Words connected with tourism

boat (n) ★★★	/bəʊt/
excursion (n)	/ɪk'skɜːʃ(ə)n/
guide book (n)	/'gaɪdˌbʊk/
hotel (n) ★★★	/həʊ'tel/
luggage (n)	/'lʌgɪdʒ/
package holiday (n)	/ˌpækɪdʒ 'hɒlɪdeɪ/

passport (n) ★	/'pɑːspɔːt/
plane (n) ★★★	/pleɪn/
sightseeing (n)	/'saɪtˌsiːɪŋ/
tickets (n) ★★★	/'tɪkɪts/
train (n) ★★★	/treɪn/
trip (n) ★★	/trɪp/

Transport

boat (n) ★★★	/bəʊt/
bus (n) ★★★	/bʌs/
car (n) ★★★	/kɑː/
coach (n) ★	/kəʊtʃ/
helicopter (n)	/'helɪˌkɒptə/
lorry (n)	/'lɒri/
motorbike (n)	/'məʊtəˌbaɪk/
plane (n) ★★★	/pleɪn/
scooter (n)	/'skuːtə/
ship (n) ★★★	/ʃɪp/
taxi (n) ★★★	/'tæksi/
train (n) ★★★	/treɪn/
tram (n)	/træm/
Underground, the (n)	/'ʌndəˌgraʊnd/
van (n) ★	/væn/

Other words and phrases

ago (adv) ★★★	/ə'gəʊ/
annual (adj) ★★	/'ænjuəl/
bag (n) ★★★	/bæg/
basis (n) ★	/'beɪsɪs/
brilliant (adj) ★	/'brɪljənt/
cheap (adj) ★★★	/tʃiːp/
connection (n) ★★★	/kə'nekʃ(ə)n/
cool (=great) (adj) ★★★	/kuːl/
creator (n)	/kri'eɪtə/
document (n) ★★★	/'dɒkjʊmənt/
dynamic (adj)	/daɪ'næmɪk/
flag (n)	/flæg/
foreign (adj) ★★★	/'fɒrɪn/
general election (n)	/ˌdʒen(ə)rəl ɪ'lekʃən/
global (adj) ★★	/'gləʊb(ə)l/
honeymoon (n)	/'hʌniˌmuː(n)/
in business (phr)	/ˌɪn 'bɪznəs/
land (n) ★★★	/lænd/
last (adj) ★★★	/lɑːst/
meeting (n) ★★★	/'miːtɪŋ/
monument (n)	/'mɒnjʊmənt/
nightlife (n)	/'naɪtˌlaɪf/
nowadays (adv) ★★	/'naʊəˌdeɪz/
on the cheap (phr)	/ˌɒn ðə 'tʃiːp/
podcast (n)	/'pɒdˌkɑːst/
price (n) ★★★	/praɪs/
rich (adj) ★★★	/rɪtʃ/
route (n) ★★	/ruːt/
sail (v) ★★	/seɪl/
sales (n)	/seɪlz/
shilling (n)	/'ʃɪlɪŋ/
sight (=see the sights) (n) ★★★	/saɪt/
success (n) ★★★	/sək'ses/
town (n) ★★★	/taʊn/
travel destination (n)	/'trævəl destɪˌneɪʃ(ə)n/
useful (adj) ★★★	/'juːsf(ə)l/
via (prep) ★	/'vaɪə, 'viːə/
vote (v) ★★★	/vəʊt/
yesterday (adv) ★★★	/'jestədeɪ/
yesterday (n)	/'jestədeɪ/

Gateway to exams, Units 5–6

barbecue (n)	/'bɑːbɪˌkjuː/
service (n) ★★★	/'sɜːvɪs/
vegetarian (n)	/ˌvedʒə'teəriən/
youth hostel (n)	/'juːθ ˌhɒst(ə)l/

Unit 7

Places of work

clinic (n)	/'klɪnɪk/
factory (n) ★★★	/'fæktri/
garage (n) ★	/'gærɑːʒ, 'gærɪdʒ/
hospital (n) ★★★	/'hɒspɪt(ə)l/
office (n) ★★★	/'ɒfɪs/
outdoors (adv)	/ˌaʊt'dɔːz/
restaurant (n) ★★★	/'rest(ə)rɒnt/
shop (n) ★★★	/ʃɒp/
studio (n) ★★	/'stjuːdiəʊ/

Jobs and work

actor (n) ★★★	/'æktə/
actress (n)	/'æktrəs/
artist (n) ★★	/'ɑːtɪst/
builder (n)	/'bɪldə/
bus/taxi/lorry driver (n) ★★★	/bʌs/'tæksi/'lɒri ˌdraɪvə/
businessman (n)	/'bɪznəsmæn/
businesswoman (n)	/'bɪznəsˌwʊmən/
cleaner (n)	/'kliːnə/
cook (n)	/kʊk/
dentist (n)	/'dentɪst/
doctor (n) ★★★	/'dɒktə/
engineer (n) ★	/ˌendʒɪ'nɪə/
farmer (n)	/'fɑːmə/
footballer (n)	/'fʊtbɔːlə/
hairdresser (n)	/'heəˌdresə/
journalist (n) ★★	/'dʒɜːnəlɪst/
mechanic (n)	/mɪ'kænɪk/
nurse (n) ★★	/nɜːs/
secretary (n) ★	/'sekrətri/
shop assistant (n)	/'ʃɒp əˌsɪst(ə)nt/
singer (n)	/'sɪŋə/
waiter (n)	/'weɪtə/
waitress (n)	/'weɪtrəs/

Culture and entertainment

art (n) ★★★ /ɑːt/
ballet (n) /ˈbæleɪ/
composer (n) /kəmˈpəʊzə/
dancer (n) ★★ /ˈdɑːnsə(r)/
director (n) ★★★ /dəˈrektə, daɪˈrektə/
film (n) ★★★ /fɪlm/
literature (n) ★★ /ˈlɪtrətʃə/
musician (n) ★ /mjuˈzɪʃ(ə)n/
novelist (n) /ˈnɒvəlɪst/
opera (n) /ˈɒp(ə)rə/
painter (n) /ˈpeɪntə/
poet (n) /ˈpəʊɪt/
poetry (n) ★ /ˈpəʊɪtri/
singer (n) /ˈsɪŋə/
theatre (n) ★★ /ˈθɪətə/
writer (n) ★★★ /ˈraɪtə/

Other words and phrases

architecture (n) /ˈɑːkɪˌtektʃə/
blame (v) ★★ /bleɪm/
blonde (n) /blɒnd/
ceremony (n) ★ /ˈserəməni/
competition (n) ★★★ /ˌkɒmpəˈtɪʃ(ə)n/
course (n) ★★★ /kɔːs/
cruise (=ship) (n) /kruːz/
cut (v) ★★★ /kʌt/
decoration (n) /ˌdekəˈreɪʃ(ə)n/
dress up (v) /ˌdres ˈʌp/
entertainment (n) ★★ /ˌentəˈteɪnmənt/
express (v) ★★★ /ɪkˈspres/
finalist (n) /ˈfaɪn(ə)lɪst/
for free (adv) /ˌfə ˈfriː/
gentleman (n) ★ /ˈdʒent(ə)lmən/
get divorced /ˌget dɪˈvɔː(r)st/
give up (v) /ˌgɪv ˈʌp/
grieve (v) /griː(v)/
guilt (n) /gɪlt/
happen (v) ★★★ /ˈhæpən/
hold somebody back (v) /ˌhəʊld ˈbæk/
honey (n) /ˈhʌni/
influence (v) ★★★ /ˈɪnfluəns/
legend (n) /ˈledʒ(ə)nd/
lie (=not tell the truth) (v) ★★★ /laɪ/
limousine (n) /ˌlɪməˈziː(n)/
look after (v) /ˌlʊk ˈɑːftə/
medieval (adj) /ˌmediˈiːv(ə)l/
moon (n) ★★ /muːn/
news (n) ★★★ /njuːz/
newspaper (n) ★★★ /ˈnjuːzˌpeɪpə/
nominate (v) /ˈnɒmɪˌneɪt/
not mind (v) /ˌnɒt ˈmaɪnd/
on your own /ˌɒn jɔː ˈəʊn/
paint (v) ★★ /peɪnt/
period (n) ★★★ /ˈpɪəriəd/
physical (adj) ★★★ /ˈfɪzɪk(ə)l/
popularity (n) /ˈpɒpjʊˈlærəti/
prize (n) ★★ /praɪz/
production company (n) /prəˈdʌkʃ(ə)n ˌkʌmp(ə)ni/
repair (v) ★ /rɪˈpeə/
romance (n) /rəʊˈmæns/
royal family (n) ★ /ˌrɔɪəl ˈfæm(ə)li/
style (n) ★★★ /staɪl/
successful (adj) ★★★ /səkˈsesf(ə)l/
waste (v) ★★ /weɪst/
willing (adj) ★★ /ˈwɪlɪŋ/

Unit 8

Feelings

angry (adj) ★★★ /ˈæŋgri/
bored (adj) ★★ /bɔːd/
excited (adj) ★★ /ɪkˈsaɪtɪd/
happy (adj) ★★★ /ˈhæpi/
interested (adj) ★★★ /ˈɪntrəstɪd/
relaxed (adj) ★ /rɪˈlækst/
sad (adj) ★★ /sæd/
surprised (adj) ★★ /səˈpraɪzd/
tired (adj) ★★★ /ˈtaɪəd/
worried (adj) ★ /ˈwʌrid/

Personality

cheerful (adj) /ˈtʃɪəf(ə)l/
hard-working (adj) ★ /ˈhɑː(r)dˌwɜː(r)kɪŋ/
intelligent (adj) ★★ /ɪnˈtelɪdʒ(ə)nt/
kind (adj) ★ /kaɪnd/
lazy (adj) ★ /ˈleɪzi/
quiet (adj) ★★★ /ˈkwaɪət/
responsible (adj) ★★★ /rɪˈspɒnsəb(ə)l/
serious (adj) ★★★ /ˈsɪəriəs/

Social problems

crime (n) ★★★ /kraɪm/
homelessness (n) /ˈhəʊmləsnəs/
hunger (n) /ˈhʌŋgə/
pollution (n) ★★ /pəˈluːʃ(ə)n/
poverty (n) /ˈpɒvəti/
unemployment (n) ★★ /ˌʌnɪmˈplɔɪmənt/
violence (n) ★★ /ˈvaɪələns/

Other words and phrases

authority (n) ★★ /ɔːˈθɒrəti/
bad mannered (adj) /ˌbæd ˈmænəd/
chore (n) /tʃɔː/
citizenship (n) /ˈsɪtɪz(ə)nʃɪp/
critic (=person) (n) ★ /ˈkrɪtɪk/
cry (=have tears) (v) ★★★ /kraɪ/
diary (n) ★★ /ˈdaɪəri/
disrespect (n) /ˌdɪsrɪˈspekt/
effort (n) ★★★ /ˈefət/

far (adj) ★★★	/fɑː/
gadget (n)	/ˈɡædʒɪt/
IQ (n)	/ˌaɪ ˈkjuː/
mark (=out of ten) (n) ★★★	/mɑːk/
near (prep, adj) ★★★	/nɪə/
opposite (n) (=someone or something completely different from another person/thing)	/ˈɒpəzɪt/
orchestra (n) ★	/ˈɔːkɪstrə/
own (adj) ★★★	/əʊn/
peace (n) ★★★	/piːs/
process (n) ★★★	/ˈprəʊses/
quotation (n)	/kwəʊˈteɪʃ(ə)n/

Gateway to exams, Units 7–8

award (n) ★★	/əˈwɔːd/
charity (n) ★★	/ˈtʃærəti/
citizen (n) ★★	/ˈsɪtɪz(ə)n/
condition (n) ★★★	/kənˈdɪʃ(ə)n/
hurricane (n)	/ˈhʌrɪkən, ˈhʌrɪkeɪn/
independence (n) ★★	/ˌɪndɪˈpendəns/
refugee (n)	/ˌrefjʊˈdʒiː/
victim (n) ★★★	/ˈvɪktɪm/

Unit 9

Wild animals and insects

alligator (n)	/ˈælɪˌɡeɪtə/
bear (n)	/beə/
bee (n)	/biː/
bite (v) ★★	/baɪt/
bite (n)	/baɪt/
eagle (n)	/ˈiːɡ(ə)l/
jellyfish (n)	/ˈdʒeliˌfɪʃ/
lizard (n)	/ˈlɪzəd/
scorpion (n)	/ˈskɔːpiən/
shark (n)	/ʃɑːk/
snake (n)	/sneɪk/
spider (n)	/ˈspaɪdə/
sting (v)	/stɪŋ/
sting (n)	/stɪŋ/
tiger (n)	/ˈtaɪɡə/
wolf (n)	/wʊlf/

The natural world

field (n) ★★★	/fiːld/
flowers (n) ★★★	/ˈflaʊəz/
forest (n) ★★★	/ˈfɒrɪst/
grass (n) ★★★	/ɡrɑːs/
hill (n) ★★★	/hɪl/
island (n) ★★★	/ˈaɪlənd/
lake (n) ★★	/leɪk/
mountain (n) ★★★	/ˈmaʊntɪn/
river (n) ★★★	/ˈrɪvə/
sky (n) ★★★	/skaɪ/
valley (n) ★	/ˈvæli/
waterfall (n)	/ˈwɔːtəˌfɔːl/

The weather

cloud (n) ★★★	/klaʊd/
cloudy (adj)	/ˈklaʊdi/
cold (adj) ★★★	/kəʊld/
dry (adj) ★★★	/draɪ/
fog (n)	/fɒɡ/
foggy (adj)	/ˈfɒɡi/
hot (adj) ★★★	/hɒt/
ice (n) ★★	/aɪs/
icy (adj)	/ˈaɪsi/
rain (n) ★★★	/reɪn/
rain (v) ★	/reɪn/
rainy (adj)	/ˈreɪni/
snow (n) ★★	/snəʊ/
snow (v)	/snəʊ/
snowy (adj)	/ˈsnəʊi/
storm (n) ★★	/stɔːm/
stormy (adj)	/ˈstɔːmi/
sun (n) ★★★	/sʌn/
sunny (adj)	/ˈsʌni/
warm (adj) ★★★	/wɔːm/
wet (adj) ★★★	/wet/
wind (n) ★★★	/wɪnd/
windy (adj)	/ˈwɪndi/

Other words and phrases

alone (adj & adv) ★★	/əˈləʊn/
arrange (v) ★★★	/əˈreɪndʒ/
bite (v) ★★	/baɪt/
bit (v)	/bɪt/
cub (=young wolf) (n)	/kʌb/
cure (n) ★	/kjʊə/
danger (n) ★★★	/ˈdeɪndʒə/
demographic (adj)	/ˌdeməˈɡræfɪk/
distribution (n) ★	/ˌdɪstrɪˈbjuːʃ(ə)n/
east (n) ★★★	/iːst/
fang (n)	/fæŋ/
fight (v) ★★★	/faɪt/
free (adj) ★★★ (=with nothing to do)	/friː/
gold (n) ★★	/ɡəʊld/
handwriting (n)	/ˈhændˌraɪtɪŋ/
headmaster (n)	/ˌhedˈmɑːstə/
hunt (v)	/hʌnt/
lie (=recline) (v) ★★★	/laɪ/
miss (v) ★★★	/mɪs/
mostly (adv) ★★	/ˈməʊs(t)li/
north (n) ★★★	/nɔːθ/
out (adv) ★★★ (=to be out of the house)	/aʊt/
parachute (n)	/ˈpærəˌʃuːt/
pet (n) ★	/pet/

pick up (v)	/ˌpɪk 'ʌp/
powerful (adj) ★★★	/'paʊəf(ə)l/
proud (adj) ★	/praʊd/
province (n)	/'prɒvɪns/
reach down (v)	/ˌriːtʃ 'daʊn/
sleepy (adj)	/'sliːpi/
smell (v) ★	/smel/
south (n) ★★★	/saʊθ/
space (=outer space) (n) ★★★	/speɪs/
square kilometre (n)	/ˌskweə(r) kɪ'lɒmɪtə(r)/
sure (=yes) (adv) ★★	/ʃɔː, ʃʊə/
survival (n) ★	/sə'vaɪv(ə)l/
survive (v) ★★★	/sə'vaɪv/
take place (phr)	/ˌteɪk 'pleɪs/
temperature (n) ★★★	/'temprɪˌtʃə/
west (n) ★★★	/west/

Unit 10

Clothes

blouse (n)	/blaʊz/
boots (n)	/buːts/
coat (n) ★★★	/kəʊt/
dress (n) ★★	/dres/
jacket (n) ★★	/'dʒækɪt/
jeans (n) ★★	/dʒiːnz/
jumper (n)	/'dʒʌmpə/
shirt (n) ★★★	/ʃɜːt/
shoes (n)	/ʃuːz/
shorts (n)	/ʃɔːts/
skirt (n) ★★	/skɜːt/
socks (n)	/sɒks/
suit (n) ★★	/suːt/
tie (n) ★	/taɪ/
tights (n)	/taɪts/
top (n) ★★★	/tɒp/
trainers (n)	/'treɪnəz/
trousers (n) ★★	/'traʊzəz/
T-shirt (n)	/'tiː ˌʃɜːt/

Accessories

belt (n) ★	/belt/
cap (n) ★★	/kæp/
glasses (n)	/'glɑːsɪz/
hat (n) ★★	/hæt/
jewellery (n) ★★	/'dʒuːəlri/
scarf (n)	/skɑːf/
sunglasses (n)	/'sʌnˌglɑːsɪz/
watch (n) ★★	/wɒtʃ/

Shops

bakery (n)	/'beɪkəri/
bank (n) ★★★	/bæŋk/
bookshop (n)	/'bʊkˌʃɒp/
butcher's (n)	/'bʊtʃəz/
chemist's (n)	/'kemɪsts/
clothes shop (n)	/'kləʊðz ˌʃɒp/
department store (n) ★★	/dɪ'pɑːtmənt ˌstɔː/
electrical goods shop (n)	/ɪlektrɪk(ə)l 'gʊdz ˌʃɒp/
greengrocer's (n)	/'griːnˌgrəʊsəz/
jeweller's (n)	/'dʒuːələz/
newsagent's (n)	/'njuːzeɪdʒənts/
post office (n) ★★	/'pəʊst ˌɒfɪs/
shoe shop (n)	/'ʃuː ˌʃɒp/
sports shop (n)	/'spɔːts ˌʃɒp/
stationery shop (n)	/'steɪʃən(ə)ri ˌʃɒp/
supermarket (n) ★	/'suːpəˌmɑːkɪt/

Other words and phrases

adapt (v)	/ə'dæpt/
address (n) ★★★	/ə'dres/
almost (adv) ★★★	/'ɔːlməʊst/
application form (n) ★★	/æplɪ'keɪʃən ˌfɔːm/
arrival (n) ★★	/ə'raɪv(ə)l/
be worth (adj)	/bi wɜːθ/
birth (n) ★★	/bɜːθ/
clip (=on YouTube) (n)	/klɪp/
designer clothes (n)	/dɪˌzaɪnə(r) 'kləʊðz/
documentary (n)	/ˌdɒkjʊ'ment(ə)ri/
domesticated (adj)	/də'mestɪˌkeɪtɪd/
employment (n) ★★★	/ɪm'plɔɪmənt/
essential (adj) ★★★	/ɪ'senʃ(ə)l/
fashion designer (n)	/'fæʃ(ə)n dɪˌzaɪnə(r)/
forever (adv) ★	/fər'evə/
gender (n)	/'dʒendə/
hit (=on the Internet) (n) ★	/hɪt/
magic (n) ★	/'mædʒɪk/
no way (phr)	/ˌnəʊ 'weɪ/
nowadays (adv) ★★	/'naʊəˌdeɪz/
present (n) ★★★	/'prez(ə)nt/
previous (adj) ★★★	/'priːviəs/
racket (n)	/'rækɪt/
remember (v) ★★★	/rɪ'membə/
reunion (n)	/riː'juːniən/
signature (n) ★	/'sɪgnətʃə/
skill (n) ★★★	/skɪl/
stamp (n) ★★	/stæmp/
stuff (n) ★★★	/stʌf/
surname (n)	/'sɜːˌneɪm/
too much (adv)	/tu 'mʌtʃ/
wedding (n) ★★	/'wedɪŋ/

Study skills

Unit 1

GRAMMAR: Using the grammar reference

- The *Grammar reference* section appears at the end of every unit. It gives information about the grammar you study in the unit. Use the *Grammar reference* to revise and check that you understand the grammar.
- Then use the *Grammar practice* to see if you can use the grammar.

LISTENING: Understanding the basic information in a text

- The first time that you listen to a text, it is good to understand the basic information in the text. It isn't necessary to understand everything. The second time you listen, listen for more detail.

Unit 2

READING: Prediction

- Look at photos, pictures and titles that go with a text. They help you to know things about the text before you read.

SPEAKING: Learning to speak English

- To speak English, you need to practise. Use every opportunity to speak in class (and outside!).
- Speak in a loud, clear voice. Look at the person you are speaking to. Don't think about mistakes all the time. The important thing is to speak.

Unit 3

VOCABULARY: Keeping a record of new vocabulary

- To learn new vocabulary, you need to revise it regularly. To be able to do this, write the new words down in a vocabulary notebook or in a list.
- Remember vocabulary by writing words in groups. One word in a group helps you to remember other words in the same group. For example, make two lists from page 40 in Unit 3: *Rooms* and *Household objects and furniture*.

LISTENING: Before you listen

- Always look at the pictures before you listen to a text. They help you to know what the situation is.
- Read the questions too. They give you ideas about what comes in the text. They help you to know what is important in the text and what isn't. Underline the words in a question that you think are important.

Unit 4

READING: Understanding the gist of a text

- The first time that you read a text, read quickly. Don't stop when there are new words. The idea is to understand the basic information in the text. We call this understanding the 'gist' of a text.
- When we read the text again, we start looking at specific details.

SPEAKING: How to know if you are doing well

You and your partner are doing a speaking activity well when:

- You are speaking in English all the time.
- You can understand your partner.
- Your partner can understand you.
- You finish the task successfully.

Unit 5

READING: Using a dictionary

- A lot of English words have two, three, or more different meanings. Sometimes the meanings can be very different. The same word can be different types of word (e.g. noun, verb, adjective, adverb ...).
- Do not just read the first definition of a word when you look it up in a dictionary. It is possible that the first definition is not the one you want. Look at all the definitions and look at the word in context to decide the probable meaning.

LISTENING: First listening, second listening

- The first time you listen, the important thing is to get a general understanding of what you hear. If there is something you don't understand, don't worry. You usually listen twice.
- The second time you listen, you can listen for specific information and listen to check your ideas from the first listening.

Unit 6

GRAMMAR: Learning spelling

Here are some ideas to help you learn the spelling of new words.

- Write all words down in a vocabulary list, even the ones you know the meaning of. Look at your list frequently to learn the spelling.
- Test yourself. Look at a word, cover it, try to spell it, and check it. Or ask a partner to read out words and you try to spell them.
- When there are rules, learn them, e.g. regular past form *-ed* endings.
- Use a dictionary to check your spelling when you write in English.
- Read lots of English. When you see a word again and again, it becomes easy to remember the spelling.

WRITING: Planning before you write

- Before you write in English it is always a good idea to plan. This helps you to think of ideas. It helps you to organise the information in a clear, logical way. It also helps you not to repeat yourself.
- Planning takes a little time, but it saves time when you start to write. It also helps you to write a good, interesting text.

Unit 7

LISTENING: Listening outside the classroom

Listen to as much English as possible. Apart from listening in class, try to listen to:

- CDs or MP3s that come with books or readers
- The original versions of films
- DVDs in English (with or without subtitles)
- Songs
- Radio or Internet radio

WRITING: Paragraphs

- A paragraph is made up of different sentences which talk about one main topic.
- Paragraphs help you to organise and structure your writing. This makes your composition easy to understand. When there are no paragraphs, compositions can be confusing and repetitive.

Unit 8

READING: Guessing new words from context

- When there are words in a text that you do not understand, look carefully at the context to help you to guess the meaning.
- Look at the sentences and words just before and just after the word. This can help you to find out the type of word (noun, verb, adjective, etc.) and the meaning.

WRITING: Knowing who the reader is

- When we write to friends and family we use informal expressions and contractions.
- We use formal expressions when we write to somebody that we do not know personally, such as to a newspaper, a company or a school, university or hospital. In these cases, we do not usually use contractions.

Unit 9

READING: Reading outside the classroom

- Reading is a great way to learn more English. Outside the classroom you can read reviews, novels/readers, poems, the words to songs, web pages, comics, newspapers and magazines.
- We read different types of text in different ways. When we read a telephone directory, we look quickly to find specific information.
- When you read longer texts, like readers or novels, don't worry about every new word. Try to get a general understanding of the text. Only look up words that seem very important or common.

SPEAKING: Speaking English better

- Some people speak very correct English, but they speak slowly. In that case, relax. Don't worry too much about mistakes. Practise speaking for longer periods without stopping.
- Some people speak a lot, and fast, but they make lots of mistakes. When there are a lot of bad mistakes it can be difficult for other people to understand you. Slow down. Correct yourself if you know that you made a mistake.
- Listen to lots of English. The more you listen, the easier it is to speak.

Unit 10

GRAMMAR: Evaluating your progress

- When you learn a language, it's useful to think about your own progress. What can you do better now? What do you need to do to continue making progress?
- The end of the course is a good time to evaluate your progress. Remember to be realistic in your evaluation and your ambitions!

SPEAKING: Intonation

- In English, HOW we say something is very important. If we use the correct intonation, we can sound interested and polite. If we don't, we can sound bored or rude and we can make people angry.
- In public situations, the intonation usually goes up and down more than usual. Try to use the correct intonation to create a good impression.

Exam success

Unit 1

READING: True/False/Not mentioned activities

In this exercise, decide if the sentences are true, false or if the information does not appear in the text. It is essential to find the information in the text. Do not answer with your opinion.

Step 1: Read the whole text quickly.

Step 2: Read the true/false/not mentioned sentences.

Step 3: Read the parts where you think the answers are. Read slowly and carefully.

Step 4: Answer all the questions. Put *Not mentioned* if you cannot find the information when you read the text.

SPEAKING: Giving personal information

The first part of a speaking exam is often asking questions about personal information such as your name, your age, where you are from, where you live, your school, your favourite subjects, your typical routine, your likes and dislikes and your hobbies.

- Practise talking about these topics.
- Practise speaking loudly and clearly.
- Say a lot of things. The examiner wants to hear you speak!
- If you don't understand the examiner, ask them to repeat the question.

Unit 2

LISTENING: Matching

- In listening exams, read the questions and information BEFORE you listen. This helps you to know what words and ideas appear in the conversation.
- In matching exercises there are, for example, five people but eight pieces of information. Sometimes the extra pieces of information appear in the conversation but they are not the correct answers.
- The names are usually in the order that they appear in the conversation.

WRITING: Answering the question

In writing exams, you can write a text with no grammar or spelling mistakes and not pass the exam. It is essential to answer the question.

- Put all the necessary information in your text.
- Write the correct number of words. Texts that are very long or very short do not usually get good marks.

Unit 3

USE OF ENGLISH: Multiple-choice cloze activities

In this type of exercise, there is a text with gaps. You complete the gaps in the text with one of three words on the page. The words are often:

- prepositions (e.g. *in, on, next to,* etc.)
- articles (e.g. *a/an, the, 0*)
- auxiliary verbs (e.g. *be, have, got, do*)
- question words (e.g. *who, what, why*)
- pronouns (e.g. *he, him, his*)
- linkers (e.g. *and, but, because*)

First, read the complete text. Don't stop to think about the gaps. This is to get a general understanding of the text.

WRITING: Checking your work

It is normal to make mistakes when we write. That is why it is important to read your work carefully when you finish, especially in exams. Check for mistakes with:

- punctuation
- word order
- tenses
- capital letters
- spelling
- agreement between the subject and verb.

Unit 4

READING: Multiple-choice activities

- In exams, always answer all the questions. You do not usually lose marks for incorrect answers.
- In multiple choice activities, cross out any answers which you know are incorrect.
- Look again at the section of the text where you think the answer comes. Read it slowly and carefully and choose one answer.

SPEAKING: Negotiating

In information role-plays, you have to communicate specific information.

- The examiner explains the situation and the information that you need to ask for and give. It is essential in the exam that you communicate this information.
- If you don't understand what the examiner or your partner says, ask them in English to repeat or to speak more slowly. Use expressions like: *'Sorry, can you say that again?'* or, *'Sorry, could you speak more slowly?'*

Unit 5

SPEAKING: Missing sentences in a dialogue

In this activity, you have a dialogue and sentences. You must put the sentences in the correct place in the dialogue. There are usually more sentences than spaces.

Step 1: Read the complete dialogue. This helps you to understand the general situation.

Step 2: Put an answer for each question. Do not leave any answers blank.

Step 3: Cross out each answer when you use it so that you don't use the same answer twice.

WRITING: Style

- When you write texts in English, it's important to remember who you are writing to. We do not write in the same way to a friend as to a company director.
- In informal texts we use contractions (*don't/aren't*). We use short, direct sentences (*Please come./Don't be late.*). We use informal expressions (*Hi./All the best.*)
- In formal texts we do not use contractions (*do not/are not*). We use long, polite structures (*I would love you to come./We would be grateful if you could arrive on time*). We use formal expressions (*Dear Mr/Mrs/ Yours sincerely*).
- In exams, you get more marks when you write in the correct style.

Unit 6

LISTENING: True/False/Not mentioned activities

- In True/False/Not mentioned exercises, you should read the statements BEFORE you listen. The statements help to give you an idea of what you are listening for.
- Be careful. The words in the statements are not always exactly the same in the listening text. They often express the same idea but in a different way.
- Put *Not mentioned* if you do not hear the information when you listen to the text.

SPEAKING: Reporting past events

- Before doing a speaking exam where you have to report past events, check that you know as many regular and irregular past forms as possible.
- Learn and use words or expressions of time (*yesterday, then, two weeks ago* ...) to explain when things happened.
- Use fillers like *Well, Hmm* or *Let me think* to give you time to think of what you want to say next.
- Use basic question words like *Who? What? When? Where? How? Why?* to help you think of more things to say.

Unit 7

READING: Matching activities

Step 1: In this type of activity, first read all the texts or parts of the text quickly to get a general understanding.

Step 2: Read the piece(s) of information that you need to find. Look for important words that help you to find the text or the part of the text which contains the information. Read that specific text or part of the text again slowly and carefully.

Step 3: If you are not sure that you have found the correct answer, read other parts of the text again in more detail.

LISTENING: Completing notes

- In this type of activity, do not write down the first thing you hear. Make sure that your answers are relevant to the question.
- Be careful with spelling. You should spell simple words correctly. If not, you could lose marks.
- Write an answer for each space. Do not leave answers blank.

Unit 8

USE OF ENGLISH: Cloze activities

In this type of activity, you have a text with gaps. You must complete the text with words which are grammatically correct and are logical. Usually the words are prepositions, articles, auxiliary verbs, pronouns, or linking words (*and, but, because* ...).

Step 1: Read the complete text. Don't stop to think about the gaps. This is to get a general understanding of the text.

Step 2: Look again at the gaps and especially the words which come just before and after the gap. Fill in the gap with the word that you think is best.

Step 3: Read the sentence again with your answer in the gap to check it.

SPEAKING: Describing a photo

When you describe a photo:

- Do not worry too much about vocabulary. If you don't know a word for something, explain it with other, simple words. Remember that you do not have to describe every small detail in the photograph.
- Use the present continuous tense to talk about what people are doing.
- Use prepositions and expressions like *On the right/left* and *In the middle* to say where people and things are.
- Use *I think, maybe, perhaps, It looks* ... when you are not 100% sure and you are making a guess.

Unit 9

SPEAKING: Pair activities

When you do a speaking exam in pairs, remember:

- It is important to listen to what your partner says. In a conversation, we listen to the other person and then respond to what they say to us.
- In some activities you need to give and receive information. Be careful that you give and receive the correct information.
- In some activities you discuss ideas and opinions and then come to a decision. In this type of activity there isn't usually a right or wrong answer. The examiner wants to hear you speaking English.
- If you don't understand what your partner says, ask them in English to repeat or to speak more slowly. Use an expression like '*Sorry, can you say that again?*'.

WRITING: Handwriting and presentation

- Sometimes we forget that good handwriting and presentation are very important in writing exams. If examiners find it difficult to read your work or if they can't understand, you will lose marks.
- Give yourself enough time in writing exams to write clearly or do a final, clean version of your text.

Unit 10

LISTENING: Multiple-choice activities

In this type of activity, you choose the best answer from three or four different answers.

- You usually hear the text twice. The questions are usually in the same order as you hear them in the recording.
- Read the different answers before you listen. They can give you ideas about the topic of the text and the vocabulary you are going to hear in it.
- When you listen, do not write the answers too quickly. Sometimes the speaker says one thing and then changes what they say or adds new information.
- Do not panic if you do not understand information the first time. If you don't hear the answer to one question, start listening immediately for the answer to the next question.

USE OF ENGLISH: Conversation activities

In this multiple-choice activity, you have five short dialogues. You choose the right answer to complete a short dialogue.

Step 1: /First, decide where each dialogue is taking place.

Step 2: /Then decide who each person is (*a shop assistant, a customer, a doctor, a patient* ...). Incorrect answers will usually be illogical because they are not right for the situation or the person who replies.

Communication activities

Unit 3

Developing speaking page 48 Exercise 7a

Student B:

You call your friend Monica. Ask if she is there. Invite her to a party at your house on Saturday. Leave a message if she isn't at home. Your partner starts the conversation.

Unit 4

Developing speaking page 60 Exercise 6b

Student B:

You are at the bus station. You want to go to the art gallery. Ask your partner for directions. If you don't understand, ask your partner to repeat.

Unit 9

Developing speaking page 126 Exercise 6

Student B:

You want to go to a safari park or to the sports centre. You do not want to go to the park. You are free only on Tuesday and Thursday. The other days you have to look after your little brother.

⇨ see also p167

Spelling rules

The third person singular

We usually add **s** to the verb.

like – likes
walk – walks

We add **es** to verbs that end in **-s**, **-sh**, **-ch** or **-x**.

watch – watches
wash – washes
kiss – kisses

We add **es** to the verbs *go* and *do*.

go – goes
do – does

With verbs that end in a consonant + **y,** we omit the **y** and add ***ies***.

go – goes
do – does

With verbs that end in a vowel + **y**, we add ***s***.

play – plays
say – says

Verb + *-ing*

We usually add ***-ing*** to the verb to form the present participle.

jump – jumping
study – studying
sleep – sleeping

When verbs end in one or more consonants + ***e***, we omit the ***e*** and add ***-ing***.

have – having
make – making
dance – dancing

When a verb has only one syllable and finishes with one vowel and one consonant (except ***w***, ***x*** or ***y***), we double the consonant and add ***-ing***.

put – putting
swim – swimming
sit – sitting

When verbs end in ***-ie***, we change the ***-ie*** to ***-y*** and add ***-ing***.

lie – lying
die – dying

Pronunciation guide

Vowels

/ɑː/	arm, large	/ɪə/	ear, here
/æ/	cap, bad	/ɒ/	not, watch
/aɪ/	ride, fly	/əʊ/	cold, boat
/aɪə/	diary, science	/ɔː/	door, talk
/aʊ/	how, mouth	/ɔɪ/	point, boy
/aʊə/	our, shower	/ʊ/	foot, could
/e/	bed, head	/u/	annual
/eɪ/	day, grey	/uː/	two, food
/eə/	hair, there	/ʊə/	sure, tourist
/ɪ/	give, did	/ɜː/	bird, heard
/i/	happy, honeymoon	/ʌ/	fun, come
/iː/	we, heat	/ə/	mother, actor

Consonants

/b/	bag, rubbish	/s/	say, this
/d/	desk, cold	/t/	town, city
/f/	fill, laugh	/v/	very, live
/g/	girl, big	/w/	water, away
/h/	hand, home	/z/	zoo, his
/j/	yes, young	/ʃ/	shop, machine
/k/	cook, back	/ʒ/	usually, television
/l/	like, fill	/ŋ/	thank, doing
/m/	mean, climb	/tʃ/	cheese, picture
/n/	new, want	/θ/	thing, north
/p/	park, happy	/ð/	that, clothes
/r/	ring, borrow	/dʒ/	jeans, bridge

Speaking bank

General

Classroom expressions

How do you spell that?
Can you repeat that, please?
What does pencil case mean?
How do you say that in English?

When you don't understand

I'm sorry, I don't understand.
Sorry, can you say that again
Sorry, could you speak more slowly?

Saying hello

What's your name? I'm ...
Nice to meet you. Nice to meet you too.
Are you English? Yes, I am./ No, I'm not.
How old are you? I'm ....

Showing interest in what someone says

Did you?/Is he?/Have they?
Really?
I see.
That's interesting.
That's incredible!
Then what happened?
Why?

Linking ideas

Addition: and
Contrast: but
Reason: because
Consequence: and so

Describing a Photo

Starting

This is a picture of _______
I can see ______

Position

On the right/left
In the middle
on, at, in front of, behind...

Tenses

Use the present continuous to say what people are doing, e.g. He's sitting down, She's asking the boy a question.

Guessing

I think
maybe
perhaps
he/she/it looks ________

Talking about the past

Time expressions

yesterday
last (night/week/year)
then
after that
two (days/weeks/months/years) ago

Past simple forms

See page 166 for the irregular past form of common verbs

Common situations

On the phone

Hello, 677 432856.
Hello, is that Ann?
Yes, speaking./No, it's Isabel.
Is Katy there?
Sorry, you've got the wrong number.
Hang on a minute. I'll get him/her.
Can I leave a message?
Do you want to leave a message?

Asking for information on the phone

I'd like some information, please.
Can you tell me what time the film starts?
How long is the film?
How much are the tickets?
Thanks for your help.

Giving information on the phone

How can I help you?
You're welcome.
Thank you for calling.

Asking for directions

Can you tell me how to get to (the cinema), please?
Excuse me, do you know where (the park) is?
Is there a (swimming pool) near here?

Giving directions

Turn right/left.
Walk along (Green Road).
Go straight on.
Go past (the bank).
It's on the right/left.
It's on the corner (of Park Street and Brown Road).
It's between (the cinema) and (the post office).
It's opposite (the school).

Ordering food: The waiter/waitress

Can I help you?
Are you ready to order?
What can I get you?
What would you like?
Would you like (a salad)?
Can I get you anything to drink?
Enjoy your meal!
That's 17.45 in total.
Here's your change.

Ordering food: The customer

Could I have the fish and chips, please?
I think I'll have the pizza.
I'd like a coke.
Have you got any lemonade?
How much is that?/Can we have the bill?

In a shop: The shop assistant

Can I help you?
Anything else?
That's (five) pounds.
Here's your change.
Would you like a bag?
You're welcome.
Sorry. We don't have any at the moment.

In a shop: The customer

Do you sell (pencils)?
Excuse me. How much is this?
I'll take it/them.
I'd like this.

Asking about somebody's plans

Do you want to (verb in the infinitive)?
Are you free (on + day/ at + time)?

Making suggestions

Why don't we (verb in the infinitive)?
Let's (verb in the infinitive).
What about (noun/verb + ing)?

Accepting suggestions

Yes, sure.
Yes, that's fine.
Okay.
Great.

Rejecting suggestions

Sorry, I can't.
Sorry, I'm busy.

Talking about a holiday

I went to (place) by (type of transport) with (people).
It took (20 minutes/two hours/ a day) to get there.
We stayed at (the Ritz Hotel/ a campsite/youth hostel/bed and breakfast).
We went to the beach.
We did some sightseeing./We went sightseeing.
We saw (a monument/bridge/tower).
We bought (souvenirs/a shirt/ a CD).
We ate (tropical fruit/typical food).
It was great/brilliant/spectacular/delicious.
I had a great time./I loved it.

Writing bank

Informal emails

page 23 (Unit 1)

Start: Hi

Style: Use contractions.

Useful expressions:

- To begin, ask questions like *How are you?* or *How are things?*.

End:
- *Write back soon, All the best.*

Content in emails giving basic personal information:

Paragraph 1: Give basic information about yourself and your family
- Paragraph 2: Give a physical description of yourself
- Paragraph 3: Write about you and your life at school
- Paragraph 4: Give information about your daily routine

Descriptions of places

page 49 (Unit 3)

Style: Adjectives are important to make our descriptions interesting.

Useful vocabulary:

To describe places: *ideal, enormous, spectacular, bright, special, old, beautiful, favourite, comfortable, cold.*

Useful grammar:

Adjectives usually come before the noun they describe (e.g. *It's a beautiful room)* or after the verb *to be*, e.g. *The room is beautiful.*

Content: Introduce the place you are going to describe. Say what it is and where it is. Describe what you can see and do there. Give your opinion of the place and explain your opinion.

Job application forms

page 139 (Unit 10)

Style: Formal. Do not use contractions. Write clearly and carefully.

Useful vocabulary to understand job application forms:

surname, date of birth, gender, marital status, address, current employment, pervious, employment, skills, any special observations, signed.

Content: Answer all the questions. Answer with just one or two words or, when necessary, give more information by writing complete sentences. Include information to show that you are a good candidate for the job.

An announcement

page 35 (Unit 2)

Start: Begin with a short question to get people interested, e.g. *Do you like . . . ?, Are you mad about . . . ?*

Style: Use short, clear sentences. Make the announcement easy, fast and interesting to read. Use imperatives to tell people what to do or what not to do (e.g. *Come!, Don't sit there!)*. Use exclamation marks.

End: Use *For more information, call/contact/visit our website . . .*

Content: Say what the club or event is that you are announcing. Include all the practical information that a reader needs to know.

Questionnaires

page 61 (Unit 4)

Useful vocabulary:

Who, Which, When, Where, Why, How, How much, How many, How often. . .

Useful grammar:

In questions, auxiliary verbs (*do, does, is, are, can. . .*) come before the subject.

Content: Give your questionnaire a title. Make all your questions relevant to the questionnaire. If possible, put the questions in order. We usually start with general questions and then we ask more specific things. The last question can ask for a general conclusion.

Informal invitation

page 75 (Unit 5)

Start: *Dear* or *Hi* with the name (not surname) of the person you are inviting.

Style: Use contractions and exclamation marks.

Useful expressions:

Would you like to come?, Can you come?, Please come, Let me know if you can/can't make it, Hope you can come, Please bring (drinks/food), Can you bring (food/drink), It's starting at (one o'clock), Don't be late.

End: *See you there! Cheers.*

Content: Say what the event is and why you are celebrating it. Say where and when it takes place. Say if people need to bring something or to confirm if they are coming.

Postcards

page 87 (Unit 6)

Start: Write the name and address of the person you are writing to on the right. On the left, write *Dear* or *Hi* and the name (not surname) of the person you are writing to. You can also write the date if you want.

Style: Informal. Use contractions and exclamation marks.

Useful expressions:

Begin *Here we are in . . ., We're having a (great/good/terrible) time.* Use *By the way* or *Anyway* to change the subject.

Useful grammar:

Use the present continuous to say what you are doing. Use the past simple to talk about things you did before writing the postcard.

End: *See you soon, Wish you were here, Bye for now.*

Content: Say where you are. Say what you are doing and if you are having a good time. Write about things you did/saw/bought/ate since the start of the holiday.

Formal letters

page 113 (Unit 8)

Start: When we do not know the name of the person we are writing to, we write *Dear Sir or Madam.*

Style: Do not use contractions.

Useful expressions in formal letters expressing opinions:

Begin: *I am writing about...*
Express your opinions with: *I agree, I disagree, I think, Personally, In my opinion, In my view.*
Finish with: *I feel very strongly about this question.*
Ask for other people's opinions with: *I am very interested in hearing other readers' opinions.*

End: When we don't know the name of the person we are writing to, use *Yours faithfully.*

Content in formal letters expressing opinions:

- Paragraph 1: Explanation of why you are writing, and quick statement of opinion
- Paragraph 2: First opinion and explanation
- Paragraph 3: Second opinion and explanation
- Paragraph 4: Ask for other people's opinions

Biographies, stories

page 101 (Unit 7)

Useful expressions:

To explain the sequence of events, use *After that, Then, Next.* To say when things happened, use, for example: *When, In 1999, The following year, At the age of 16, Two years later, When he was 12.*

Useful grammar:

Use the past simple to talk about completed actions in the past.

Content of a biography:

- Paragraph 1: Where and when the person was born and their life as a child
- Paragraph 2: The start of their career
- Paragraph 3: The important part of their career
- Paragraph 4: Their death and why they are famous now

Phone messages

page 127 (Unit 9)

Start: Just write the name of the person you are writing to.

Style: Use contractions. Use short, clear sentences. Make the note easy and fast to read.

Useful grammar:

We can sometimes leave out articles (*a, an, the*), subject pronouns (*I, he*), prepositions (*at, in*), auxiliary verbs (*am, is, does, will*). We cannot leave out nouns, main verbs, adjectives. If you are not sure that you can leave a word out, it is better to include it.

End: Write your name

Content: Include all the practical information necessary – who called, what they wanted, what the person needs to do.

Checking your writing

All units

Check for mistakes with:

- punctuation
- capital letters
- word order
- spelling
- tenses
- agreement between the subject and verb (e.g. He works. NOT He work.)
- style
- content

Irregular verbs

Infinitive	Past simple	Past participle
be	was/were	been
beat	beat	beaten
become	became	become
begin	began	begun
break	broke	broken
bring	brought	brought
build	built	built
burn	burnt	burnt
buy	bought	bought
catch	caught	caught
choose	chose	chosen
come	came	come
cost	cost	cost
cut	cut	cut
do	did	done
draw	drew	drawn
drink	drank	drunk
drive	drove	driven
eat	ate	eaten
fall	fell	fallen
feel	felt	felt
find	found	found
fly	flew	flown
forget	forgot	forgotten
forgive	forgave	forgiven
get	got	got
give	gave	given
go	went	gone
grow	grew	grown
hang out	hung out	hung out
have	had	had
hear	heard	heard
hide	hid	hidden
hit	hit	hit
hurt	hurt	hurt
keep	kept	kept
know	knew	known
lay	laid	laid
leave	left	left
learn	learned/learnt	learned/learnt

Infinitive	Past simple	Past participle
let	let	let
lie	lay	lain
lose	lost	lost
make	made	made
mean	meant	meant
meet	met	met
pay	paid	paid
put	put	put
read	read	read
ride	rode	ridden
ring	rang	rung
run	ran	run
say	said	said
see	saw	seen
sell	sold	sold
send	sent	sent
set up	set up	set up
shine	shone	shone
shoot	shot	shot
show	showed	shown
sing	sang	sung
sit	sat	sat
sleep	slept	slept
speak	spoke	spoken
speed	sped	sped
spell	spelt	spelt
spend	spent	spent
split up	split up	split up
stand up	stood up	stood up
steal	stole	stolen
swim	swam	swum
take	took	taken
teach	taught	taught
tell	told	told
think	thought	thought
understand	understood	understood
wake up	woke up	woken up
wear	wore	worn
win	won	won
write	wrote	written

Unit 1

Developing speaking page 22 Exercise 5a/b

Student B:

Name:	Amy Smith
From:	Dublin, Ireland
Parents' names:	Joe and Holly
Brothers and sisters:	Carl – 16 years old – studies at this school Robert – 8 years old – studies at primary school
Favourite subjects:	English, Spanish ➜ have got a Spanish friend
Don't really like:	art, music
After school:	play computer games, don't watch TV ➜ don't like it!

Student A:

Name:	Max Taylor
From:	San Francisco, USA
Parents' names:	Brad and Lily
Brothers and sisters:	Hannah – 22 years old – works Daniel – 19 years old – studies at university
Favourite subjects:	physics, chemistry
Don't really like:	history, P.E. ➜ don't like sport
After school:	do homework, don't play ➜ don't have time!

Unit 3

Developing speaking page 48 Exercise 7a

Student A:

The phone rings in your house. Answer it. Give your number (660 718 2469). Your sister Monica is not at home. Find out if the caller wants to leave a message. You start the conversation by giving your number.

Unit 4

Developing speaking page 60 Exercise 6b

Student A:

You are at the bus station. You want to go to the shopping centre. Ask your partner for directions. If you don't understand, ask your partner to repeat.

Unit 9

Developing speaking page 126 Exercise 6

Student A:

You want to go the park or the sports centre. You do not want to go to a safari park. You prefer to go out on Wednesday. You are free only on Wednesday and Thursday. The other days you have to work in your parents' shop.

⇨ see also p160

Macmillan Education
Between Towns Road, Oxford OX4 3PP
A division of Macmillan Publishers Limited
Companies and representatives throughout the world

ISBN 978-0-230-72338-2
ISBN 978-0-230-41759-5 (plus Gateway Online)

Page make-up by eMC Design
Illustrated by Kathy Baxendale (9, 13, 40, 60, 70, 77, 121), Moreno Chiacchiera (81), Stephen Dew (133), Stephen Elford (6, 20, 37, 51, 71, 123), Janos Jantner (15, 43, 69, 77, 108, 118, 141), Richard Jones (52), Joanna Kerr (9, 14, 25, 40, 42, 50, 60, 129), Peter Lubach (10, 11, 16, 21, 47, 68, 92, 104, 132), Julian Mosedale (11, 17, 20, 33, 55, 95, 115, 124), Mark Ruffle (13, 14, 25, 43, 46, 63, 106, 137), Martin Sanders (122) and Mark Turner (45)
Cover design by Andrew Oliver
Cover photographs from Corbis, Corbis/ Tom Stewart, Image Source, Photolibrary/ Bill Stevenson, Photolibrary/ Nicole Hill

Author's acknowledgements
I would like to thank the whole Macmillan team in Oxford for their dedication and hard work during the creation of this book. A big thanks also to all the students that I have had the pleasure of teaching at Colegio Europeo Aristos, Getafe and to my colleagues there. Finally, writing this book would not have been possible without the support of my wonderful family. All my love and thanks to Gemma, Jamie and Becky.

The publishers would like to thank all of those who reviewed or piloted Gateway: Benjamin Affolter, Evelyn Andorfer, Anna Ciereszynska, Regina Culver, Anna Dabrowska, Ondrej Dosedel, Lisa Durham, Dagmar Eder, Eva Ellederovan, H Fouad, Sabrina Funes, Luiza Gervescu, Isabel González Bueno, Jutta Habringer, Stela Halmageanu, Andrea Hutterer, Nicole Ioakimidis, Mag. Annemarie Kammerhofer, Sonja Lengauer, Gabriela Liptakova, María Cristina Maggi, Silvia Miranda Barbara Nowak, Agnieska Orlińska, Anna Orlowska, María Paula Palou Marta Piotrowska, N Reda, Katharina Schatz, Roswitha Schwarz, Barbara Ścibor, Katarzyna Sochacka, Joanna Spoz, Marisol Suppan, Stephanie Sutter, Halina Tyliba, Prilipko, Vladyko, Pia Wimmer, Katarzyna Zadrożna-Attia, and Katarzyna Zaremba-Jaworska.

The authors and publishers would like to thank the following for permission to reproduce their photographic materials:
Advertising Archive/ Image courtesy of The Advertising Archives p79; **Alamy/** Stephen Oliver p7(bm), Alamy/ Patrick Eden p8(r), Alamy/ Geoff du Feu p10(m), Alamy/ B. O'Kane p26(c), Alamy/ Alex Segre pp29(a), 61, 81(c), Alamy/ Clair Dunn p29(e), Alamy/ keith morris pp29(f), 44(d), Alamy/ Images-USA p38, Alamy/ BL Images Ltd p44(a), Alamy/ charlie stroke p44(b), Alamy/ The Photolibrary Wales p56, Alamy/ mediablitzimages (uk) Limited p72(t), Alamy/ A ROOM WITH VIEWS p81(a), Alamy/ Justin Kase zsixz p81(b), Alamy/ David R. Frazier Photolibrary, Inc. p81(d), Alamy/ Ben Pipe p81(e), Alamy/ Motoring Picture Library p81(g), Alamy/ Stuart Kelly p83(bm), Alamy/ Ian Dagnall p86(b), Alamy/ Geoffrey Robinson p107(c), Alamy/ David R. Frazier Photolibrary, Inc. p126(tl), Alamy/ Adrian Sherratt p126(b), Alamy/ ACE STOCK LIMITED p131(l), Alamy/ Paul Wood p131(m), Alamy/ PYMCA p131(r), Alamy/ David Bagnall p136; **BANANASTOCK** pp80, 99(l); **BRAND X** pp82(background), 86(a), 118(c), 120(br), 121;**COMSTOCK IMAGES** p66(l, r and d), 69(c); **Corbis** p122(background), Corbis/ Rubberball p10(l), Corbis/ Doable/amanaimages p15, Corbis/ Peter Dench/In Pictures p19(t), Corbis/ Leo Mason p19(m), Corbis/ Fabio Cardoso p26(a), Corbis/ Tom Stewart p26(d), Corbis/ Ariel Skelley p26(f), Corbis/ David Zimmerman p29(d), Corbis/ Jim Craigmyle p41(b), Corbis/ Radius Images p41(t), Corbis/ Richard Leo Johnson/Beateworks p49, Corbis/ Lynn Goldsmith p57, Corbis/ Duomo p58(b), Corbis/ GUILLAUME HORCAJUELO/epa p59(2), CORBIS p66(a), 85(b), 86(tm), 120(tl), Corbis/ Jim Vecchi p81(f), Corbis/ Svenja-Foto p86(d), Corbis/ Luis Claraco / Ipa Press /Retna Ltd. P93(r), Corbis/ Leon/Retna Ltd. P94(l), Corbis/ Bettmann p98(lmc), Corbis/ DOMENECH CASTELLO/epa p100(a), Corbis/ Daniel Hambury/epa p108, Corbis/ EVERETT KENNEDY BROWN/ epa p116(tr), Corbis/ ANDY RAIN/epa p117, Corbis/ Matthias Kulka p134(l); **CREATAS** pp84, 90(t); **DigitalStock p124(m); DIGITAL VISION** pp31(bml), 118(d), 120(bl); **Getty/** Commercial Eye p7(bl), Getty/ DreamPictures p7(br), Getty/ The FA Collection p8(bl), Getty/ Jetta Productions p22, Getty/ Ron Levine p26(b), Getty/ Seth Kushner p26(e), Getty/ Jamie Grill p27, Getty/ Dag Sundberg p29(b), Getty/ Stella p29(c), Getty/ David Rogers p31(b), Getty/ Wire Image p31(d), GETTY pp31(bl), 32, 55(a-d), 70, 73, 120(t), 134(r), 142, Getty/ Jupiterimages p48, Getty/ AFP p59(3), Getty/ Flying Colours Ltd p64, Getty/ Frank Herholdt p65, Getty/ Kutay Tanir p69(e), Getty/ Dorling Kindersley p78(d and g), Getty/ AFP p85(ml), Getty/ SSPL p85(tl), Getty/ SambaPhoto/Felipe Reis p86(e), Getty/ Cassio Vasconcellos p86(c), Getty/ LatinContent p94(r), Getty/ SuperStock p96(b), Getty/ Contour by Getty Images p87, Getty/ Time & Life Pictures p98(b), Getty/ Hulton Archive p98(tm), Getty/ Redferns p99(r), Getty/ Evan Agostini p101(l), Getty/ Time & Life Pictures p101(r), Getty/ Ryan McVay p105(l), Getty/ Retrofile p105(r), Getty/ Leon Neal/ AFP p111(r), Getty/ Noel Hendrickson p112(a), Getty Images p116(tl), Getty/ Indeed p130(tl), Getty/ Jack Hollingsworth p130(tm), Getty/ Michael Blann p138; **IMAGE SOURCE** pp31(br), 66(b and c), 67(t), 69(f), 87, 113, 118(a); **Lonely Planet Images/** Paul Kennedy p30(l), 82(top and bottom), LP/ Christine Osborne p86(br); **MACMILLAN AUSTRALIA** pp30(r), 125; **Macmillan Publishers Ltd/** Haddon Davies pp66(e), 69(d and g), 72(b); Macmillan Publisher Ltd/ David Tolley p66(f); **Mary Evans Picture Library** pp96(a), 116(b); **PHOTOALTO** pp110, 120(tr); **PHOTODISC** pp70, 118(b), 120(tm), 124(t, b) ; **Photolibrary/** Pixtal Images p10(r), Photolibrary/ Britain on View p19(b), Photolibrary/ Comstock p23, Photolibrary/ Photoalto p31(bmr), Photolibrary/ Ken Graham p44(c), Photolibrary/ Bill Stevenson p53, Photolibrary/ Peter Hatter p59(1), Photolibrary/ Tim Hill p67(b), Photolibrary/ White p75, Photolibrary/ Charles Bowman p83(t), Photolibrary/ Roy Rainford p83(br), Photolibrary/ JW. Alker JW. Alker p86(tl), Photolibrary/ Julian Love p86(tr), Photolibrary/ Dave Bartruff p86(bl), Photolibrary/ Chris Gascoigne p90(b), Photolibrary/ Dheeraj Dixit p100(c), Photolibrary/ A Chederros p107(bl), Photolibrary/ Denis Meyer p107(a), Photolibrary/ Bildagentur RM p107(b), Photolibrary/ Petteri Kokkonen p107(d), Photolibrary/ Jochen Tack p112(b), Photolibrary/ Britain on View p126(tr), Photolibrary/ Nicole Hill p130(r); **Reuters/** Steve Crisp p59(4); **Rex Features/** Sipa Press p11, Rex/ Everett Collection p31(a), Rex/ Kyle Rover p31(c), Rex/ David Rowland p31(e), Rex/ MATT BARON / BEI p31(f), Rex/ TM & copyright 20th Century Fox p34(a), Rex/ Alex Sudea p42, Rex/ Skyline Features P85(bl), Rex/ Kazden p93(l), Rex/ TM & copyright 20th Century Fox p99(t), Rex/ Alex Oliveira p100(b), Rex/ Stewart Cook p119, Rex/ NICK RAZZELL p134(t), Rex/ Derek Cattani p135; **Robert Harding World Imagery/** Gavin Hellier p30(m); **STOCK DISC** p69(a); **SUPERSTOCK** pp7(ml, t, mr, br, bl), 30(t), 55(e), 78(a, b, c, e, f, h, i), 85(br),
The Picture Desk/ CASTLE ROCK ENTERTAINMENT / THE KOBAL COLLECTION p34(b), The Picture Desk/ TWENTIETH CENTURY-FOX FILM CORPORATION p34(c), The Picture Desk/ Collection Dagli Orti / Fondation Chopin Varsovie / Alfredo Dagli Orti p96(c), The Picture Desk p85(tr), The Picture Desk/ 20TH CENTURY FOX / THE KOBAL COLLECTION p98(tr), The Picture Desk/ THE KOBAL COLLECTION p98(rmc), The Picture Desk/ PARAMOUNT / THE KOBAL COLLECTION p109, The Picture Desk/ Kobal/ TOUCHSTONE p111(l); **THINKSTOCK** p107(tl).

Photo p58(t) courtesy of Marise Vitti/ Fédération Internationale de KIN-BALL.
Photo p83(bl) courtesy of Shakeaways.

The authors and publishers would like to thank the following for permission to reproduce the following copyright material:
LACRYMOSA – Words and Music by Terry Balsamo and Amy Lee copyright © 2006 SWEET T 666 MUSIC (ASCAP) Administered by BUG MUSIC, DWIGHT FRYE MUSIC INC. (BMI) and PROFESSOR SCREWEYE PUBLISHING (BMI). All Rights Reserved. Used by Permission. Reprinted by permission of Hal Leonard Corporation;
We Got The Beat – Words & Music by Charlotte Caffey © 2009 Copyright BMG Songs Limited. Universal Music Publishing MGB Limited. All Rights Reserved. International Copyright Secured. Used by permission of Music Sales Limited & Hal Leonard Corporation;
United Agents for the poem "The Orange" by Wendy Cope, published in Serious Concerns. Reprinted by permission of United Agents on behalf of Wendy Cope;
Random House Group Limited for an extract from 'Mission survival: Sands of the Scorpion' by Bear Grylls adapted from www.beargrylls.com/books_videos.html published by Red Fox Children's Books, June 2009. Reprinted by permission of The Random House Group Ltd.

Dictionary extracts taken from Macmillan Essential Dictionary copyright © Macmillan Publishers Limited 2003 and Macmillan English Dictionary 2nd Edition copyright © Macmillan Publishers Limited 2007

Printed and bound in Thailand

2014 2013 2012 2011
5 4 3 2 1

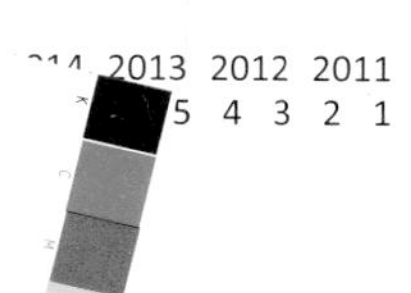